CREATIVE ARTS
FOR THE SEVERELY
HANDICAPPED

(Second Edition)

CREATIVE ARTS
FOR THE SEVERELY
HANDICAPPED

Edited by

CLAUDINE SHERRILL

Texas Woman's University
Denton, Texas

CHARLES C THOMAS • PUBLISHER
Springfield • Illinois • U.S.A.

Published and Distributed Throughout the World by

CHARLES C THOMAS • PUBLISHER

Bannerstone House

301-327 East Lawrence Avenue, Springfield, Illinois, U.S.A.

© *1979, by* CHARLES C THOMAS • PUBLISHER

ISBN 0-398-03908-9

Library of Congress Catalog Card Number: 78-31721

With THOMAS BOOKS *careful attention is given to all details of manufacturing and design. It is the Publisher's desire to present books that are satisfactory as to their physical qualities and artistic possibilities and appropriate for their particular use.* THOMAS BOOKS *will be true to those laws of quality that assure a good name and good will.*

Printed in the United States of America
V-OO-2

Library of Congress Cataloging in Publication Data

Main entry under title:
  Creative arts for the severely handicapped.

  Bibliography: p. 251
  Includes index.
  1. Handicapped and the arts--Addresses, essays,
lectures. I. Sherrill, Claudine.
NX180.H34C73 1979   371.9′044   78-31721
ISBN 0-398-03908-9

CONTRIBUTORS

Ollie M. Brown, M.S.
Assistant Professor
Department of Health, Physical Education, and Recreation
Jackson State University
Jackson, Mississippi

Rosann McLaughlin Cox, Ph.D.
Dance Coordinator
Arts Magnet High School
Dallas, Texas
Adjunct Professor
Texas Woman's University
Denton, Texas

Wynelle Delaney, M.A., DTR
Registered Dance Therapist in private practice
Houston, Texas
Instructor
Texas Woman's University
Houston, Texas

Sandra Ervin, B.S.
Special Education Teacher
Dallas, Texas

Lee Fuller, B.A.
Austin State School
Austin, Texas

Barbara E. Gench, Ed.D.
Assistant Professor
Coordinator, Undergraduate Professional Programs
Department of Health, Physical Education and Recreation
Kansas State University
Manhattan, Kansas

Marilyn M. Hinson, Ph.D.
Professor and Acting Dean, College of Health, Physical Education and Recreation
Biomechanics Advisor to TWU Dance Repertory Theatre
Texas Woman's University
Denton, Texas

Terry Lawton, Ph.D.
Assistant Professor
Department of Physical Education
Texas Woman's University
Denton, Texas

Michal Anne Lord, B.S.
Supervisor, Adaptive Programs
Austin Parks and Recreation Department
Austin, Texas

Ellen Lubin, Ph.D.
Assistant Professor
University of Arkansas
Little Rock, Arkansas

Joan M. Moran, Ed.D.
Associate Professor
College of Health, Physical Education, Recreation, and Dance
Texas Woman's University
Denton, Texas

David Morgan, M.A.
Recreation Center for the Handicapped
San Francisco, California

Wendy Perks, M.A.
Executive Director
National Committee, Arts for the Handicapped
Washington, D.C.

Wanda Rainbolt, M.A.
Assistant Professor
Physical Education and Dance
Chadron State College
Chadron, Nebraska

Margie Reesing, B.S.
Music Teacher
Special Education Department
Fort Worth State School
Fort Worth, Texas

Marsha A. Reid, M.S.
Recreation Leisure Studies Faculty
Southwest Missouri State University
Springfield, Missouri

C. Warren Robertson, Ph.D.
Assistant Professor, Speech
University of Southern Mississippi
Hattiesburg, Mississippi

Philip Roos, Ph.D.
Executive Director
National Association for Retarded Citizens
Arlington, Texas

Barbara K. Ross, M.A.
Austin State School
Austin, Texas

Lauren Gossett Routon, M.A.
Creative Arts Specialist
BEH Training Project on Physical Education and Recreation
for the Handicapped
Texas Woman's University
Denton, Texas

J. Randy Routon, M.A.
Coordinator, BEH Project on Arts for Handicapped
Texas Women's University
Denton, Texas

Donna Russell, M.A.
Consultant, Adapted and Developmental Physical Education
Birdville Public Schools
Coppell, Texas

Michael Schneider, M.A.
Director, Teaching-Research Project on Asthma and Exercise
Garland Public Schools
Garland, Texas

Claudine Sherrill, Ed.D.
Professor
College of Health, Physical Education, Recreation, and Dance
Texas Woman's University
Denton, Texas

Ellen Simon Uhler, Ph.D.
Director of Special Education
Forth Worth State School
Fort Worth, Texas

Jacquelyn L. Vaughan, M.S.
Assistant Professor of Recreation
California State University at Northridge
Northridge, California

Peter Wisher, D.Ed.
Professor and Chairperson
Department of Physical Education and Athletics
Gallaudet College
Washington, D.C.

ACKNOWLEDGMENTS

THE editor wishes to express appreciation to the following people:

Dr. Edwin Martin and Mr. William Hillman at the Bureau of Education for the Handicapped, Washington, D.C., for their advocacy;

The severely handicapped children at the Denton ARC Developmental Center, the Denton State School, the Fort Worth State School, and the Special Care School of Farmers Branch who have allowed us to test the appropriateness of our arts activities with them and, in so doing, have enriched our lives;

Hayes Prothro, Don Weston, Don Partridge, Philip Manning, Fillmore Hendrix, and Ewell Sessom at the Texas Education Agency, whose creative leadership in the implementation of P.L. 94-142 gives us hope;

Dr. Ellen Uhler, Director of Special Education at the Fort Worth State School, Dr. Chris Kallstrom, Director of TreeTop School in Arlington, and Mrs. Ruth Tompkins, Executive Director of the Denton Association for Retarded Citizens, for their inspiration and long-standing support in the implementation of dreams;

Rae Allen, for her photography, darkroom work, and artistic assistance.

C.S.

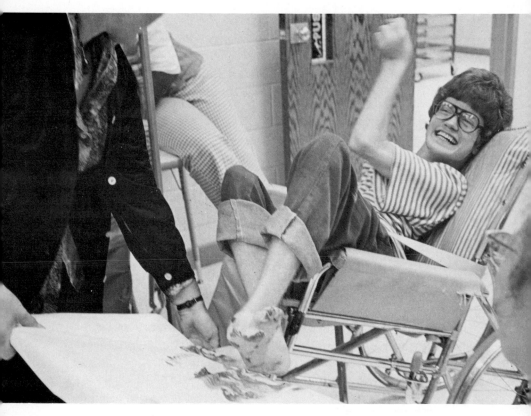

Structure 1. Nonverbal adolescent, with spastic cerebral palsy so severe that he cannot use his hands, learns to express thoughts and feelings through "finger painting" with his feet.

A CREDO

We believe:

That there are more than 8 million handicapped children and youth in the United States; that the special educational needs of such children, especially the severely handicapped, are not being fully met;

That these educational needs include training for wise, healthy, and productive use of leisure time now and for the adult years;

That handicapped persons, because of problems in securing employment, often have an abundance of leisure time;

That the creative and/or expressive arts can offer viable learning experiences that enrich the quality of life;

That the creative and/or expressive arts should be an integral part of special education, including physical education and related services as described in P.L. 94-142;

That no architectural, attitudinal, nor aspirational barriers should deny handicapped citizens of America the educational services needed for enjoyment of and participation in the creative arts.

Claudine Sherrill

CONTENTS

CREATIVE ARTS
FOR THE SEVERELY
HANDICAPPED

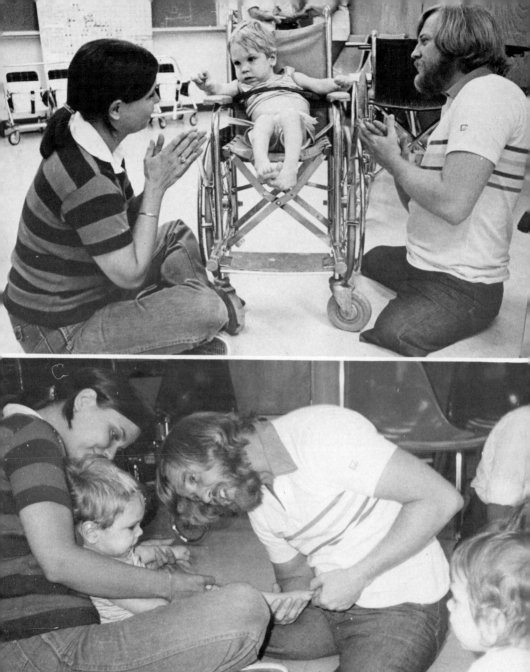

Structure 2. Teacher training in art, music, dance, and drama, as well as special education and its related services, should include classroom experiences in creative/expressive movement with handicapped children and youth. Handicapped adults make excellent teachers of teachers.

Chapter 1

PERSONNEL PREPARATION IN CREATIVE ARTS FOR THE HANDICAPPED: IMPLICATIONS FOR IMPROVING THE QUALITY OF LIFE

CLAUDINE SHERRILL AND ROSANN COX

> Every child is a gift of God and every child of God has a potential for talent; a capacity for creativity; and a right to enjoy to the fullest the beauty and vitality of the arts.
>
> The talent of every child is precious to us all — the creativity of every child can enrich us all. The joy of every child exposed to the arts is a blessing to us all.
>
> Only when every child in our society can be assured the opportunity to share in an appreciation of the arts, can all of us claim a share in the wonder of the talent, the creativity, and the joy of every child.
>
> Jean Kennedy Smith
> *from her acceptance speech,*
> *New York Humanities conference*

CREATIVE arts programs for the handicapped must be approached with the belief that the arts have a contribution to make to all students and that the handicapped have needs common to all children. Every child should be allowed to explore his talents and skills and learn to shape his thoughts and feelings into a form of artistic expression. Exposure to the arts as a spectator is undeniably important and culturally enriching, but the acts of participating, discovering, feeling, sharing, and shaping his ideas are necessary in order for the child to become an active participant in the creative arts.

3

Research Findings Concerning Creativity

Little research has been conducted on handicapped children's potential for creativity. Yet over a decade ago Torrance (1960), Getzels and Jackson (1962), and Wallach and Kogan (1965) indicated that there was little relationship between creative thinking ability and the generalized ability measured by intelligence tests.

Pioneers in research on the creativity of mentally retarded children include Tisdall (1962), Stern (1964), Kelson (1965), Rouse (1965), Smith (1967), Pollack, Pollack, and Tuffli (1973), and Sherrill and Rowe (1975). While the research designs and specific methods of collecting data vary for these investigators, there seems to be general agreement on two findings: (1) children of normal intelligence score significantly higher than retarded children on verbal measures of creativity, and (2) there are no significant differences between retarded and nonretarded children on nonverbal measures of creativity. This latter finding forms a strong rationale for use of the creative arts in the education of the mentally retarded, particularly if we believe in individualized educational planning based on the strengths rather than the weaknesses of children.

The nonverbal measures of creativity reported in the more recent research with mentally retarded children are either drawings or gross body movements. Most often used are adaptations of the incomplete Figures and Circles subtests of the Torrance Tests of Creativity (1966). The first subtest involves adding lines to incomplete figures in an effort to develop interesting objects or pictures. In the circles subtest, the subject is challenged to make objects or pictures from thirty-six circles, each about the size of a quarter. The Wyrick Tests of Motor Creativity (1968) include such challenges as moving the body back and forth between two parallel lines in as many ways as possible, moving in as many ways as possible from one end of a balance beam to the other with the hips always held higher than the head, and moving balls toward a wall in as many different ways as possible. Both the Torrance and Wyrick tests focus upon recognized components of creativity: originality, fluency, flexibility, and elaboration.

Pollack, Pollack, and Tuffli (1973) suggest that fluency may provide the best base for determining creativity abilities at all intelligence levels. They agree, however, with other researchers who stress that fluency alone is insufficient for measuring creativity and state that teachers should assess other traits involved in the total process of creativity.

Facilitation of Creative Behaviors

Personnel preparation in creative arts for the handicapped

Table 1-I

CLIENT BEHAVIORS IN THE CREATIVE PROCESS*

Behavior	Meaning
Cognitive	
1. Fluent Thinking To think of the most	Generation of a quantity, flow of thought, number of relevant responses
2. Flexible Thinking To take different approaches	Variety of kinds of ideas, ability to shift categories, detours in direction of thought

3. Original Thinking
    To think in novel
    or unique ways
	Unusual responses, clever ideas, production away from the obvious

4. Elaborative Thinking To add on to	Embellishing upon an idea, embroidering upon a simple idea or response to make it more elegant, stretching or expanding upon things or ideas
Affective	
1. Risk Taking To be challenged	Expose oneself to failure or criticisms, take a guess, function under conditions devoid of structure, defend own ideas
2. Complexity To have courage	Seek many alternatives, see gaps between how things are and how they could be, bring order out of chaos, delve into intricate problems or ideas
3. Curiosity To be willing	Be inquisitive and wonder, toy with an idea, be open to puzzling situations, ponder the mystery of things, follow a particular hunch just to see what will happen
4. Imagination To have the power	Visualize and build mental images, dream about things that have never happened, feel intuitively, reach beyond sensual or real boundaries

*From the *Total Creativity Program* by permission of the author Frank E. Williams. This program, comprised of several volumes, packets, and tape cassettes, is distributed by Educational Technology Publications, 140 Sylvan Avenue, Englewood Cliffs, New Jersey 97632.

should begin with an understanding of creativity, what it is, and how it can be fostered. Table 1-I describes pupil behaviors in the creative process; they are well accepted by both researchers and educators.

Applications of the content of Table 1-I to the movement exploration approach to teaching creativity are discussed by Sherrill (1976 — Chap. 3). Bundschuh, Carter, and Richmond (1973) and Sherrill and Rowe (1975) have adapted the Wyrick Tests for Motor Creativity to mentally retarded children. The University of Georgia study involved children, ages seven to sixteen, in motor creativity experiences with ropes, hula hoops, parallel lines, pasteboard box, maze, tin cans, ball-wall, Frisbee®, ball-hoops, and paper plates. The Texas Woman's University study involved children ages two to seven in motor creativity experiences on the Lind Climber®, a novel play apparatus. The Lind Climber motor creativity research design is now being replicated with the Trestle Tree® movement education apparatus from London (Sherrill, Lubin, and Routon, 1977).

The creative arts provide a unique opportunity for success for handicapped children because there is no right or wrong way to fulfill an assignment in terms of artistic expression. The sense of success is an important consideration in any endeavor, but it is especially valuable to the handicapped who meet failure regularly. The handicapped child can become aware of new possibilities for expression through the creative arts. Two illustrations of the self-expression activities of children in special education provide evidence of their relatively untapped creative potential. The first focuses on painting while the second describes a collection of poems and pictures.

Stabler, Stabler, and Karger (1977) report a study in which paintings by 11 severely retarded children (mean IQ=23.4; mean age=18.4), 11 moderately retarded children (IQ=57.5; mean age=14.9), and 15 nonretarded children (IQ=115.0; mean age=16.6) were evaluated by 80 judges with and without art training. Each subject did a total of five paintings, one during each painting session. The resulting 185 paintings were photographed in color for slides that were presented in random sequence to the judges. Statistical findings showed that judges with art training did not differentially rate the art of nonretarded and retarded persons. The researchers conclude —

> Engaging in painting allows a person to "do something" with his experience, disciplines him to see and integrate internal and external realities, provides a chance to transmit an emotional truth that may be impossible to verbalize, and generally facilitates self-actualization. These benefits are universal and do not depend on intelligence, technical ability, or number of paintings that one can sell or is invited to exhibit.

The other illustration of artistic talent is a book of thirty-eight poems and eleven drawings entitled *Choose to Be Good or Bad*. The poems and pictures were created by students in special education classes at the McEvoy Educational Center as part of the Poet-Artist in the Schools program, a pilot program of New York State Council on the Arts. What better·way to enhance the self-concept of children than to provide reinforcement of artistic expression by putting their works in print?

In one of the many IRUC (Information and Research Utilization Center) publications funded by the Bureau of Education for the Handicapped, Julian Stein (1975) presents many other illustrations of arts for the handicapped, including excellent bibliographies. Additional materials to be used in professional preparation in arts for the handicapped can be obtained* from National Arts and the Handicapped Information Service, a joint project of the National Endowment for the Arts and the Educational Facilities Laboratories.

The widely accepted concepts of zero-reject and appropriate education in the least restrictive environment should be applied to creative arts education. Teachers, recreators, and parents need specialized training for the development of teaching competencies in the creative arts and the full utilization of community resources for providing arts experiences.

Emphases in Professional Preparation

While the specific competencies to be achieved in personnel preparation will vary according to the length of the inservice or

---

*ARTS, Box 2040, Grand Central Station, New York, NY 10017.

preservice training provided, the following topics should be addressed as they relate to the generic roles that personnel may assume.

1. Assess, appraise, or diagnose the needs of handicapped children and youth with particular emphasis upon leisure time practices: How does the handicapped child spend his nonschool hours? How will he spend his nonwork time as an adult? What knowledges, skills, understandings, and appreciations about the arts does he possess already? Which ones necessitate individualized educational planning?

2. Leisure counseling, both individual and family, necessitates further appraisal skills in answering such questions as — How does a handicapped child affect family recreation and/or use of leisure time? Which arts activities can be engaged in at home, at school, at community facilities?

3. Purposive intervention of an educational, recreational, or therapeutic nature to change behaviors (including attitudes) in a positive way facilitates increased involvement in the creative arts and improved quality of life for the handicapped child as well as for his family members.

4. Mainstreaming role includes tasks inherent in integrating handicapped children in the creative arts in the least restrictive environments possible, i.e. community resources whenever possible. This task generally focuses upon the elimination of architectural, attitudinal, and aspirational barriers.

5. Resource room role includes individual and small group learning experiences in the creative arts when the mainstream setting is not sufficient for optimal growth and development.

6. Evaluation role is continuous and entails human management skills in that it is achieved through multidisciplinary input from all groups involved. Evaluation may be of a child, his family, the teacher or personnel providing learning experiences, or the creative arts program as a whole.

7. Administrative role implies organization of all resources (human, physical facilities, etc.) to provide optimal learning

experiences in the creative arts for handicapped children.
8. Advocacy role encompasses use of legislation and litigation to achieve rights of handicapped, also extending these rights in legislation to more emphatically include the arts as well as an improved quality of leisure.
9. Research (of an *action* nature) entails adapting creative arts activities to the interest and skill level of the handicapped; developing, testing, and validating assessment tools in the creative arts as well as learning modules; and determining behavioral changes in handicapped children that result from creative arts training.

Jean Kennedy Smith, in the opening quotation, implies that the quality of life for all of us will be enriched when professional preparation enables us to "share in the wonder of the talent, the creativity, and the joy of every child." Philosophers almost from the beginning of time have told us that the humanness of life depends above all on the quality of man's relationships to man, on our capacity to share the things we love, and on our success in utilizing the creative potential of all.

William Hillman, advocate for the arts in the Bureau of Education for the Handicapped, Washington, D.C., applies these concepts to professional preparation:

> Developing a leadership that will do its best to improve the "quality of life" for the consumer takes on many faces. These faces include sound professional preparation in an institution of higher learning, strong practicum and field work experiences and good articulation with other professionals... To paraphrase John W. Gardner, the struggle begins with the preservation of our resources both natural and human. It further extends to the use of leisure and to the pace of human life.

BIBLIOGRAPHY

Appell, Louise S. "Enhancing Learning and Enriching Lives: Arts in the Education of Handicapped Children." *Teaching Exceptional Children*, 1979, *11*, 74-76.

Carter, Kyle R.; Richmond, Bert O.; and Bundschuh, Ernest. "The Effect of Kinesthetic and Visual-Motor Experiences in the Creative Development of Mentally Retarded Students." *Education and Training of the Mentally Retarded*, 1973, *8*, 24-28.

Getzels, J. W., and Jackson, P. W. *Creativity and Intelligence: Explorations with Gifted Students*. New York: Wiley, 1962.

Hillman, William A. "Therapeutic Recreation and the Quality of Life." *Therapeutic Recreation Journal*, 1974, *7*, 3.

Kelson, F. "An Assessment of Creativity in the Retarded Child." Unpublished doctoral dissertation, Yeshiva University, 1965.

Lubin, Ellen. "Motor Creativity of Preschool Deaf Children." Unpublished doctoral dissertation, Texas Woman's University, 1978.

Pollack, Sally; Pollack, Donald; and Tuffli, Christian. "Creativity in the Severely Retarded." *The Journal of Creative Behavior*, 1973, *7*, 67-72.

Rouse, Sue. "Effects of a Training Program on the Productive Thinking of Educable Mental Retardates." *American Journal of Mental Deficiency*, 1965, *69*, 666-673.

Rowe, Joanne. "Motor Creativity of Mildly Mentally Retarded Preschool Children." Unpublished doctoral dissertation, Texas Woman's University, 1976.

Sherrill, Claudine. *Adapted Physical Education and Recreation: A Multidisciplinary Approach*. Dubuque, Iowa: Wm. C. Brown, 1976.

Sherrill, Claudine; Lubin, Ellen; and Routon, Lauren. "Motor Creativity of Mainstream Preschool Children on the Trestle Tree Apparatus." Unpublished study funded by faculty institutional research grant, Texas Woman's University, 1977.

Sherrill, Claudine, and Rowe, Joanne. "Changes in Sensory-Motor Fluency of Young Mentally Retarded Children Engaged in a Space-Oriented Learning Program." *Proceedings of the Research Council, Southern District, American Alliance for Health, Physical Education, and Recreation*, Mobile, Alabama, 1976. Funded by faculty institutional research grant, Texas Woman's University, 1975.

Smith, Robert M. "Creative Thinking Abilities of Educable Mentally Handicapped Children in the Regular Grades." *American Journal of Mental Deficiency*, 1967, *71*, 571-575.

Stabler, John; Stabler, Joan; and Karger, Rex. "Evaluation of Paintings of Nonretarded and Retarded Persons by Judges With and Without Art Training." *American Journal of Mental Deficiency*, 1977, *81*, 502-503.

Stein, Julian (Ed.): *Materials on Creative Arts for Persons with Handicapping Conditions*. Washington, D.C.: American Alliance for Health, Physical Education, and Recreation, 1975.

Stern, A. "Divergent Thinking in Educable Mentally Retarded Children Compared with Average and Superior Children." *Dissertation Abstracts*, 1964, *24*, 2791-2792.

Taba, Hilda. "Opportunities for Creativity in Education for Exceptional

Children." *Exceptional Children,* 1963, *29,* 247-256.

Tisdall, W. J. "Efficacy of a Special Class Program on the Productive Thinking of Educable Mentally Retarded Children." *Exceptional Children,* 1962, *29,* 36-41.

Toor, Marcelle; Lang, Jon; and DjaniKian, Greg. *Choose to Be Good or Bad.* Cortland, New York: University Press, 1975. Funded through the New York State Council on the Arts.

Torrance, E. P. "Educational Achievement of the Highly Intelligent and the Highly Creative: Eight Partial Replications of the Getzels-Jackson Study." Minneapolis: Bureau of Educational Research, University of Minnesota, 1960.

Torrance, E. P. *Torrance Tests of Creative Thinking.* Princeton: Personnel Press, 1966.

Wallach, M. A., and Kogan, N. *Modes of Thinking in Your Children: A Study of Creativity-Intelligence Distinction.* New York: Holt, 1965.

Wyrick, Waneen. "The Development of a Test of Motor Creativity." *Research Quarterly,* 1968, *39,* 756-765.

Structure 3. In Public Law 94-142, the arts are included under *related services*, which are required to assist handicapped pupils to benefit from special education; here puppetry is used to motivate a preschooler with spina bifida to learn and practice crutchwalking.

Chapter 2

PUBLIC LAW 94-142 AND THE ARTS

CLAUDINE SHERRILL

PUBLIC Law 94-142, the Education for All Handicapped Children Act, was signed by President Gerald Ford on November 29, 1975. Almost two years later, on August 23, 1977, the final rules and regulations for implementing this law were published in the *Federal Register*, Vol. 42, No. 163. Thus a new era began. What are the implications of this law for the arts? What understandings and appreciations must educators and therapists in music, dance, art, and drama have in order to implement the law? This chapter will attempt to answer such questions.

Purpose of the Law

The intent of Congress in passing P.L. 94-142 was to assure quality education for the estimated 8 million handicapped children, ages three to twenty-one, in the United States. The following statement comes directly from the law: "It is the purpose of this Act to assure that all handicapped children have available to them, within the time periods specified, a free appropriate public education which emphasizes special education and related services designed to meet their unique needs." (Public Law 94-142, 1975, Sec. 3, c) Congress conceived of P.L. 94-142 as a Bill of Rights for Handicapped Children. Inherent in this law are four basic rights:

- Right to Free Public Education
- Right to Nondiscriminatory Evaluation
- Right to an Appropriate Education
- Right to Due Process of Law

P.L. 94-142 places responsibility for implementation of the goal of *full educational opportunity* for all handicapped children on the state education agency. In most instances, the special education division of the state educational agency will be the driving force behind the goal attainment. It is imperative, therefore, that arts advocates and/or arts teachers or therapists become knowledgeable about special education, thoroughly conversant with state and local priorities, and personally acquainted with their community's decision-making special educators.

Achieving the Purpose

One way to achieve this task is to join special education professional organizations so that arts advocates are always highly visible at various gatherings. A list of names and addresses of such organizations appears in the appendix. On the other hand, organizations pertaining to arts, music, dance, and drama should invite special educators to participate in their meetings and conferences and should ascertain that key special educators are on their mailing lists. Only by frequent, cooperative sharing of perceptions concerning the meanings of *full educational opportunity* will special educators and arts personnel reach common understandings.

P.L. 94-142, like most legislation, is written in the broadest of terms. Whereas arts advocates may view *full educational opportunity* as including experiences in the arts, others may have entirely different perceptions. Clearly, each state education agency, through cooperative planning activities, must develop its own priorities.

Full educational opportunity, as used in P.L. 94-142, simply reflects a civil rights principle. No meaning can be read into the phrase other than the obligation of the public schools to provide free education for all children, ages three to twenty-one by September 1, 1980 (except in instances where the education of the three to five and eight to twenty-one age ranges would be inconsistent with state law or practice or any court decree). P.L. 94-142 mandates that public schools must find ways to meet the educational or training needs of all children regardless of the severity of their handicap. Public schools of the future will have nonambulatory, nonverbal, non-toilet-trained children who in the past were considered uneducable. No longer will parents have to pay for special training programs in private or residential schools, nor will they have to provide transportation for severely handicapped children unable to use regular school or city buses. This is the essence of the meaning of full educational opportunity.

References to the Arts in the Rules
and Regulations

In developing the official rules and regulations for implementation of P.L. 94-142, two years were devoted to gathering input from all groups that might be affected. Arts advocates, among others, worked arduously to convince decision makers that specific reference to artistic and cultural activities should appear in the rules and regulations. Success in achieving such reference would lend considerable valence to subsequent cooperative planning of curricula at local levels.

As a result of these efforts, the following appears in the comments section of the *Federal Register,* August 23, 1977, following the presentation of *Full Educational Opportunity Goal* (121a. 304).

> *Comment.* In meeting the full educational opportunity goal, the Congress also encouraged local educational agencies to include artistic and cultural activities in programs supported under this part, subject to the priority requirements under 121a.320-121a.324. This point is addressed in the following statements from the Senate Report on Pub. L. 94-142:
>
> The use of the arts as a teaching tool for the handicapped has long been recognized as a viable, effective way not only of teaching special skills, but also of reaching youngsters who had otherwise been unteachable. The Committee envisions that programs under this bill could well include an arts component and, indeed, urges that local educational agencies include arts in programs for the handicapped funded under this Act. Such a program could cover both appreciation of the arts by the handicapped youngsters and the utilization of the arts as a teaching tool per se.

This statement gives arts advocates considerable leverage when interpreting the intent of Congress to local townspeople and soliciting their support in cooperative planning of educational programs for handicapped children. The comment, however, cannot be interpreted as a mandate. It appears only to expand and broaden the awareness of local programmers. Once such awareness exists, tremendous effort is still required to translate it into action.

Another specific mention of the arts appears under *Program Options,* 121a.305, in the *Federal Register,* August 23, 1977:

> Each public agency shall take steps to insure that its handicapped children have available to them the variety of educational programs and services available to non-handicapped children in the area served by the agency, including art, music, industrial arts, consumer and homemaking education, and vocational education.

Those school systems that employ art, music, dance, and drama specialist-teachers for instruction within the regular education curriculum must now provide the same variety of program options within special education to be in compliance with the law. Handicapped children must be accorded the right to try out for chorus or band, for a role in the school play, and to submit their original art products in various school contests. Sensitive educators, knowledgeable about the variables that affect self-concept, will insure not only the right to try out but also the right to succeed, at least within the framework of the same normal probability that governs the chance of nonhandicapped children. The law, however, cannot mandate success; this outcome depends entirely upon the value systems and humanistic philosophy of teachers and administrators.

It should be noted that the law does not specify *who* shall provide such program options nor *what* instructional arrangements shall be made available. Nor does it indicate that specially designed and separate arts programs must be developed specifically for the handicapped. In many instances, mainstream arts programs can be expanded to include the handicapped. A new part can be added to the school play or a dance choreography to create a role for a nonverbal or nonambulatory pupil. Musical instruments can be fitted with special adaptations so that physically disabled children can learn to play them. Writing, choreographing, producing, and directing talents can be developed among handicapped children who show creative potential. For pupils who seem to lack both creativity and performance potentials, but who still yearn for involvement, numerous other tasks can be shared: ushering, selling tickets, constructing scenery, moving props, even cooking the traditional after-performance meal.

The Arts in Special Education and in Related Services

The rules and regulations for P.L. 94-142 make only one other specific reference to the arts. To understand it, one must be familiar with the distinction made in the law between *special education* as opposed to *related services*.

Special education is defined as

> ... specially designed instruction at no cost to parents or guardians, to meet the unique needs of a handicapped child, including classroom instruction, instruction in physical education, home instruction, and instruction in hospitals and institutions. (Sec. 121a.14)

Related services is explained as

> ... transportation and such developmental, corrective, and other supportive services as are required to assist a handicapped child to benefit from special education, and includes speech pathology and audiology, psychological services, physical and occupational therapy, recreation, early identification and assessment of disabilities in children, counseling services, and medical services for diagnostic and evaluation purposes. The term also includes school health services, social work services in schools, and parent counseling and training. (Sec. 121a.13)

Arts advocates tried but failed to gain a specific reference to the arts within the official definition of related services. They did, however, succeed in achieving a mention within the comments following the definition:

Comment. With respect to related services, the Senate Report states: . . . the list of related services is not exhaustive and may include other developmental, corrective, or supportive services (such as artistic and cultural programs, and art, music, and dance therapy) if they are required to assist a handicapped child to benefit from special education.

This comment opens the door for the arts as well as their related therapies, provided their proponents can convince local educational programmers that such arts services are requisite to a particular child's benefiting from special education. The comment also provokes consideration of the meanings of such words as *developmental, corrective,* and *supportive,* which appear to be the determining criteria for inclusion of the arts in the curriculum under the related services provision.

In summary, P.L. 94-142 mandates for all handicapped children *specially designed instruction* to meet their unique needs and *related services* required to assist handicapped pupils to benefit from special education. Clearly, most handicapped children do not need specially designed instruction in all curricular areas; they can spend some time in the mainstream. Likewise, not all handicapped children require related services as defined in the law.

What then determines whether or not a child is receiving an appropriate education? Specifically, how can the arts become an integral part of *specially designed instruction* or of *related services?*

The Individualized Educational Program

The right to an appropriate education is guaranteed by P. L. 94-142 by the provision that each handicapped child's specially designed instruction shall evolve from an *individualized education program* (IEP) written specifically for him. A meeting must be held at least once a year for the specific purpose of reviewing this IEP and, if appropriate, revising its provisions. The public agency must insure that this meeting includes the child's teacher, one other school representative who is knowledgeable about special education, one or both parents, the child when appropriate, and other individuals at the discretion of the parent or agency.

The right to appropriate education then is protected by cooperative planning and review of the handicapped child's specially designed instruction and requisite related services. P.L. 94-142 specifies the content the resulting IEP must include as follows:

(a) A statement of the child's present levels of educational performance;

(b) A statement of annual goals, including short-term instructional objectives;

(c) A statement of the specific special education and related services to be provided to the child, and the extent to which the child will be able to participate in regular educational programs;

(d) The projected dates for initiation of services and the anticipated duration of the services; and

(e) Appropriate objective criteria and evaluation procedures and schedules for determining, on at least an annual basis, whether the short-term instructional objectives are being achieved. (Sec. 121a.346)

The extent to which the arts appear within the components of the individualized educational program is entirely dependent upon the participants in the cooperative planning and review process. Teachers and parents aware of the values of the arts for their own sake and/or as preliminary activities or teaching tools may infiltrate the IEP with specific short-term instructional objectives in the arts. They may write in specially designed arts instruction to meet unique needs and/or they may specify a certain percentage of time each day or week in mainstream arts instruction. In the case of a nonverbal autistic child, they may write in the related services of a dance, music, or art therapist. In the case of a teenager with severe socialization deficits that prevent academic learning, they may write in the related services of a recreation specialist skilled in the use of the arts to facilitate improved social skills.

The potential within the IEP for prescribing the arts as content and/or as process is subject to only the boundaries of human vision. Full realization of such possibilities rests with school systems in which arts specialists, parents, and special educators have learned and shared together for many years. Much caring, trusting, and compromising occur in cooperative planning endeavors leading to some of the new integrated arts approaches to learning. Territorial hostilities among the separate disciplines of art, music, dance, and drama must disappear. The dichotomy between education and therapy must be resolved.

Preservice and Inservice Training Needs

The old adage, "a journey of a thousand miles begins with a single step," seems appropo. If the arts are to become an integral part of the education of handicapped children, preservice and inservice training of teachers and paraprofessionals must be drastically changed. Special educators must be expected to develop understandings, appreciations, and skills in the arts and the creative process.

Arts educators and/or therapists must achieve competencies in evaluation and assessment, in describing present levels of educational performance, in writing short-term instructional objectives, in teaching handicapped children in the mainstream and a variety of other instructional arrangements, and in evaluating the behavioral changes that occur in handicapped children as a result of participation in the arts and the creative process.

The many tasks involved in direct service delivery within the arts can be organized under three broad areas as depicted in Table 2-I: learner assessment and counseling, program implementation and evaluation, and artist-educator community leadership. These roles, whether actualized by educators, artists, recreators, or parents, can be adapted to the home or residential facility, the school, or the creative arts facilities in the community.

Table 2-II is an illustrative taxonomy of tasks associated with the three broad areas of roles. These tasks can serve as the basis for developing learning modules for inclusion in inservice education workshops and leadership institutes.

Table 2-I

CHART DEPICTING BROAD AREAS OF PERSONNEL ROLES IN CREATIVE
ARTS EDUCATION FOR THE HANDICAPPED

Learner Assessment & Education Planning	*Program Implementation and Evaluation*		*Community Leadership*
Assessment of present level of creative arts performance: Participating Discovering Feeling Sharing Shaping	**SCHOOL**		Identification and utilization of arts resources
	Mainstream Regular education setting or least restrictive environment	*Resource Room* Individual instruction Small group instruction	Advocacy
	COMMUNITY		Elimination of barriers
Assessment of present level of creative arts appreciations	*Mainstream Regular* Attending performances Participating in creative arts	*Special Resource* Attending performances given especially for handicapped Participating in activities especially for handicapped	Legislation Litigation Consumer involvement
Assessment of leisure time preferences and practices	**HOME**		Employment of handicapped
Leisure counseling Individual Family Significant others IEP Tasks	*Family Creative Arts* Activities in which handicapped child participates	*Individual Creative Arts* Endeavors by handicapped person alone or one supportive family member or friend	Action Research

Table 2-II

TAXONOMY OF TASKS ASSOCIATED WITH PERSONNEL ROLES
IN CREATIVE ARTS EDUCATION FOR HANDICAPPED
CHILDREN AND YOUTH

Tasks Associated with the Role of Assessment and Counseling

1.1 Utilizes effective procedures for collecting information about present level of creative arts performance and leisure preferences and practices of each student (client) and his family members.

   1.11 Makes effective use of informal procedures: oral questionnaires, preferences and practices inventories, and interviews on video and audio tapes; anecdotal records; pictorial checklists.

   1.12 Utilizes standardized test data when appropriate for severely handicapped.

   1.13 Constructs new instruments or modifies and/or adapts old ones to performance levels of severely handicapped.

1.2 Uses the appropriate leisure counseling orientation and extends existing identifiable models to include and/or focus on the creative arts.

   1.21 Adapts avocational, recreation, and activities models to severely handicapped.

   1.22 Adapts developmental-educational models to severely handicapped.

   1.23 Adapts normalization models to severely handicapped.

1.3 Assists student (client) and significant others (including family members) in understanding and appreciating self and creative arts potential.

   1.31 Cooperatively explores potential for participating, discovering, feeling, sharing, and shaping ideas in creative/expressive arts.

   1.32 Cooperatively explores potential for attending, observing, enjoying, appreciating, understanding, and criticizing art performances and products of others.

1.4 Works effectively with specialized services and resources.

   1.41 Encourages community recreation personnel to identify and share resources for creative arts education.

   1.42 Encourages civic organizations to help with transportation, cost, volunteer instruction, etc.

   1.43 Encourages artistic and administrative directors of museums, studios, and other facilities to extend services to handicapped.

1.5 Uses IEP (Individualized Educational Planning) model as described in P.L. 94-142 to structure creative arts assessment and planning into a viable instructional program.

   1.51 Includes in IEP a statement of present levels of creative arts performance.

   1.52 Includes in IEP a statement of annual goals for creative arts education and leisure time use, including short-term specific behavioral objectives.

   1.53 Includes in IEP a statement of the creative arts services to be provided.

   1.54 Includes in IEP the projected date for initiation of creative arts services and anticipated duration of such services.

   1.55 Includes in IEP evaluation procedures for determining discrepancy between objectives and actual performance after set periods of purposive intervention (instructional, recreational, therapeutic).

Tasks Associated with the Role of Program Implementation and Evaluation

2.1 Adapts principles of growth and development to planning of creative arts activities.

   2.11 Recognizes psychomotor prerequisites to creative arts participation: head and neck control, sufficient muscle tonus; grasp and release mechanisms; fine muscle coordination.

   2.12 Adapts creative arts materials and media accordingly.

2.2 Plans teaching-learning creative arts situations in accordance with acceptable principles of learning.

    2.21 Provides for effective and continuing motivation.

    2.22 Utilizes a variety of learning experiences broken down according to level of difficulty.

    2.23 Helps student (client) make application of his learning experiences to varied leisure settings at home and in the community.

2.3 Demonstrates professional level in instructional competence.

    2.31 Provides evidence that instruction changes student's level of creative arts performance.

    2.32 Provides evidence that learning experiences increase breadth and/or depth of leisure preferences.

    2.33 Provides evidence that learning experiences change leisure time practices in a positive manner.

2.4 Provides physical environment that facilitates creative arts learning.

    2.41 Adapts musical instruments, arts and crafts equipment and supplies, and other creative arts media and materials to special needs of learner.

    2.42 Controls heat, light, ventilation.

    2.43 Provides adequate structure and eliminates irrelevant stimuli.

    2.44 Eliminates architectural barriers.

2.5 Evaluates continuously as an integral part of instructional process.

    2.51 Involves students and significant others in evaluation of self, teacher, and program.

    2.52 Uses resulting data to improve creative arts learning experiences.

2.6 Uses community resources to enhance and reinforce creative arts learnings.

    2.61 Uses handicapped adults in the community as role models and artist-educators.

    2.62 Takes advantage of creative arts expertise of volunteers in the community.

    2.63 Solicits help from professional organizations like NARC and civic organizations like Jaycees and Shakespeare Club.

    2.64 Ascertains that students have direct access to all creative arts resources in community.

    2.65 Develops in students responsibility for caring for and protecting art products found in the community.

    2.66 Helps students acquire value systems that cherish and protect the arts as an essential right of all American citizens.

Tasks Associated with the Role of Leadership in the Community

3.1 Participates in the definition and solution of community problems relating to creative arts for the handicapped.

3.2 Interprets to others legislation, and possible litigation, that protects rights of the handicapped.

3.3 Acts as an advocate for the severely handicapped and works for extension of his educational-vocational-leisure opportunities to include increasing amounts of the creative arts.

3.4 Works closely with the press and other media in presenting and interpreting the educational and leisure needs and potentials of the severely handicapped to the public.

3.5 Initiates and carries through research pertaining to discrepancies between creative arts education and services received by handicapped versus nonhandicapped populations; pertaining to behavioral changes in handicapped after exposure to creative arts education; pertaining to attitudinal changes of selected groups concerning creative arts potential and performance of the severely handicapped; etc.

Structure 4. The National Committee, Arts for the Handicapped, encourages special education and arts personnel to try team teaching in providing integrated arts curricula and Very Special Arts Festivals for handicapped children and youth.

Chapter 3

SELF-EXPRESSION THROUGH THE ARTS: A HUMAN RIGHT

Wendy Perks

WE are living in a world of excesses. As we drive down highways, our senses are bombarded by sights, sounds, smells, tastes, movements. An endless stream of sensory stimulation attacks our systems. In education, we talk about skill development, socialization, behavior modification, mainstreaming, cognitive growth, psychomotor coordination, affective behavior, career education, individual education plans, leisure education, a basic education — the list is endless. Why then consider the arts where there is already *too much*? Are the arts another panacea for all the problems surrounding those people afflicted with emotional, physical, and mental handicapping conditions?

I believe the arts encompass something larger than all these issues, and at the same time smaller than all these issues. They are larger, because the arts involve a basic human need — the need to create. It is the basic right of all men to create meaningful forms of self-expression. Indeed, man's ability to express himself through the arts — to create meaningful forms of self expression — is what separates him from all other animals. The arts are smaller than all these issues, because the arts essentially involve people working with the material objects that surround them. Multi-million dollar buildings are not necessary. The resources are available for creative arts experiences to occur in every school in this nation. Administrators and teachers must simply activate the artistic process.

Thomas Wolfe, in *Story of a Novel,* makes an eloquent statement about the creation of a novel. His thoughts reflect the nature of man's basic need to create:

It seemed that I had inside me, swelling and gathering all

25

the time a huge black cloud and that this cloud was loaded with electricity, pregnant, crested, with a kind of hurricane violence that could not be held in check much longer; that the moment was approaching fast when it must break. Well all I can say is that the storm did break. It came in a torrent, and it is not over yet.

A storm has broken across the nation. Handicapped people are demanding their human rights. They are demanding rights to recreation, medical services, education, legal protection, and building access through Section 504 of the 1973 Rehabilitation Act. This is indeed an important "Bill of Rights" for handicapped people.

We know that 12 percent of the estimated 8 million handicapped children in this country have no opportunity to experience the arts. (No statistics are available for the adult population.) The arts are man's most basic means of self-expression and communication. To deny man this right is to deny his human rights. The arts offer each human being the opportunity to make his mark, to say "I am."

Recognizing that the arts can strongly affect the quality of life for all handicapped children and realizing the need to provide expanded arts opportunities for all handicapped children and youth, the National Committee, Arts for the Handicapped was established. The National Committee, Arts for the Handicapped is composed of leaders from major national arts organizations, organizations representing handicapped citizens, general education organizations, and private foundations. Funding support from the Alliance for Arts in Education; Bureau of Education for the Handicapped; Department of Health, Education and Welfare — Division of Arts and Humanities; and Joseph P. Kennedy, Jr. Foundation has allowed the Committee to focus its attention on three major national goals:

1. To research and disseminate information about curriculum and instruction in the arts for the handicapped.
2. To exemplify model arts programs that may be successfully used with the handicapped.
3. To increase the number of handicapped students served by arts programs by 200,000 per year for five years.

During 1976-1977, the National Committee fostered the growth of arts programs for handicapped children and youth through three major implementation strategies:

1. *Very Special Arts Festivals:* NCAH selected twenty pilot sites to develop and implement Festival programs. Each site reflected a strong capability to provide quality arts experiences for handicapped people.
2. *Model Site Programs.* NCAH identified and supported model arts programs. Each model site emphasized a particular aspect of arts programming, as well as provided a wide range of arts experiences for all handicapped children and youth.
3. *National Awareness Program.* Through publications, media presentations, and a series of special projects, NCAH developed a greater public awareness of the need for expanded opportunities in the arts for handicapped children and youth.

As an arts advocate I believe that music, dance, drama, and art are man's natural and essential means for self-expression. They assist in leading man to an understanding of himself and the world in which he lives. Man expresses his dreams, fears, desires, awe, and wonder of life through the arts. Since the arts are integral to man, they must be central in the educational and life experiences of all people. Creative arts experiences can be a powerful vehicle for providing beauty and joy to people burdened by physical, emotional, or mental handicapping conditions. Arts programs for handicapped people assist in developing a heightened awareness of self in relationship to others and life.

I believe another storm has broken across the nation. There is a rebirth of an ancient wisdom; there is a national recognition of man's basic need and right to create. There is a growing awareness and acceptance of handicapped people as creative, productive, and artistic human beings.

Victor Lowenfeld (*Creative and Mental Growth,* Chapter XII) clearly addresses this issue:

> It is one of my deepest innermost convictions that wherever

there is a spark of human spirit — no matter how dim it may
be — it is our sacred responsibility as humans, teachers, and
educators to fan it into whatever flame it conceivably may
develop. I venture to say that the ethical standard of a society
can be measured by its relationships to the handicapped. We
as human beings have no right whatsoever to determine
where to stop in our endeavors to use all our power to develop the uppermost potential abilities in each individual.
We all are by nature more or less endowed with intrinsic
qualities and no one has the right to draw a demarcation line
which divides human beings into those who should receive
all possible attention in their development and those who are
not worth all our efforts. One of these intrinsic qualities is
that every human being is endowed with a creative spirit.
Soon after birth he begins to investigate and explore and use
this ability for new adventures. New findings in psychology
consider this one of the "basic drives," a drive without which
we cannot exist; the ability to create is probably what distinguishes man most decisively from the animal. Man creates;
the animal does not.

With dedication and cooperation each state can provide
quality art experiences for those children who have been denied
the opportunity to paint the sunset, hear the verse, move with
the wind, or play the melody.

BIBLIOGRAPHY

Lowenfeld, V., and Brittain, L. *Creative and Mental Growth,* 4th ed. New
    York: Macmillan, 1964.
Wolfe, Thomas. *Story of a Novel.* New York: Charles Scribner's Sons, 1936.

Structure 5. Nonambulatory four-year-old with cerebral palsy, too handicapped to move much on his own, benefits therapeutically from the vestibular sensory input of whirling and experiences the feeling of "dancing" as teacher whirls him around.

Chapter 4

THE SEVERELY HANDICAPPED: WHO ARE THEY? WHAT CAN THEY DO?

CLAUDINE SHERRILL

IMAGINE a child, age two or three, whose physical growth and development are so slow that he still cannot walk. His world is that of a playpen, or cradle, or some ambulation device controlled by another. He does not talk, although often he can communicate by grunts, noises, and gestures. His typical posture is lying, probably because he lacks head and neck control and trunk strength to sit alone. He seems to pay little attention to the things about him but does respond with smiles and gurgles when he is touched or cuddled.

Picture this same child fifteen to twenty years later. With his exercise group, he can walk well over a mile in forty-five minutes (Ross, 1975). He recognizes and responds to his name and to simple commands such as "Look at me," "Stand up," and "Come here." He still has no speech but can hum songs such as "Old McDonald" and communicates quite well through signing, gestures, and babbles. With supervision, he can dress and undress himself but cannot yet manage buttons, zippers, or shoe laces. He is conditioned well in meal time procedures. He remains in the meal line, picks up his tray, carries it to the table, sits down appropriately, and eats with a spoon. He is also toilet trained (regulated) although he has occasional night-time accidents.

This is one example of a profoundly mentally retarded person. In the average community, there is one severely or profoundly retarded child for every 1,000 schoolage youngsters. In the past, most of these persons have been institutionalized, but there is a trend toward more and more parents keeping such offspring home and relying upon the public schools to provide educational services. Public Law 94-142, passed in 1975, specifies that all handicapped children have the right to a free, appropriate, public education.

Such legislation, with subsequent litigation to ensure enforcement, has drastically changed special education approaches to curricular planning. Not until the 1960s was sufficient research conducted with the severely and profoundly handicapped to show their learning potential. Among the pioneers in such research were behaviorists Fuller (1949); Bensburg, Colwell, and Cassel (1965); and Rice and McDaniel (1966). The training of teachers for the severely and profoundly handicapped is now recognized as a number one priority by the Bureau of Education for the Handicapped and other special education agencies.

The Mentally Retarded Population

The mentally retarded comprise the largest group of severely/profoundly handicapped. Classifications within retardation are based upon definitions established by the American Association on Mental Deficiency (Grossman, 1977). The classifications most often used appear in Table 4-I.

Table 4-I

PERCENTAGE OF MENTALLY RETARDED POPULATION
LISTED BY LEVEL AND INTELLIGENCE QUOTIENT

Level	% of Retarded Population	Stanford-Binet IQ Range
Mild	89.0	52 - 68
Moderate	6.0	36 - 51
Severe	3.5	20 - 35
Profound	1.5	0 - 19

It is important to note that only 5 percent of all mentally retarded persons fall into the severely/profoundly handicapped classification. Assignment to a classification is based upon three criteria: (1) subaverage general intellectual functioning as shown in the Table; (2) deficits in adaptive behavior; and (3) developmental period.

Deficits in adaptive behavior refer to problems of maturation, learning, and/or social adjustment that result in the individual's failure to meet standards of personal independence and social responsibility expected of his age and cultural group. Adaptive behavior is measured by such standardized instruments as the Vineland Social Maturity Scale, the Gesell Developmental Schedules, and scales similar to that depicted in Table 4-II.

Developmental period, the third criterion for classification,

Table 4-II

LEVELS OF ADAPTIVE BEHAVIOR USED IN
CLASSIFICATION OF MENTAL RETARDATION*

	Pre-School Age 0-5 Maturation and Development	School Age 6-21 Training and Education	Adult Age 21 and Over Social and Vocational Adequacy
Level I Mild	Can develop social and communication skills; minimal retardation in sensorimotor areas; often not distinguished from normal until later age.	Can learn academic skills up to approximately sixth grade level by late teens. Can be guided toward social conformity. "Educable"	Can usually achieve social and vocational skills adequate to minimum self-support but may need guidance and assistance when under unusual social or economic stress.
Level II Moderate	Can talk or learn to communicate; poor social awareness; fair motor development; profits from training in self-help; can be managed with moderate supervision.	Can profit from training in social and occupational skills; unlikely to progress beyond second grade level in academic subjects; may learn to travel alone in familiar places.	May achieve self-maintenance in unskilled or semiskilled work under sheltered conditions; needs supervision and guidance when under mild social or economic stress.
Level III Severe	Poor motor development; speech is minimal; generally unable to profit from training in self-help; little or no communication skills.	Can talk or learn to communicate; can be trained in elemental health habits; profits from systematic habit training.	May contribute partially to self-maintenance under complete supervision; can develop self-protection skills to a minimal useful level in controlled environment.
Level IV Profound	Gross retardation; minimal capacity for functioning in sensorimotor areas; needs nursing care.	Some motor development present; may respond to minimum or limited training in self-help.	Some motor and speech development; may achieve very limited self-care; needs nursing care.

* *The Problem of Mental Retardation.* U.S. Department of Health, Education, and Welfare, Office of the Secretary, Secretary's Committee on Mental Retardation, Washington, D.C., Government Printing Office, 1969.

specifies that the subaverage intellectual functioning and deficits in adaptive behavior are severe enough that they are identified within the first eighteen years of life. For instance, it is possible for an adult automobile accident victim to exhibit deficits similar to that of the severely retarded; however, the disability classification is *brain injured* rather than mentally retarded because the deficit did not occur as part of the developmental period.

Ramey, in preparing case studies of ten randomly selected profoundly mentally retarded males, ages ten to nineteen, summarized their characteristics as follows:

> ... Of the ten subjects, only three had any speech. These three could say only one or two words, usually "mama" or their own names. Most of the subjects were observed displaying the rocking mechanism at some time. Other mannerisms included wiggling the fingers, "skating across the floor," rumination, and head banging.
>
> Most of the subjects were at least fairly skilled in the self-help categories. Eight were toilet trained, and only five of these had occasional accidents. All of the subjects could feed themselves and dress and undress themselves with varying degrees of supervision.

Concerning basic movement skills, Ramey reported that walking was the only one that all of the profoundly retarded boys could perform more or less efficiently without assistance. With respect to running, three boys ran for twenty-five yards, two more-or-less jogged for a few seconds, and five took running steps when pulled manually by the arms. Only two of the group could lift their bodies into the air in a jumping pattern, and none could execute such simple dance and/or rhythmic steps as the gallop, skip, and hop.

An understanding of such basic movement characteristics enables the creative arts specialist to adapt activities in a realistic manner while aspiring always to improve performance. Ross, in a chapter later in this book, differentiates between the creative arts behaviors usually exhibited by the severely retarded as opposed to the profoundly retarded.

Recent federal guidelines do not, however, distinguish be-

tween severe and profound levels of retardation. The two classifications are lumped together and symbolized by the abbrevia-
tion S/PH (severely/profoundly handicapped).

Other Severely Handicapped Persons

Not all severely/profoundly handicapped persons are mentally retarded. The current definition of the severely/pro-
foundly handicapped as stated by the Bureau of Education for
the Handicapped is as follows:

> A severely handicapped child is one who, because of the
> intensity of his physical, mental, or emotional problems, or a
> combination of such problems, needs educational, social, psy-
> chological, and medical services beyond those which have
> been offered by traditional regular and special educational
> programs, in order to maximize his full potential for useful
> and meaningful participation in society and for self fulfill-
> ment. Such children include those classified as seriously emo-
> tionally disturbed (schizophrenic and autistic), profoundly
> and severely mentally retarded, and those with two or more
> serious handicapping conditions such as the mentally
> retarded-blind and the cerebral palsied-deaf.

Each state has autonomy in establishing its own definition of
severely handicapped. Additionally, a nationwide search called
CHILD FIND has been underway for some time now to locate
such children and begin educational programming.

Seriously Emotionally Disturbed

It is conservatively estimated that approximately 2 to 3 percent of the school age population is so severely emotionally
disturbed that special education provisions are required. This
encompasses 1,100,000 to 1,650,000 children between the ages of
five and nineteen. *Schizophrenic disorders,* the most common
of the psychoses, are defined broadly as abnormal behavior
patterns involving varying degrees of personality disorganiza-
tion and less than adequate contact with reality. *Autistic behaviors* include (1) self-stimulatory and unusual movements like

rocking, head banging and rolling, tapping or twiddling the fingers; (2) muteness or inability to use speech for communication; (3) withdrawal from, or failure to become involved with, people; (4) abnormal response to one or more types of sensory stimuli, usually sound; (5) pathological resistance to change manifested by observance of rituals, excessive preoccupation with certain objects, and temper outbursts; and (6) apparent intellectual retardation.

While some children appear to have no major problems other than schizophrenia or autism, it should be noted that most severely handicapped children exhibit some autistic behaviors or tendencies. The relatively new professions of music therapy (1950), dance therapy (1966), and art therapy (1969) have each shown a special interest in developing techniques to elicit positive behavioral changes in the seriously emotionally disturbed. The journals of these professions constitute especially good resources for further information.

Cerebral Palsied

Approximately 0.50 percent or 275,000 of the school age population falls into the classification of crippled and other health impaired (COHI). Of the many physically handicapping conditions which may severely impair a child, cerebral palsy is by far the most common. The incidence of cerebral palsy is 3.5 cases per 1,000 births.

Cerebral palsy is defined broadly as a group of neuromuscular conditions caused by damage to the motor areas of the brain. For the beginning teacher, it can be generalized that most children in wheelchairs, as well as those who walk with awkward gaits, are cerebral palsied.

Almost all cerebral palsied persons have multiple handicaps. Approximately 50 to 60 percent are mentally retarded; about 33 percent have seizures; 55 to 60 percent have visual defects; 5 to 8 percent have hearing defects; and many exhibit *neurological soft signs* such as hyperactivity, hyperexcitability, distractibility, perseveration, and conceptual rigidity. Nearly all children with cerebral palsy need speech therapy. The incidence of actual speech defects varies from 30 to 75 percent, with about half able to improve with training. Many never learn to talk, but they can communicate through sign language or by pointing to appropriate pictures or words on a communication board.

In cerebral palsy, damage to the motor part of the brain is expressed in abnormal patterns of posture and movement, in association with abnormal muscle tone ranging from extreme *hypotonia* (flaccidity) to extreme *hypertonia* (tenseness or even rigidity). Many cerebral palsied persons are *nonambulatory*, i.e. they lack sufficient muscle and postural tone to sit and stand unassisted. Even when supported in a wheelchair, they may experience problems of head and neck control and consequently have difficulty focusing on or maintaining eye contact with the art product on which they are working.

Problems of hand grip and manual dexterity often cause difficulty in arts and crafts activities. When noncerebral palsied persons close their fingers, the automatic accompanying wrist extension gives optimal power to the hand closure. In contrast, the spastic and athetoid child often exhibits a weak grip because there is an associated flexion and ulnar deviation of the wrist. The opposite problem, a clenched fist, characterizes other persons with cerebral palsy. Educators who are programming children to play rhythm band or musical instruments and to engage in arts and crafts activities must learn to cope with many problems involving abnormal muscle tone and postural reflexes.

In planning dance and creative movement activities, teachers must consider gait abnormalities and balance problems. Some cerebral palsied children tend to walk on their toes, and many have a *scissors gait*, i.e. the legs turn inward at the hips, thereby causing a pigeon-toed type of walk.

Spina Bifida

Another severe orthopedic condition in which the child is often multihandicapped is spina bifida, a birth defect caused by failure of one or more of the vertebral arches in the spinal column to close. The incidence of spina bifida is 1.6 to 3 per 1,000 live births. The child with spina bifida is usually paralyzed or has severe muscle weakness from the waist down. He typically is confined to a wheelchair or wears long leg braces. Kidney infections are an everpresent danger.

Many children with spina bifida have normal intelligence. Often, however, spina bifida is accompanied by *hydrocephalus*, an abnormally enlarged head caused by an accumulation of cerebrospinal fluid. In such cases, mental retardation is present and additional balance problems are created by the increased size and weight of the head.

Deaf-Blind

Rubella epidemics affecting pregnant women left relatively large numbers of infants both deaf and blind in the 1960s. Other diseases like meningitis and scarlet fever can also result in deaf-blindness.

Any time two sensory modalities are involved, educational problems are severe. In the case of deaf-blind children, most learning must occur through proprioceptive, kinesthetic, and tactile means. An integrated arts approach, with emphasis upon sensory stimulation through movement and touch, is especially effective.

Implications for Arts Programming

Clearly art, music, dance, and drama for the severely handicapped bear little resemblance to that generally conceptualized by the artist and/or artist-educator. The emphasis in arts for the severely handicapped is on the *process* rather than the product or content. Many educators believe that the arts (appropriately adapted) comprise the best approach to teaching self-help skills, language, and socialization. Recently, research (Harrison et al., 1966; Kesler, 1974; and Metzler, 1974) is beginning to substantiate such claims.

Individualized Educational Programming

Vast individual differences characterize severely handicapped children. The talent of another Helen Keller may exist undiscovered and unexplored. In another, a fleeting visual fixation or a momentary tensing of a limb may be the strength to be capitalized on.

Creative arts programming should begin with an assessment of each child's present level of educational performance. Is he ambulatory or nonambulatory? If he is confined to a wheelchair, what kind of head and neck control does he have? Are his hand grip and manual dexterity sufficient for making things of clay? What kind of listening skills does he exhibit? How many minutes (or seconds) will he attend to a story or a puppet show? Given a piece of paper and a magic marker, how long will he attend to the task of drawing? When music with a strong beat is played, does he respond with rocking or rhythmic movements? Does he have speech? Can he imitate arm movements and facial expressions? Are certain movements, postures, or activities contraindicated?

Few assessment instruments for use with severely handicapped children encompass the arts. One which does is the BCP, or Behavioral Characteristics Progression, which is described in detail later in this book. The BCP lists thirty-four music and rhythm behaviors and thirty-three arts and crafts behaviors, each of which is checked yes or no. Illustrative of these are:

- Mimics simple gross rhythmic hand movements, e.g. claps with music
- Marches in time to repetitious beat
- Makes simple shapes from clay
- Cuts/tears paper to make designs/shapes

The present level of a child's performance in art, music, dance, or drama can perhaps best be described by stating his behaviors in brief phrases similar to those comprising the BCP.

When the baseline (initial) behaviors have been recorded, the teacher should choose the art in which the child is most likely to succeed and develop long- and short-term goals for that art.

Each goal should include a method for assessing achievement and a description of the educational services planned, i.e. answers to such questions as (1) *who* will teach and what pupil-teacher ratio is recommended; (2) *where* will instruction occur: in the mainstream or a specially designed setting; (3) *when* will instruction begin, how many sessions will be conducted, how long will each session be; and (4) *how* can the child best be taught, what behavior modification and/or reward systems must be implemented, what instructional materials are required; and (5) *what* methodology appears best? The long- and short-term goals for the art activity, of course, explain *what* is to be taught.

The who, where, when, how, and what of the individualized educational program should then be shared with the parents and others who may provide input concerning the child. The concepts of individualized educational programming can be applied on a smaller scale to the teaching of a specific art activity.

For example, we will assume that music is chosen. The baseline behaviors already recorded for a particular child include (1) seems to attend best to instrumental rather than vocal music; (2) seems to attend best to fast rather than slow music; (3) seems to attend best to music dominated by percussive instruments; (4) responds to favorite records by rocking body forward and back from waist; and (5) reveals pleasure with appropriate facial expression, e.g. smiles when record begins playing.

The teacher selects playing the maracas as the specific music activity to be taught. The first step in planning a series of guided discovery sessions is a task analysis.

Task Analysis

Task analysis essentially requires the precise delineation of skills needed to achieve a certain long-term objective, the division of these skills into their simplest component parts, and the sequencing of the skills from simple to complex. The checklist (Fig. 4-1) shows how one item on the BCP (Strand 40, Music and Rhythms; Item 7, Plays rhythm instruments) must be broken down into many easier sub-items that are prioritized into a teaching progression. Specific observable behaviors are listed in order from easy through difficult, thereby serving dually as guides for both instruction and evaluation. A criterion level for success, like 80 percent, is established to show that the child has performed the task four out of five attempts before the *yes* column is checked.

Clusters A, B, and C represent three distinct stages in learning. Items .01 to .08 comprising Cluster A are prerequisite behaviors normally achieved in infancy or early childhood:

Name of Child_____ Date_____Name of Observer_____

IEP ^{40} Music and Rhythms, 7 Rhythmic Instruments

Long-Term Objective: Given (insert name of record) of _____ minutes duration, plays (insert name of rhythm band instrument) in correct tempo, starting and stopping appropriately, and remaining in standing position on assigned floor spot.

Educational Services: Five sessions, each _____ minutes in duration, on MWF afternoons, using a pupil/teacher ration of 2:1. Beginning on _____.

Evaluation Procedure: Videotape every fifth session with recording of sound. Check appropriate box in right hand column to show achievement status with regard to each objective.

A Short Term Objectives (Criterion for Success 80%)	NO	YES With Assistance	YES Without Assistance
.01 Goes to assigned floor spot on signal			
.02 Remains in appropriate posture on this spot for duration of music			
.03 Looks at rhythm instrument when it is offered			
.04 Reaches for rhythm instrument			
.05 Grasps instrument			
.06 Maintains contact with instrument until signal for release			
.07 Experiments, i.e. shakes, strikes, etc. randomly			
.08 Gets quiet when given signal, appears to listen to instructions and/or look at demonstration			
B .09 Attends to (watches) leader			
.10 Mimics leader in up and down shaking movements			
.11 Mimics leader, responding accurately to even 4/4 tempo			
.12 Mimics leader, shifting rhythm in accordance with changes in tempo			
.13 Starts on signal			
.14 Stops on signal			
C .15 Shows understanding of rhythm instrument by shaking it to music without demonstration, but may be off beat			
.16 Plays rhythm instrument, responding accurately to 4/4 tempo			
.17 Reproduces various short rhythm patterns (8 beats)			
.18 Plays accent beat of music on rhythm instrument			

Figure 4-1.

responding appropriately to changes in environment like going to a phonograph or television receiver when it is turned on; staying in one place instead of aimlessly wandering about the room; having sufficient attention span to attend to a task; and reaching, grasping, holding, and manipulating when an object is offered. Many severely handicapped children appear frozen at the level of Cluster A behaviors and require special training programs like behavior modification and operant conditioning to achieve.

Cluster B encompasses mimicry, imitation, and follow-the-leader skills, i.e. the ability to learn from a teacher-demonstration. Items .09 through .14 can be expanded to include imitations of movements of different body parts, in varying directions (up, down, circular, right, left); at varying speeds (fast, slow); at different levels (high, low); in varying rhythmic patterns (even, uneven). Severely handicapped children (unless blind) generally learn better through demonstration than verbal instructions. Often, in early stages, two teachers per child are needed: one to demonstrate and one to move the child's limbs manually through the desired imitative movement.

Cluster C entails behaviors dependent upon *conceptualizing* skills, i.e. the child recognizes a rhythm instrument and demonstrates its appropriate use. He understands that his rhythmic pattern is determined by the record on the phonograph. In this stage also he can reproduce a short series of sounds or movements, i.e. a rhythmic pattern like —

long   short-short   long   short-short   long   short-short

Principles of Teaching

In guiding severely handicapped children in arts activities, the teacher should consider the following principles.

1. Learning should proceed in small steps from the known to the unknown. This principle is based upon the teacher's

skill in task analysis and sensitivity in assessing the readiness of the child to move on to a more difficult or complex step. It is sometimes known as the principle of progression.

2. An appropriate level of methodology should be applied. Bruner (1966) specified three levels: (a) *enactive* — physical guidance of the child through motor activity; (b) *iconic* — careful demonstration of activity to child before his attempt; and (c) *symbolic* — verbal explanation of task prior to child's attempt.

3. Optimal use of the pupil's sense modalities should be used with attention to how he learns best: visually, auditorially, kinesthetically, tactilely (through taste, smell, vibration, or massage).

4. Learning attempts should be reinforced immediately and consistently through praise, hugs, candy, or whatever reward seems to work best. The reinforcers used in arts activities should be consistent with those used in the rest of the educational program.

5. Brief practice periods, rather than long ones, should be conducted, and the activity should be halted soon after the child experiences his first success.

6. Overlearning results in longer retention. Overlearning should be planned for through the provision of frequent review and the opportunity to repeat pleasurable activities over and over again.

7. Relevancy should be assured by providing opportunities for the child to practice newly acquired arts skills at home in an atmosphere of sympathetic understanding and encouragement. Hopefully, other family members engage in the arts so that the child feels the relevancy of school learnings in the home setting.

BIBLIOGRAPHY

Bensburg, G. J.; Colwell, C. N.; and Cassell, R. H. "Teaching the Profoundly Retarded Self-Help Activities by Behavior Shaping Techniques." *American Journal of Mental Deficiency* 69(5) (March 1965): 674-679.

Bruner, Jerome S. *Toward a Theory of Instruction.* Cambridge: Harvard University Press, 1966.

Fuller, P. R. "Operant Conditioning of a Vegetative Human Organism." *American Journal of Psychology* 62 (October 1949): 587-590.

Grossman, Herbert J. (Ed.). *Manual on Terminology and Classification in Mental Retardation,* 6th ed. Washington, D.C.: American Association on Mental Deficiency, 1977.

Harrison, W.; Lecrone, H.; Temerlin, M. K.; and Trousdale, W. W. "The Effect of Music and Exercise Upon the Self-Help Skills of Nonverbal Retardates." *American Journal of Mental Deficiency* 71 (September 1966): 279-282.

Kesler, E. B., Jr. "The Effects of Music Training Program on the Music Production Skills and Social Development of Severely and Profoundly Retarded Institutionalized Children and Adolescents." *Dissertation Abstracts International* 34A (January 1974): 3991-3992.

Luckey, Robert E., and Addison, Max R. "The Profoundly Retarded: A New Challenge for Public Education." *Education and Training of the Mentally Retarded* 9 (October 1974): 123-130.

Metzler, R. K. "The Use of Music as a Reinforcer to Increase Imitative Behavior in Severely and Profoundly Retarded Female Residents." *Journal of Music Therapy* 11 (Summer 1974): 97-110.

Ramey, Marsha. "Development of Materials for Professional Preparation in Physical Education for the Profoundly Mentally Retarded." M.A. thesis, Texas Woman's University, 1974.

Rice, H. K., and McDaniel, M. W. "Operant Behavior in Vegetative Patients." *Psychological Record* 16 (July 1966): 279-281.

Ross, Barbara. "Changes in Profoundly Mentally Retarded Adult Females During a Walking Program." M.A. thesis, Texas Woman's University, 1975.

Stainback, Susan; Stainback, William; and Maurer, Steven. "Training Teachers for the Severely and Profoundly Handicapped: A New Frontier." *Exceptional Children* 42 (4) (January 1976): 203-210.

Stephens, Beth; Baumgartner, Bernice B.; Smeets, Paul M.; and Wolfinger, William. "Promoting Motor Development in Young Retarded Children." *Education and Training of the Mentally Retarded* 5 (October 1970): 119-124.

Structure 7. Public Law 94-142 requires that handicapped children be taught in the least restrictive educational setting; mainstreaming handicapped with their nonhandicapped peers in creative arts learning experiences is often the least restrictive educational placement.

Chapter 5

MAINSTREAMING SEVERELY AND PROFOUNDLY HANDICAPPED CHILDREN IN CREATIVE ARTS

Joan M. Moran

ALL too frequently, architectural, attitudinal, and aspirational barriers have prevented and/or denied the severely and profoundly handicapped an opportunity for exposure to or involvement in the various art media. Yet, all human beings have a normal probability, capacity, and potential for talent and creativity in the arts. In "one nation under God," everyone has a basic human right to enjoy, to the fullest extent possible, the beauty and vitality obtainable through exposure to and participation in these various media. Such opportunities in the arts can contribute to, improve, and enrich the quality of leisure experiences for the handicapped.

Creativity is a condition of man that inspires the feelings necessary to produce, form, or bring to pass a work of thought or imagination that is new or different (Moran, 1977). It is based on man's total past experiences with people, things, and events. Although expressive forms and levels may differ, man is endowed by nature with the ability to express himself creatively. Therefore, all human beings have a normal probability of being creative and talented in one or more of the various expressive art forms. According to Lowenfeld (1964): "Creativity is an instinct all men possess. . . . It is an instinct we primarily use to solve and express life's problems."

Creative abilities begin to emerge in human beings by the end of babyhood (two to three years) as the child engages in imitative and symbolic play. Play experiences used by the child to test his cognitive and affective powers can be likened to the creative experiences of the mature artist who also tests and

47

experiments in the process of producing an artistic endeavor. The artistic impulse is universal in children, who are instinctively creative, curious, and interested in exploring their environment. Regretfully, the child's need for exposure to and experience with a variety of play environments, although frequently observable, is often disregarded. This lack of exposure exists despite the fact that philosophers, psychologists, sociologists, anthropologists, and educators have all written of the value and importance of play in the early developmental stages of man. Following are but two of the many existing endorsements of play:

> ... in teaching children, train them by a kind of game and you will be able to see more clearly the natural bent of each. (Plato, 380 BC)

> Therefore as I said before, our children from their earliest years must take part in all the more lawful forms of play, for if they are not surrounded with such an atmosphere they can never grow up to be well conducted and virtuous citizens. (Socrates, 420 BC)

The truly creative child (handicapped or nonhandicapped) at play often does not fit into society's mold. This problem is intensified by school systems that do not reward (in the form of grades) creative behavior because it is inconsistent with the serious work of learning. Such naturally creative talents are, therefore, often thwarted, ignored, or tossed aside by adults on the grounds that they work against long established human traditions. Yet, creativity in play is a necessary aspect in the total developmental sequence of the maturing child. Freud (1953) observed the creative aspects of play when he wrote:

> We ought to look in the child for the first traces of imaginative activity. The child's best loved and most absorbing occupation is play. Perhaps we may say that every child at play behaves like an imaginative writer, in that he creates a world of his own or, more truly, he arranges the things of his world and orders it in a new way that pleases him better. It would be correct to say that he does not take his world seriously; on the contrary, he takes his play very seriously and expends a great deal of emotion on it. The opposite of play is not

serious occupation, but reality. Notwithstanding the large affective catharsis of his play world, the child distinguishes it perfectly from reality; only he likes to borrow the objects and circumstances that he imagines from the tangible and real world. It is only this linking of it to reality that still distinguishes a child's "play" from "daydreaming."

According to Piaget (1962), creative play through art expression is the vehicle for spanning the transition between a child's play and the intelligent constructive activity of work. He describes the deliberate conscious illusion characteristic of both play and art as "Play is accompanied by a feeling of freedom and is the herald of art which is the following of spontaneous creation."

Because art is skill in performance that is acquired by experience, study, or observation, anything done well is an art (Moran, 1977). For the severely handicapped child it may be an artistic achievement to perform a simple skill, such as moving the fingers to produce a few marks on a finger painting surface. The finger movements employed by a nonhandicapped child engaged in the same task may produce more patterns but with less effort or thought. Because the beauty of art is in the eye of the beholder, who can say which is the greater artistic endeavor, especially if one remembers that anything done well, in accordance with the individual's ability to perform, is an art.

If the creative potentials of the severely and profoundly handicapped are to be developed in the various art media, this segment of our population must receive early and frequent exposure to a variety of aesthetic and cultural activities that provide stimulation and enrichment. They must have opportunity to experiment with, feel, and explore rich and varied sensory inputs. The end of babyhood and the beginning of early childhood is the most appropriate time to begin developing the creative potential of both handicapped and nonhandicapped children. At the same time, such viable learning experiences can contribute to the affective, cognitive, and psychomotor development of these children.

Noncategorical, integrated play environments, if properly

structured, can provide all children with the exposure needed to develop and nurture their innate powers to be creative. This is especially true when one considers that *all* children have common developmental needs. The only fundamentally different environmental feature for the handicapped, as opposed to the nonhandicapped, is the need for extra sensory input to stimulate creative output.

Developmentally, the child progresses from imaginative play, to fantasy play, and finally creative play. Frequently, the handicapped child's play is not as imaginative as that of the nonhandicapped child's play. Instead, it is mechanical and repetitious. Constructive play experiences, however, help the unimaginative child gradually become freer and more imaginative in his play.

Development of the Imaginative Play Stage

Imaginative play is the forerunner of creativity. It promotes, within the child, an effective interaction with his environment. Through the symbolic make-believe that imaginative play provides, the child is assisted in assimilating reality at his own level. Imaginative play is an effective method for practicing various tasks and adult roles without fear of failure or excessive censure.

The proper selection of toys and play objects is imperative if imaginative play is to be developed fully in children. All children are great mimics. They can be encouraged to imitate good demonstrations, imitate actions of people, or pretend to be animals. It may be necessary at first to provide the child with extra input in the form of sensory stimulation, including kinesthetic experiences, and to allow time for him to repeat and practice his efforts at imaginative play. Such efforts will facilitate within the child the development of perceptual and cognitive skills.

Development of the Fantasy Play Stage

Fantasy play provides the child with a concrete method of expressing his feelings and aspirations. In addition, the playacting of fantasy play assists the child in overcoming the pain and fear experienced in his real world.

Children, especially the handicapped, long for constancy in their lives. They need a safe, accepting, predictable environment. If anything changes this, nonhandicapped children will, in all probability, bring it back through play. Frequently, handicapped children lack the daring and energy to remake their world in play. They may be afraid of make-believe. To them, it may be a means of lowering their guard and leaving themselves vulnerable to the threats of the real world. Such children need to be taught the skills of fantasy play as a means of expressing the fears, hopes, and needs not satisfied in their everyday lives. When such fantasy play skills are developed, the children will be better prepared to adjust to difficult life experiences.

The development of fantasy play, like imaginative play, depends upon the proper selection of toys and play objects. Paint, clay, sand, and water are useful media for fantasy play. These materials can be used by the child symbolically as a means of expressing his fears, hopes, and needs. If this is going to succeed, however, the teacher must be sensitive to the child and his feelings. He must accept the child's attitudes and convey to the child a consistent and sincere belief in him. The teacher must respect the child as he is and permit the child to express himself freely.

At first the child may express diffused and undifferentiated emotions. His feelings may be negative. He may have lost contact with the people and situations that originally aroused his feelings of frustration, anger, fear, or guilt. The child's emotions may frequently be magnified, generalized, easily stimulated or evoked, and no longer tied to reality.

The handicapped child may see himself as an inferior person, unloved, inadequate, and afraid of the consequences of his behavior. He may be threatened by criticism and punishment. Reward and approval may be perceived as attempts to change or modify him. Punishment and disapproval may be reminders and reflections of his past inadequacies, reinforcing his feelings of insecurity or terrifying him. However inadequate his feelings may be, and in spite of all allurements, he may struggle to maintain his own picture of himself.

The teacher should not attempt to modify the child or pressure him to change. He should respect and accept the child entirely. If the child feels secure and unthreatened, he can begin to express himself fully without feeling ashamed or guilty. The child will eventually learn to make decisions and to act spontaneously and confidently. He will grow within himself and gain a more realistic impression of himself. Eventually, the process of depicting his imaginary and real life through fantasy play will enable the handicapped child to resolve his emotional problems and interpersonal conflicts. He will have a socially acceptable method for the release of his emotional tensions.

Development of the Creative Play Stage

Creative play is thoughtful, exploratory play with materials, objects, feelings, and ideas. As the child manipulates, transforms, and explores these materials and objects with meaning and purpose to convey or fulfill his intent, he provokes an effective interaction with the environment and engages in the creative process. Creative play increases the child's insight and sensitivity by cultivating the senses and promoting the sensory involvement necessary for symbol formation. It encourages learning through exploration, experimentation, manipulation, and transformation, thus developing the child's interest and readiness for further discovery. The creative process expands the child's potential as it develops curiosity, flexibility, improvisation, commitment, and the courage to risk. With this freeing of the imagination, which results in a relaxation from inhibition, the child gains greater psychological and physiological control. Psychologically, the child refines his fantasy play into healthful and constructive creative play. Physiologically, the child refines and enhances the development of his fine and gross motor abilities as he manipulates his entire body or its various parts. Thus, eye-hand coordination improves, visual skills required for reading and writing improve, the mental set for learning symbolic language is developed, and the problem-solving behavior which leads to learning, coping, and adaptation to change is promoted.

All children have creative potential. Creative play behavior can be nurtured in children. Rich and varied sensory inputs, including kinesthetic experiences, form the necessary basis for symbol formation and optimal cognitive development.

Developmental Stages in Symbol Formation and Creative Growth

Lowenfeld (1964) has identified six developmental stages in symbol formation and creative growth that correspond to Piaget's cognitive stages:

1. *Scribbling Stage:* Two to four years. Dawn of symbol formation and self-expression. Piaget's sensorimotor and preoperational stage.
2. *Preschematic Stage:* Four to seven years. First representative attempts. Conceptual realism is projected through universal symbols. Piaget's intuitive stage.
3. *Schematic Stage:* Seven to nine years. Achievement of a form concept is realized through self-devised schemas. These schemas are modifiable expressive symbols for man and his environment. Piaget's preconceptual stage.
4. *The Gang Stage:* Nine to eleven years. Dawning realism is projected through representational symbols. Piaget's concrete operational stage.
5. *Pseudo-Naturalistic Stage:* Eleven to thirteen years. Optical naturalism and realistic symbols replace conceptual realism. Continuation of Piaget's concrete operational stage.
6. *Adolescence:* Thirteen to eighteen years. Period of crisis and decision. Representational or personal symbols. Piaget's stage of formal operations and deductive thought.

According to Michelman (1971), there are three stages of development in the creative process. The first is a manipulative stage that satisfies the child's tactile and emotional impulses. This is followed by an exploratory stage during which the child experiments and plays with the materials in his environment to discover their potential. The final level of development is a stage of form consciousness in which the child employs the materials in his environment to fulfill his intent and desire for expression.

Implications for Educators and Recreators

Teaching techniques, methods, procedures, and materials may, of necessity, have to be modified or changed to permit the free and spontaneous utilization of the creative abilities of each and every handicapped and nonhandicapped child. The most important factor to remember is that *all* children should be free to explore and experiment with shapes, colors, textures, and three-dimensional forms in an enriched, sensory-filled environment. The toys, raw materials, and physical objects used to engage the senses should be easily accessible to *all* children.

Typical art materials are attractive and educational because they leave children free to follow their imaginations wherever they may lead and provide varied and immediate sensory experiences. Scribbling and drawing activity should be encouraged. Finger paints are probably the most sensuous of all art materials. By using art materials the child learns a sense of color and the way colors can be combined to form new ones. Collage is an excellent art form in which the child pastes together paper, cloth, and other materials of different shapes and sizes, colors and textures to create a work of art. Sand, clay, blocks, water, and other media should be accessible.

Prefabricated stencils, molds, copying, or coloring books should *not* be used as they deaden the imaginative spirit and block creative growth. Meaningless repetition should be avoided. Because enforced controls discourage curiosity and inhibit spontaneous exploration of colors, shapes, and new materials, they should *not* be imposed on the children.

Creative play activity can be structured by limiting the number and kind of materials available to the child, specifying dimensions for the working surface, or setting time limits. On occasion the child should be permitted to struggle with self-imposed problems.

Creative art experiences contribute to the child's drive for mastery and understanding of himself and of the world's complexities. They also provide the child with a safe arena to exercise curiosity, flexibility, commitment, and improvisation. Such experiences initiate multi-sensory investigation of the physical world; stimulate imaginative exploration; provide endless opportunities for flexible approaches, change, and modifications; and provide necessary inputs to compensate for deprivations and deficiencies within self and the environment.

The strategy of choices and alternatives involved in creative art performance tasks promote involvement, flexibility, the beginnings of self-affirmation, and planned rehearsal for exercising judgment and decision-making. The child is an innate creator, designer, and inventive builder. He expends energy spontaneously in painting, drawing, modeling, or constructing. The art process is multi-faceted. It involves the child in perceiving the world he lives in; reacting to what he sees and feels; selecting, interpreting, and reforming elements; and communicating his emotions and insights through a variety of sensory art media. In turn, the child's creative expression mirrors how he feels, thinks, sees, and imagines. The interaction between self and the environment is the foundation for abstract intellectual processes. This interaction is a basic part of all creative experience.

As a result of federal legislation, architectural barriers are beginning to disappear. Regretfully, attitudinal and aspirational barriers that prevent total integration of the severely and profoundly handicapped cannot easily be removed with a hacksaw or bulldozer. Noncategorical, integrated play environments, however, can begin to hack away at prejudice as *all* children begin to accept one another because of their individual abilities and contributions rather than their disabilities. Such play environments, if properly structured, can also provide *all* children with the tools and materials necessary for the development of their inherent capacity and potential for creative and artistic expression.

BIBLIOGRAPHY

Freud, Sigmund. "The Relationship of the Poet to Daydreaming." *Collected*

Papers, Vol. 4. London: Hogarth Press, 1953, pp. 173-174.

Gross, Karl. *The Play of Man.* New York: D. Appleton, 1908.

Huizinga, Johan. *Homo Ludens* (Man the Player). Boston: Beacon Press, 1950.

Lowenfeld, V., and Brittain, L. *Creative and Mental Growth,* 4th ed. New York: Macmillan, 1964.

Michelman, Shirley. "The Importance of Creative Play." *American Journal of Occupational Therapy,* 1971, 25(6), 285-290.

Moran, Joan M. *Leisure Activities for the Mature Adult.* Minneapolis: Burgess, 1979.

Moran, Joan M., and Kalakian, Leonard. *Movement Experiences for the Mentally Retarded or Emotionally Disturbed Child,* 2nd ed. Minneapolis: Burgess, 1977.

Piaget, Jean. *Play, Dreams and Imitation in Childhood.* London: Routledge and Kegan Paul, 1962.

Structure 8. Ballet for handicapped children is a *normalization* experience that can be provided through community recreation classes; wearing a leotard and going to dance lessons is part of the "normal" growing up experience in America; handicapped children need and want the same recreation activities as their peers.

Chapter 6

SENSITIVITY IN RECREATION PROGRAMMING, NOT TOKENISM

MICHAL ANNE LORD

Each of us was made as a precious, unique individual full
of the power and glory and majesty that is us ... being
human means being imperfect. Only a God can be perfect. So
we need to accept our imperfections and realize that the
reason we were given our particular set of imperfections is a
mystery we must accept, and know we can never understand
... that while we must accept what we are and while we
cannot change what we are, we can change the things we do
and so we have a large degree of control over our lives
through the control of our actions.

Jess Lair

EACH of us as a unique individual has the
need for self-expression — to explore, to experience, to say who
we are. Recreation can provide these opportunities. Increasing
numbers of community parks and recreation departments, hos-
pitals, residential facilities, and special schools are employing
therapeutic recreation specialists to help persons develop the
attitudes, appreciations, and skills needed to derive optimal
values from use of leisure time.

A relatively new helping profession, *therapeutic recreation* is
defined as a process utilizing recreation services for purposive
intervention in some physical, emotional, and/or social behavior to bring about a desired change in that behavior and to
promote growth and development of the individual. Therapeutic recreation specialists belong to the National Therapeutic
Recreation Society (NTRS), a branch of the National Recreation and Park Association (which has its headquarters at 1601
North Kent Street, Arlington, Virginia 22209).

Gunn and Peterson state that the three major components of

therapeutic recreation services are (1) *therapy* for persons in treatment programs who lack the basic functional skills to play; (2) *education* for persons who possess fundamental play skills but who need help expanding leisure understandings, appreciations, and skills; and (3) *recreation* for persons who need assistance in finding and optimally utilizing opportunities for socioleisure participation. While most persons could probably benefit from such services, handicapped children and youth particularly need leisure education.

Tague and Humphrey (1976) state in this regard:

> When an individual is ill or handicapped, the problem of leisure is compounded. Behavioral impairments, functional loss, or social barriers have frequently caused limited exposure or participation in leisure experiences. The majority of handicapped individuals have an even greater abundance of free time than the average American and many are confined to institutional settings. The need for leisure education is imperative if these individuals are to reach their potential in independent living and thus achieve for themselves, as individuals, a meaningful and purposeful life.

Public Law 94-142, the Education of All Handicapped Children Act, recognizes the potential values of recreation as a viable part of special education by including it among the related services, i.e. "such developmental, corrective, and other supportive services as are required to assist a handicapped child to benefit from special education." Thus recreation may be prescribed in the child's individualized educational program (IEP) in the same way as are occupational therapy, physical therapy, and speech therapy. According to the *Federal Register* (1977), recreation includes

1. Assessment of leisure function;
2. Therapeutic recreation services;
3. Recreation programs in schools and community agencies; and
4. Leisure education.

Special education personnel in public schools may therefore look to recreators for assistance in teaching handicapped children and youth wise use of leisure time. The 1975 report of the National Advisory Committee on the Handicapped makes a strong case for strengthening leisure education in the schools. In it the deputy commissioner of the Bureau of Education for the Handicapped states:

> Only 21 percent of the handicapped children leaving schools in the next four years will be fully employed or go on to college.
>
> Another 40 percent will be underemployed, and 26 percent will be unemployed. An additional 10 percent will require at least a partially sheltered setting and family, and 3 percent will probably be almost totally dependent.

In light of these statistics, there can be little doubt that handicapped children and youth should be exposed to a wide variety of program areas such as music, art, dance, drama, literature, horticulture, and sports in an effort to develop a lifestyle that can be rich and satisfying in spite of limited employment opportunities. Vocational training within the special education curricula must be balanced by socioleisure training in order to realistically prepare handicapped children and their families to cope with the future as well as the present.

Of the many program areas encompassed by recreation, the creative arts are perhaps the most successful in providing channels for discovery and expression of one's uniqueness. Everyone has the power to create and the need for self-expression to feel good about himself. Maynard (1976) states four goals in the creative developmental process that the recreator should consider when programming for the disabled:

1. Developing an understanding and sensitivity to various art forms in the environment.
2. Encouraging the outlet for creative expression.
3. Providing opportunities for the development of coordination and manipulative skills.
4. Promoting situations for creative problem-solving and communication of ideas, feelings, and attitudes.

To pursue creative growth, one must start at the level where there is interest — to meet the participants where they are, where they live, at their existing ability level.

In community-based recreation programs for the handicapped, the initial response to involving the handicapped in recreation programs is often to get them into an arts and crafts class, because of the ease of adapting the activity or integrating the participants. This is outright tokenism. A viable alternative is to provide a diverse, well-rounded arts program that provides exposure to a broad range of activities and experiences within the arts.

The cost factor can be kept to a minimum by using volunteers from art organizations or groups (Civic Chorus, Civic Theatre, Art Guild) as well as individual artists rather than paid professionals. Creating an awareness and sensitivity to art experiences within the existing staff is another means of beating the cost of specialized program personnel. Many creative experiences can be performed with little or no cost for materials. Many discarded items from around the house can become valuable materials for exploration activities within the arts.

By becoming sensory sensitive to everyday items and activities, one has the impetus for creative experiences at his fingertips. Art is the intermingling of fantasy and reality. Awareness of sensory input can sharpen one's expressive ability: through exploring, one stores a wealth of information that can be called on during any creative experience. A typical application of usually discarded household items follows. What can you do with a paper towel roll? What sounds can you make with it? What does it look like, feel like, taste like? The next step in the creative process is to make the paper roll into another object. This can be done as an arts and crafts activity or a creative dramatics activity by acting out the use of the object that the paper roll has become, i.e. the paper roll can become a peashooter with the participant miming the acts of putting a pea in his mouth, blowing it out the shooter, and hitting the target. Variations of this activity are achieved by setting limits or boundaries — the objects that you are creating must be of the same size or used for a particular holiday or occasion.

Often, our own imagination as recreation leaders limits the creative experience for a participant. As leaders we must display a willingness to accept their ideas. By accepting their ideas there is success for the participant and beginnings of creative growth and receptiveness for future exploration and stimulation. There are other imposed limitations to the handicapped individual in his efforts to explore family, institutions, and society. Many handicapped individuals, particularly the severely handicapped, are sensory starved and lack exploration experiences because parents and family members have been overprotective rather than encouraging exploration or any form of self-expression for fear the child might hurt himself or be the victim of ridicule or failure.

Institutions, private and public, have limited handicapped individuals by either setting a low expectation level of what they can do and thereby limiting stimulation and opportunities for exploration and self-expression, or because exposure to the arts and creative experiences are low priorities of the training, education, or rehabilitation services. Society has also placed limitations by not making the arts accessible — architecturally, attitudinally, or financially. For too long, the arts have been for the "able-bodied" — able to walk upstairs, able to appreciate, and able to afford.

As professionals, particularly those professionals in community-based recreation programs, we therefore have the responsibility to not only provide the opportunities for exploration and creative experiences, but also to provide a positive environment for self-expression and creative growth — to make it accessible, stimulating, and fun. Through acceptance of one's uniqueness there is discovery and purpose. One's uniqueness is one's right to life!

BIBLIOGRAPHY

Corcoran, Eileen L., and French, Ronald W. "Leisure Activity for the Retarded Adult in the Community." *Mental Retardation* 15 (April 1977):21-23.

Federal Register, Part II, August 23, 1977. Vol. 42, No. 163, p. 42479.

Gunn, Scout Lee, and Peterson, Carol Ann. "Therapy and Leisure Education." *Parks and Recreation* 12 (November 1977):22-25.

Hutchison, Peggy, and Priddy, Penny. "Beginning Recreation Integrated in a Community." *The Journal of Leisurability* 4 (3) (1977):7-12.

Lair, Jess, and Lair, Jacqueline Carey. *Hey God, What Should I Do Now?* Greenwich: Fawcett Publications, Inc., 1973.

Maynard, Marianne. "The Value of Creative Arts for the Developmentally Disabled Child: Implications for Recreation Specialists in Community Day Service Programs." *Therapeutic Recreation Journal* 10 (1976):10-13.

Public Law 94-142, 94th Congress, November 29, 1975.

Tague, Jean, and Humphrey, Fred. "Leisure Education/Leisure Counseling: A Continuum in Therapeutic Recreation Services." Unpublished paper, National Leisure Education Conference, New York City, February 1976, p. 1.

Structure 9. Illustrations of paintings done by mentally retarded persons and submitted to the National Association for Retarded Citizens for its annual Art Design Contest.

Chapter 7

ADVOCATING FOR
MENTALLY RETARDED PEOPLE

PHILIP ROOS

ILLUSTRATIVE of the many parent-professional organizations that advocate for handicapped children and youth is the National Association for Retarded Citizens (NARC; formerly the National Association for Retarded Children), which was founded in 1950. Each year this organization recognizes the creative abilities of retarded persons by sponsoring an annual Art Design Contest. The winning designs are used on Christmas cards and calendars and sold throughout the country, thereby increasing awareness of American citizens concerning the creative talents of retarded persons.

Today, increasing efforts are being exerted by NARC in such areas as governmental affairs, public information and education, advocacy and monitoring, and litigation. The basic principles that guide these activities are appropriate for creative arts programming.

Basic Principles

Through the years, NARC has advocated fundamental principles that have governed its policies and objectives. One of these principles is that mentally retarded children and adults are just as worthwhile as any other people. It follows that they are entitled to the same basic rights and advantages. They have the same human needs as others. In addition, many retarded people have special needs resulting from their handicaps, which may require extraordinary services.

Another basic assumption underlying many of NARC's efforts is that, although mentally retarded people are worthwhile human beings, mental retardation is an undesirable condition that impairs functioning to a greater or lesser degree. Hence, it should be prevented whenever feasible, and its effects should be minimized to the greatest extent possible.

More recently, NARC has endorsed the concept of a developmental model of mental retardation as fundamental to all services for retarded people (Addison, Luckey, and McCann, 1972; Roos, McCann, and Patterson, 1970; Roos, in press). According to this concept, all retarded persons have potentials for growth, learning, and development, regardless of the severity of their handicap. All services should be designed to foster development. Program goals should be selected so as to (1) increase the retarded person's control over his environment; (2) increase the complexity of his behavior; and (3) maximize his human qualities, i.e. those behaviors culturally defined as "human," "normal," or "desirable."

A related concept is that retarded persons should be treated as much like normal persons as possible. Usually referred to as normalization, this principle has become increasingly popular (Nirje, 1969; Wolfensberger, 1972). It has sensitized those working with retarded persons to the danger of fostering deviancy as a result of labeling, segregation, and isolation of the retarded from the mainstream of society. Accordingly, NARC has advocated retaining retarded people within the community, as close to their families as possible and served by generic services to the greatest degree practical. Recourse to specialized services should occur only in those instances where generic services fail to meet extraordinary needs.

NARC has also emphasized the importance of recognizing the uniqueness of each retarded person (Roos and McCann, 1977; Roos, in press). Thus, individualized programming has become a cornerstone of services for the mentally retarded and is now incorporated in national standards and federal legislation.

A related concept is NARC's emphasis on the importance of providing every retarded person with the maximum opportunity to make his own decisions and shape his individual future. This requires not only direct involvement of retarded people (or, where unrealistic, their parents or advocates) in all decisions that directly affect them, but it also underlines the necessity of providing options for choice among desirable alternatives (Roos and McCann, 1977; Roos, in press).

Leisure Activities

The association has long recognized the importance of providing retarded people of all ages and levels of handicap with services and conditions that will foster as full and rewarding a life as possible. While education, employment, residential services, and health care have received major emphasis, the need for meaningful leisure activities has long been recognized as an essential and often neglected area. Recreational and artistic activities have been found highly gratifying to most retarded people, and indeed, many have excelled in specific recreational or artistic endeavors.

It is not surprising that recreational programs were among the first services developed by many local ARC units, and they have remained a key ingredient in the comprehensive array of services advocated by the units for all retarded people. Hence, in October 1964, the NARC Board of Directors adopted the following statements to emphasize the importance of leisure time programs for retarded people:

1. Recreation is a vital factor in contributing to the total growth and welfare of the mentally retarded individual.
2. The mentally retarded are entitled to be included in public and community recreation programs. Special programs geared to meet the varying needs, ages, intellectual levels, etc., should be provided for those who find it difficult to participate in the existing community programs.
3. Recreation programs for the mentally retarded should be under the supervision of professional recreation leaders who have an optimistic insight into the expectations possible with the mentally retarded as well as their limitations.
4. Recreation programs sponsored by associations for retarded children should, wherever possible, be established and operated on a demonstration basis with the objective of involving the appropriate agency in the community at

the earliest possible date.

5. Institutions of higher education should be encouraged to include courses related to recreation and physical education for the mentally retarded in their special education, physical education, and recreation curricula.

6. NARC units have the responsibility to cooperate with and encourage the local directors of existing recreation programs for the mentally retarded to establish the best possible standards of operation. The National Association for Retarded Children/Citizens will cooperate actively with the National Recreation and Park Association, the American Camping Association, and other public and private agencies to achieve this goal.

7. The recreation program for the mentally retarded should encompass a wide spectrum of activities as offered in programs for all citizens of the community. The program should include year-round activities (scouting, canteens, hobbies, etc.) as well as seasonal ones (camping and baseball).

8. Both the professional staff and volunteers should be given orientation prior to the start of the recreation program. In addition, provision should be made for inservice training to be given to both the volunteers and professional staff.

Fostered by NARC's national Recreation Committee, which deals with artistic programs as well as other forms of recreation, the association's voting delegates adopted a formal resolution at the 1972 annual convention. The thrust of the resolution was that retarded people should have equal access to publicly supported recreational facilities and that public recreation agencies should exert every effort to adapt their facilities to the needs of mentally retarded and other handicapped persons.

During that same year, NARC's Board of Directors established two annual awards in recreation. One of these awards gives recognition to a local ARC unit that has been most successful in using community resources in fostering the development of recreation for retarded people. The second award recognizes a non-ARC organization or agency that has made outstanding contributions toward providing recreational services to the mentally retarded.

During the 1970s, several publications were developed under the aegis of NARC's Recreation Committee to assist state and local units in expanding and monitoring recreational services. A basic handbook outlined how recreation committees should be organized and function at the state and local level. A mass distribution flyer, *Retarded Citizens Need Recreation, Too* (1975), alerted recreational professionals and the general public to the recreation needs of retarded people. Most recently, NARC published a booklet, *The Fullest Life* (1976), highlighting innovative recreation programs for retarded people throughout the United States.

Cultural Arts Activities

With the help of funds from the President's Committee on Mental Retardation, NARC conducted cultural arts planning sessions at each of its six Regional Conferences in 1974. It was concluded on the basis of those sessions that the development of leisure activities was an important area of need for retarded people. Concern was expressed, however, that normalization should not be impeded by the development of special programs in the areas of art, music, dance, and drama, which might further isolate retarded individuals from the nonretarded. Furthermore, it was stressed that the responsibility for implementing cultural programs should rest with NARC's local units, working either independently or in concert with other community groups and organizations.

Based on those regional conferences, NARC's Board of Directors issued in October 1975 the following resolution:

> Now, therefore, it is hereby resolved that during the Bicentennial Year the National Association for Retarded Citizens convene a National Arts and Skills festival at which cultural skills of retarded citizens may be featured, such convocation to be held with adequate safeguards against competitiveness and special awards; and that this national endeavor be combined with local interest and effort to the end that community cultural resources and organizations include the mentally retarded within their service programs and activities.

As a followup to this resolution a program was presented at the 1976 NARC Annual Convention in Indianapolis involving mentally retarded performers and artists.

For many years, NARC has promoted the creative abilities of retarded people through its annual Art Design Contest. Since the project's inception in 1969, more than 45,000 paintings and drawings have been entered in the national contest. Retarded artists of all ages have submitted art forms from pen and ink to watercolors and oil.

Entries are judged locally and exhibited at suitable community events. Local winners compete in statewide contests. State winning designs are then submitted for the national competition, where they are evaluated by a panel of distinguished judges. The winning designs are used each year to create Christmas cards and calendars which are sold throughout the country. Each card and calendar identifies the winning artists as being mentally retarded. Brochures, news releases, and magazine articles highlight the artists. The program has been highly successful in educating the public regarding the capabilities of mentally retarded people.

In summary, since NARC's early beginning, it has recognized the importance of leisure activities in the total programming for retarded people. In most instances, retarded individuals can use existing community facilities and services. Nonetheless, the need continues to help retarded people avail themselves of these resources and teach them the skills that will enable them to achieve personal fulfillment.

BIBLIOGRAPHY

Addison, M.; Luckey, R.; and McCann, B. *Residential Programming for Mentally Retarded Persons: Developmental Programming in the Residential Facility.* Arlington, Texas: National Association for Retarded Children, 1972.

National Association for Retarded Citizens. *Retarded Citizens Need Recreation, Too.* Arlington, Texas: National Association for Retarded Citizens, 1975.

National Association for Retarded Citizens. *The Fullest Life.* Arlington, Texas: National Association for Retarded Citizens, 1976.

Nirje, B. "The Normalization Principle and Its Human Management Implications." In Kugel, R., and Wolfensberger, W. (Eds) *Changing Patterns in Residential Services for the Mentally Retarded.* Washington, D.C.: The President's Committee on Mental Retardation, 1969.

Roos, P. "Parent Organizations." In Wortis, J. (Ed.) *Mental Retardation — An Annual Review,* Vol. 3. New York: Grune and Stratton, 1970.

Roos, P. "Parents of Mentally Retarded People." *International Journal of Mental Health,* 1977, 6, 96-119.

Roos, P. "Action Implications of the Developmental Model." In Smith, D. and St. Louis, B. (Eds.) *Proceedings of a Symposium on Early Intervention: Steps in the Prevention of Developmental Handicaps.* Parsons, Kansas University Affiliated Facility, 1978.

Roos, P.; McCann, B. and Patterson, G. A Developmental Model of Mental Retardation. Arlington, Texas: National Association for Retarded Citizens, 1971.

Roos, P., and McCann, B. "Major Trends in Mental Retardation." *International Journal of Mental Health,* 1977, 6, 3-20.

Wolfensberger, W. *The Principle of Normalization in Human Services.* Toronto: National Institute on Mental Retardation, 1972.

Structure 10. Imitation of a child's movement, called *mirroring* or *reflecting*, is a technique frequently used in dance therapy and adapted/developmental dance. Here the group mirrors the arm movements, postures, and facial expressions of a boy with Down's Syndrome.

Chapter 8

THE DANCE OF CHILDHOOD:
FOCUS ON WELLNESS,
NOT EMOTIONAL DISTURBANCE

LEE FULLER

Probably in no other field do we have to reckon with so many unknown quantities and nowhere do we become more accustomed to adopting methods that work, even though for a long time we may not know why they work. The irrational fullness of life has taught me never to discard anything, even when it goes against all our theories or otherwise admits of no immediate explanation.

Carl G. Jung

MOVEMENT is nonverbal and yet communicates, and movements never lie. All children, especially severely disturbed children, explore, discover, understand, and cope with their world primarily on a preverbal level. The inherent needs of the severely disturbed child in growing and developing are the same as those of any child, even though the development may be arrested or slow.

Movement is for growing and is essential for physical and mental well-being. A very young child discovers movements and experiments with them instinctively as he stretches, turns, rocks, climbs, and falls. He begins to discover the potentials inherent in his body. As his coordination increases and his needs and desires grow, he starts to experiment. In this way he learns how to alter the speed, dimension, direction, flow, and energy of his movements to suit his purposes. For a child, every experience involves physical exploration.

As a child grows older, he learns to internalize the control of his body and to manipulate his environment in a more self-directed, self-disciplined manner. The other side of the coin

75

must not be forgotten as the child is learning to internalize control. Spontaneity must be encouraged, nourished, and given a supportive environment in which to grow. As the growth and integration of these polar opposites develop, the child learns that he can use movement to express himself in ways uniquely his own. He grows in awareness and perception through each new discovery. His self-confidence increases as he realizes his ability to organize, alter, and develop what he has discovered. His rate of personal development is directly related to the amount of freedom he is given for exploration and the degree to which he is encouraged to use his own ideas and imagination.

Unforced, spontaneous movement is the dance of childhood. If he is permitted, the child will dance out spontaneously the compelling impulses of his life. And if given the opportunity to do so, he will feel gratification and pleasure in the experience of being able to express them so vividly with his body.

The use of dance and rhythmical movements can provide special children with such opportunities. Dance or movement therapy utilizes techniques of creative movement, spontaneous dance, pantomime, and other aspects of creativity. I contend, however, that when working with severely disturbed/psychotic children, dance/movement therapy is a *more* appropriate means to an end than would be an educational approach to creative movement.

Authentic movement responses (spontaneous, involved movement resulting from body awareness and accompanied by a readiness to move) are capable of eliciting unconscious material that will involve experiencing and relating on a feeling level. When this material starts to emerge from within the person, the phenomenon is much like a corked bottle being uncorked and tipped over. What flows forward is not a consciously selective process; it *all* comes forth. A trained dance/movement therapist must be prepared to guide and interact with this flow, to observe and interpret the movements, and nurture and foster that all-important central aspect, the relationship between therapist and child.

Dance and movement, as therapy, require intentional therapeutic intervention based on a relationship between child and therapist, with dance activities being specifically designed to promote the healthy integration of mind and body. What is dance/movement therapy? What are its purposes, aims, goals, and objectives? What are its elements when modified for severely emotionally disturbed children? The answers to these questions will be the focus of this chapter.

What Is Dance/Movement Therapy?

Dance/movement therapy is a form of psychotherapy in which the therapist utilizes movement interactions as the primary means for accomplishing therapeutic goals. The dance therapist extrapolates those ingredients from dance that enable the child to move toward a healthier functioning; movement is the medium used in creating a new dance — a dance of health.

Movement can acquaint the child with his physical self as the *source* of his felt-experiencing process. It thereby puts the child in touch with what his actual felt experience is. Movement then allows an opportunity to express outwardly and confirm these inner felt processes in a safe manner. Perhaps the child will eventually be able to achieve the next step, which is verbalization of these experiences, thereby clarifying further the ambivalent personal feelings, explicitly validating his experience and acknowledging full responsibility.

Dance therapy emphasizes rhythmical, expressive movement as a means of establishing initial contact with children who have lost that capacity. Sometimes the first step towards socialization is the moving in unison that occurs in a group hello.

First, of course, a child must have a sense of identity, and this requires the existence of another by whom one is known. Direct imitation of the child's movement, called reflecting or mirroring, can help to establish this crucial aspect of development. Dance therapy provides a safe and constructive atmosphere in which children can go through developmental stages, thereby increasing their trust and self-image. A cardinal rule under which dance therapists operate in order to create this safe and supportive atmosphere is to realize that no movement is "bi-

zarre" or wrong. Each child is accepted where he is. All movement is acceptable and the dance therapist can reflect this by
taking on the movement of the child, i.e. moving as the child
does.

Dance therapy is expressive, developmental, and physically
integrative. It reduces fragmentation and constriction. It is in-
clusive, meaning that the dance therapist can work with groups
or individuals; it includes verbal as well as nonverbal communication. It can be carried out in the community or the back
ward of the hospital. No group nor diagnostic category is ex-
empt from the benefits of dance therapy.

Who Is the Dance/Movement Therapist?

Who is the dance/movement therapist? She or he is usually a
person who is willing to take a job that is low paying and not
well-entrenched in institutional hierarchies. She must have an
extensive dance background. The more training one has had,
the more sensitive one becomes to relating in a kinesthetic
sense. The therapist must always work on increasing her own
movement repetoire, which will enable her to relate more
thoroughly, intuitively, and spontaneously. She must be able to
suggest alternative movement patterns. She does not perform;
she interacts and reacts. Her educational background is pre-
dominately in psychology or special education, along with
basic movement knowledge such as kinesiology and exercise
physiology.

Her observational skills must be well developed. The dance
therapist can use spontaneous dance for evaluating the needs of
the child. Several diagnostic or assessment tools have been developed for this purpose, effort-shape analysis being the most
notable.

The dance therapist often focuses on these aspects of movement while observing (1) degree of organization/disorganiza-
tion; (2) tension level; (3) action level; (4) directness/diffuseness;
(5) purposefulness; (6) degree of self-control; (7) self-injury behaviors; and (8) degree of subtleness/overtness of expression.
She is constantly sensitive to where the child is and encourages

the development of that uniqueness instead of imposing style. She is able to perceive and relate to the integrated aspects of each child in order to nurture that seed of health that exists in everyone. She is aware of the life-asserting elements of dance and its ability to renew a feeling of wholeness.

What Are the Goals of Dance Therapy?

What are the goals of dance therapy? Many practitioners have postulated various objectives and aims. The following list is a synthesis:

1. increase awareness
   a. heighten kinesthetic sensitivity
   b. increase awareness of self
   c. increase awareness of the space and its occupants around the child
2. extend flexibility of a person's movement and behavior repetoire
   a. gain skill for relating positively and satisfactorily
   b. acquire constructive coping responses to frustration and negative situations
3. acquire self-acceptance through acceptance and being accepted through the movement experiences
4. experience success in efforts to achieve, learn, and enjoy
5. release tension
6. to move from a one-to-one relationship into a group situation, thereby transfering more responsibility to the child for his own development and behavior
7. to provide an atmosphere in which conflict and hostility can be constructively channeled into body action and dance

What are the elements of a modified dance therapy program? In the beginning there must exist much structure. As awareness and trust evolve, the structure can lessen.

Sounds, instruments, and music are part of the dance therapy situation. They are used, however, only when the child indicates a readiness for such devices. It is advisable to start with a comfortably small space since the child can be overwhelmed by too much space. In a small group more interaction and observation can occur. Each therapist and her situation are unique, and by trial and error she will discover the best way to begin for her, her children, and her space.

Dressing in comfortable, flexible clothing is essential. The removing of shoes can become a ritual that can be a cue to elicit the appropriate psychological and physiological set for the child.

A circle is a natural formation for children and is one in which they can see each other sharing their movements. A feeling of unity is created. As often as possible, the therapist should try to follow the lead of the children. Those who do not wish to join can have a space left open just for them when they are ready to join. The floor is a structural limit and an awareness of this fact can help the children come together. It is the common base of support and is the surface on which they are grounded.

The therapist can use polarities or imitation very effectively. For instance, she can intersperse intense, excited movement with relaxation, again taking her cues from the children. She can move in a manner opposite to that of the child's movement or imitate it. She can exaggerate or understate the movements.

Putting all the above elements together provides a framework within which a dance therapist may work. Now, what are the methods? Delaney has summarized these methods:

1. *Spontaneous dance* allows the utilization of primitive motility reflex patterns, auditory reactions, visual activity, and spatial relationships. Giving expression to and stimulating primitive, unconscious fantasies allows children to express personal aims, capacities, and conflicts.
2. *Improvisation* allows a freedom for setting out to solve a problem by beginning with no preconception as to how it will be done and by permitting things in the immediate environment to work for the child in solving the problem.
3. Experience in *pantomime* activities offers opportunities for working with half-dance, half-acted, imitations of real actions and events through an experimenting with a mix-

ture of impersonation, dramatic movement, and dance, using large bodily movements. It helps to establish contact with reality and provides practice in the selection of appropriate movements for expressing specific emotions or feelings and necessitates a great deal of personal involvement.

4. *Dramatic play* provides children both a safety valve and an emotional catharsis. It offers opportunities for emotional control and inner self-disciplining.
5. *Movement exploration* is used as guided discovery in helping children find their own ways of working with images.
6. *Relaxation techniques* also offer ways for children to get in conscious touch with their bodies.

The task of the dance therapist is not always an onward and upward experience. There are many delays and setbacks. Progress is notoriously slow and at times the therapist can become quite discouraged. A child psychologist once told a dance therapist that she might better understand what she was doing if she saw her work thusly: "You are providing an environment in which things will happen. Your job is to make that environment a special place and time where children may come and take or give as they can. Their ability to do so depends on many factors, most of which are out of your hands. What is important is that the opportunity for them to grow and learn through movement is left open to them."

BIBLIOGRAPHY

Alperson, Erma Dosamantes. *The Creation of Meaning Through Body Movement*. Stanford, California: Stanford Press, 1974.

Delaney, Wynelle. "Dance Therapy with Emotionally Disturbed Children in a Psychoeducation Day Hospital Program." *ADTA, Monograph, No. 3*. Columbia, Maryland: ADTA Press, 1974.

Espenak, Liljan. "A Non-verbal Approach to Personality Evaluation." Lecture presented at AAMD, Region 10 Conference at Provincetown, Massachusetts, September 27-29, 1970.

Koslow, Sally Platkin. "New, Exciting Direction in Psychiatry: Dance/Music/Art Therapy." *Mademoiselle Magazine*, January 1976.

Puder, Miriam. "Dance Therapy for the Emotionally Disturbed and/or Neurological Impaired Child: A Field Study." Unpublished M.A. thesis, Newark State College, Newark, New Jersey, 1972.

Schmais, Claire. "Dance Therapy in Perspective." *Dance Therapy: Focus on Dance VII*. Washington, D.C.: AAHPER Publications, 1974.

Smallwood, Joan Chodorow. "Dance-Movement Therapy." *Current Psychiatric Therapies*, 1974, 14.

Structure 11. Wynelle Delaney leads training sessions on therapeutic relationships and dance/creative movement. Top: Group experiences trust as members lean against each other while lowering bodies in "bookends" activity. Bottom: Group practices mirroring one another's movements.

Chapter 9

FABRICS, BALLS, AND PILLOWS IN DANCE AND MOVEMENT DISCOVERY

WYNELLE DELANEY

THE physical environment of the setting in which dance and/or movement discovery takes place can be designed to elicit certain behaviors. Some materials (like yarn balls, soft fabrics, and comfortable pillows) seem more effective than others in encouraging positive growth and development.

Nylon Fabrics

— The beauty of moving with them through space. Wrapping up in to feel tightness and limitation, exploring ways to move within the tightness. Rolling up — then unrolling back out on the floor. Getting covered while standing, then turning round and round spinning them off, or having others pluck them off one by one as you turn. Getting covered while lying down to be "buried," tucked into bed, or just simply to watch the room change colors. Beautiful, flowing costumes and capes. Moving to the feeling-quality in the colors—

In response to the floating, smooth quality of colorful nylons children move rhythmically stretching, turning, reaching, and covering themselves in various ways. Their actions seem to reflect a sensuous enjoyment and an aesthetic awareness as the fabrics float and move across their bodies. Paradoxically, the soft fabrics can become a factor in spatial structuring as well. At times, when children feel extremely tense and seem to have a need for containment, being wrapped completely immobile in the full width of the fabric, by either turning when standing or rolling when lying down, will have a relaxing and quieting effect. Without speaking directly to such needs, children will ask for this kind of containment by suggesting familiar activities that have included it in other movement contexts.

Nylon fabrics also provide an intermediary focus for children who find it difficult to relate directly to other persons. Spin-arounds, with partners holding opposite ends of the fabric, aid in keeping distance yet staying together. Wrap-up spin-outs allow a moment's closeness, with access to quick and immediate freedom from nearness. Imaginative play and imagery occur with the fabric being used as such items as clothing, costumes, bedding, housing, and light-shielding to put a color glow in a darkened room. Aggressiveness is accommodated by wrapping a soft yarn ball inside one end of the fabric and throwing it as if it were a comet streaming through space. "Dodge fabric" has aggressive moments of fun and beauty combined when one or several fabrics are loosely wadded into a ball and thrown at a moving human target. The floating open of the fabric(s) while traveling in space sometimes creates unusual beauty. Children also like to lie down and be covered completely, using one fabric at a time in layering fashion. As the layers of fabrics deepen, children typically comment on the constant change of color and on the increasing dimness through the emerging thickness.

Tubular Stretch-Knit Fabric

— For crawling on, walking on, sleeping on, being pulled around on, swung on, being rolled across. For going inside, making shapes, rolling around in, being swung around in, getting stuffed into, being dragged around, going through a tunnel. Can see outside from inside but people can't see you — can fight, snarl, rage safely tucked inside, can curl up and make baby sounds. Gentle rocking-swinging to sleep for dream pantomime work —

Soft, stretchy, tubular knit fabrics approximately three yards long have soothing, protecting properties. The tubular fabrics make excellent "hammocks" on which to lie and be swung. When persons alternate in lifting ends of the fabric, causing the body to roll from one end to the other, a special sensation of being moved in space is felt. An interesting sensation of directional change is experienced when running and charging forward into a tauntly stretched fabric that "gives" then bounces the person off backwards. Stretch-tube fabrics lend themselves well to nondirected dramatic play and fantasy-action. They become roads, rivers, roofs, "ghosts," hooded persons, Roman togas, stuffed sausages, pickles, grass, and tunnels. Playing inside stretch tube fabrics adds further dimension to their use. It is a way for children to shield themselves from direct observation and physical touch contact with other persons while at the same time being able to look out through the fabric and see the persons. When working inside, the fabrics can become an open-ended tunnel to explore, or a closed and safe haven for being swung, rolled, dragged gently around the floor, or for pretending all alone in fantasy-action.

Inside the fabrics can also become a place to experiment with making different shapes and forms by bending and extending body parts against the softly resilient material. When lying outside on the fabric, being swung gently, spontaneous pantomime of "dreams" is easily evoked. These "dreams" touch deeply into children's subconscious urges and needs; the expressive body action accompanying the dream fantasies allows for safe catharsis and emotional release of tensions reflected in the dream content. The fabrics provide for rocking and swaying when children need comforting and relaxing, without working openly or directly with those needs. "Games" that have been experienced earlier when the children were simply exploring the use of the fabrics can be repeated when the need for comforting or soothing arises.

Yarn Balls

— More structured and functionally demanding activities are done with rhythmically synchronized toss, catch, and rolling games. Isolations of body parts can be experienced by bouncing the ball off different parts of the body or by contacting the ball with a specific body part before releasing and passing it on to another person. In dramatic play and fantasy-action, balls become various kinds of foods, jewels, rocks, rockets, bombs, and the "equipment" for pretend games of baseball, kickball, touch football, and bowling —

Yarn balls, about six inches in diameter, permit many varieties of throwing activities for imaginative play as well as safe release of aggressive tensions. Imaginative ideation about different ways to throw, jump with, and bat the ball stimulate alternative ways of thinking as well as encourage children to risk expressing their ideas. Warm-up stretches are executed by using different body positions to transfer the ball to the next recipient. One-to-one synchronization of full body action occurs when partners try to support a ball between them with various parts of their bodies while traveling across the room. Yarn balls can be used purposefully aggressively for "bowling" and dodge ball. There is also volleyball for competition. Balls can also be kept rolling around the floor by hand-batting vigorously back and forth.

DIRECTIONS FOR MAKING YARN BALLS: Use two stiff, cardboard discs six inches in diameter; cut a hole in the center of each two inches in diameter. Make a shuttle of a thin piece of wood about one-and-a-half to one-and-three-quarters inches wide and about twelve inches long, with each end slant-slotted knotched to hold wool that is wound on it. Use four ounces of wool, different colors, from old sweaters raveled or odds and ends of wool left from knitting, or new wool.

Wind wool on shuttle. It will not be possible to wind all of it on at one time. Place the two discs together and wind wool around the edge by passing the shuttle through the center, keeping the strands of wool even. Keep going round and round until all the wool is used. The covered disc will be about two inches thick when finished. Lay the wool-covered discs on a flat surface placing the palm of your hand flat on top (or lay the discs between two saucers and press down). Cut through the widest edge of the wool toward the two discs with a very sharp razor blade or knife. When you can freely get to the outer edge of the two discs insert a piece of heavy twine or string between them, wrapping it around the inside center twice. Pull very tight and tie securely. The wool will pop up. Remove the cardboard discs and you have a wonderfully safe toy. Remember to keep your hand or the saucers contacting the wrapped wool at all times until you have wrapped the twine in the center. If you don't wrap twine tightly the wool will work loose. Trim to circular ball after you've tossed and fluffed the ball a bit.

Multi-Colors of Velveteen Pillows

— For sitting on, standing on, jumping onto from different spots on the floor, moving around or over them in different patterns and shapes. Padded targets for jumping from high places, easy balancing on heads for walking, gliding, dancing around, for sitting down and standing up without using hands. Playing catch with as many as a person can hold at once — building up one-by-one. Portable floor mat for practicing acrobatic tricks. All sorts of make-believe objects. Softness to cuddle —

Velveteen pillows of different hues, about twelve by twelve inches in size, provide additional ways of working with gross body coordination, satisfying aggressive urges, enriching fantasy work, and simply enjoying softness and beauty. The challenge of simultaneously catching steadily increasing numbers of pillows (sometimes up to ten) changes light-hearted festivity into serious cooperative work. There is much pride when young arms can encircle a "bear hug" catch on so many pillows.

Balancing something as large and soft as a pillow on the head fosters success in walking and "dancing" around the room while maintaining the pillow above. It also creates a built-in change of pace from strong, throwing/catching movements into smoothly gentle sustained/gliding qualities of action. Further, a need is created for becoming aware of precisely where the body is and what it is doing as it moves through space. Changing of levels from standing to sitting on the floor, then rising back up again while the pillow remains on the head is quite demanding on physical skills of children. It can be fun or frustrating and requires discretion by the dance therapist for use as an activity.

Pillows can be spaced in patterns around the floor within

reaching distance of jumps, hops, or leaps. These ways of moving from pillow to pillow at different forces of strength, tempos, or directions (front, side, backwards, turning) provide a brief interlude of imaginative physical challenge. The space between the pillows can be used similarly: zigzagging around, running through, or crawling by without making physical contact with the pillows.

Placing pillows closely together in a double row makes a child-size "gym mat" for practicing front and back somersaults, front dives, walkovers, back bends, back limbers, and other beginning acrobatic/gymnastic efforts. It seems to be a relief and a release for the child to have a place to come that is free from comparative work with a larger group to practice new body actions being learned in the physical education setting.

Pillow targets aid the child in gaining courage to jump from a "high" place to the floor — the landings are softened. As expertise in jumping emerges, the number of pillows required for the landing site diminishes. Self-challenge begins taking over as self-confidence is gained, and distance as well as height become the jumping goals for the child. He experiences for brief moments the delicious feel of flying through space and landing on his own two feet. The more agile child will at times continue further and work into tagging on a forward somersault as he lands, which can end for him coming to standing up fully erect. Facial expressions of children who accomplish this kind of physical autonomy are a joy to behold.

When children are in aggressive moods, or seem to need strong moving-out efforts of energy, pillows make excellent targets at which to throw other pillows or yarn balls (a la bowling). The pillows can be teepee-stacked in twos or threes on the floor waiting to be toppled over with a throw; they can be tower-stacked to be knocked down all at once or pillow by pillow; or, they can be singly balanced against a ballet barre or any elevated supporting object to be target-practiced at like duck silhouettes in a shooting gallery. Ways that provide controlled and indirect permission for aggression seem to release muscular tension while easing anxiety about "acting out" impulses of fury or aggression.

In fantasy work, pillows become thrones for royalty, beds to sleep on, roads to walk on, rocks to fall on, fortress and castle walls to hide behind during battles, babies in abdomen, fat-people padding, stuffing for sausages inside stretch-tube fabrics, steering wheels on boats, lifejacket seats, moon rocks. Their identities seem limitless.

There are times, as well, when pillows are simply for cuddling to, staying near, or lying upon for comfort and rest, or for hiding under. Pillows go the range from being the most impersonal of the materials used in the sessions to the most comforting of things to be found. Their soothing powers with the children seem, in many ways, related to their being a substitute softness for human softness. On the other hand, they tend to reinforce distance between people by making direct relating to one another fairly difficult. In general, the use of pillows seems to be a very personal, rather than shared, thing.

Structure 12. Preschool mentally retarded children learn directions and body parts through movement exploration in circle formation as a lead-up activity to square and folk dance.

Chapter 10

SQUARE DANCING FOR AMBULATORY SEVERELY MENTALLY RETARDED CHILDREN

OLLIE BROWN

SQUARE dance is one of the most effective of the creative arts in teaching social skills. It also provides a medium through which the children can learn to respond to rhythm, follow directions, develop coordination, and learn balance. Properly taught, it can also lead to increased perceptual-motor efficiency. The activities which follow contribute specifically to laterality, directionality, and improved temporal and spatial relationships.

Laterality	Buzz Swing; Right and Left Hand Stars; Right and Left Elbow Swings
Directionality	Moving forward, backward, left, or right; Calls directed to opposites
Temporal Relationships	Stepping in place to the rhythm of the music; Walking in time to the rhythm of the music; Clapping rhythms

Teaching

Points to Remember

Select simple dances. Simple dances may not need to be modified; if so, very little modification will be necessary.

Select single and double visitation figure types. These figure types offer continuous repetition that enable children to remember their positions and direction of progression around the square. Symmetrical figures may be used with success. There is *continuous repetition* of all couples simultaneously executing

93

the same action. Individual dancers progress around the set so that each has a new partner for the repetitions of the figure, such as "Arkansas Traveler."

Demonstrate. In addition to teacher demonstration, use various couples or individuals as models.

Dance with each child. This will help the child acquire a feeling of rhythm and develop a sense of the line of direction.

Select any hoedown record. Hoedown music makes learning simple because a continuous definite rhythm is present and there is absence of a clearly defined melody.

Select records without calls. This will give the teacher latitude in calling at different speeds, modifying the figure creating, or doing whatever is necessary.

Encourage children to help each other.

Keep the class or group under control. Constantly remind the children to give their attention to what they are doing. Emphasize following directions.

Always give praise to individuals or to the class or group.

Methods and Materials

Masking tape can be used to indicate positions as shown in Figure 10-1. The tape should be placed on the floor in front of each couple's home position. This will help the children to maintain a square formation and form circles. A colorful wrist band or ribbon can be worn on the wrist to help the children to learn left and/or right. When the children are required to make whole turns or half turns, they should be instructed to focus on one object in the room that will serve as a cue to begin or stop.

When necessary, dances should be modified. This can be done by deleting original parts and creating substitute parts. For example:

Star By the Right (Traditional)	*Star By the Right* (Modified)
First couple out to the couple on the right	First couple out to the couple on the right (red)

Form a star with right hand crossed	Form a star with right (red) hand crossed
Back with the left and don't get lost	Back with the left (green) and don't get lost
Form a ring and around you go	One step in and circle right (red)

To use the command "One step in and circle right" helps the children begin and maintain a well-formed circle while moving. In executing, one step is taken to a position just in front of the guide tape before moving to the right. The colors red and green have reference to the wrist bands which may be worn to help the children learn right and/or left. The colors can be substituted in the command. If the children have difficulty forming stars with raised arms as shown in Figure 10-1, then modify by instructing them to lower the arms to the center as shown in Figure 10-2.

The methods used to teach square dance to severely mentally retarded children do not differ very much from those used to

Figure 10-1. Star by the Right.

Figure 10-2. Easier progression for Star by the Right.

teach normal children. Basically, it is a matter of modifying the dance skills and patterns of movement. Success in teaching severely mentally retarded children to dance is dependent upon an expedient and creative teacher.

BIBLIOGRAPHY

Beter, Thais, and Cragin, Wesley E. *The Mentally Retarded Child and His Motor Behavior.* Springfield: Charles C Thomas, 1972.

Fait, Hollis F. *Special Physical Education.* Philadelphia: W. B. Saunders, 1972.

Ginglend, David. *The Expressive Arts for the Mentally Retarded.* Arlington, Texas: National Association for Retarded Citizens, 1967.

Grassman, Cyrus. "Modified Folk and Square Dancing for the Mentally Retarded." *The Physical Educator,* 1958, *15*, 32-35.

Moran, Joan May, and Kalakian, Leonard Harris. *Movement Experiences for the Mentally Retarded or Emotionally Disturbed Child.* Minneapolis: Burgess, 1977.

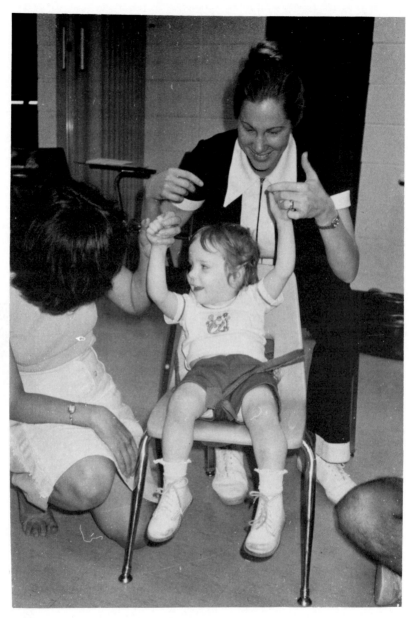

Structure 13. Dancing has many meanings. In working with the severely handicapped, dance may mean moving body parts to music. When the child can move his own arms, a helper may push the chair in rhythmical patterns about the room.

Chapter 11

WHERE THERE'S A WILL: ADAPTING WHEELCHAIR DANCE TO THE SEVERELY DISABLED

Wanda Jean Rainbolt

Asked what they preferred to do at the next meeting of their Recreation Club, the group voted unanimously for dancing. But how do you dance with someone who is so severely handicapped he cannot maneuver his own wheelchair without assistance? Some of the group members had cerebral palsy; others were disabled by spinal cord injuries, polio, or spina bifida. Like all young adults, however, they wanted to dance!

Dance or dancing has many meanings. In working with the severely handicapped, dance may mean moving body parts in a rhythmic and patterned sequence accompanied by music. The movements of the body may consist of the following: a raising and lowering of the arms, clapping the hands, raising the feet, touching the feet together, touching the hands to the thighs, touching the hands to the knees, shaking the hands, feet, head, and bending the upper body at the waist forward, to name a few.

Dancing offers many benefits for the severely handicapped: social, physical, and psychological. Social benefits derived from dance are the contact with other people who may have dance as a hobby; the opportunity to overcome shyness in order to develop new friends with common interests; a chance to mingle with individuals of the opposite sex and those with a different handicapping condition; and new experiences to teach etiquette and respect as one meets and converses with others. This is part of the socialization process that nonhandicapped individuals have experienced and taken for granted. However, many severely handicapped persons have not had the opportunity to socialize because of limited transportation, restrictive living environment, and architectural barriers.

The physical benefits are the opportunity to develop rhythm, balance, and poise. Physical fitness can be improved by a repetition of the dances, which demands continuous movement of the body and stimulates the cardiovascular system.

Another important benefit for the severely handicapped population is psychological. The participants are experiencing the satisfaction of achieving, maybe for the first time in their life. The experience may be unique with the learning of new movements and new routines. There is an opportunity for the individual to learn about his body and to find an outlet for his emotions. Dancing is a lifetime activity that should contribute toward the severely handicapped being accepted by society.

As the severely handicapped are confined to wheelchairs, there are many factors to consider when selecting a building in which to dance. Some of these considerations are the size of the room, the doors and doorways, the floor, restrooms, water fountains, and parking. The selected room should be large enough to allow movement of the wheelchairs without repeated collision of one wheelchair into another. The controls for the room such as lights should be placed within easy reach of the people in wheelchairs. Other criteria to be followed include the following:

1. The doorways should be at least thirty-two inches wide in order for the wheelchair to move easily through. The doors should open and close with ease.
2. The floors should be of a nonslippery consistency without carpeting. If carpeted, the indoor-outdoor carpet is better than a deep pile carpet, allowing better mobility.
3. The restrooms need to have an area large enough to allow the wheelchairs to be turned. One toilet stall must be of proper dimensions to accommodate a wheelchair.
4. Water fountains should be no higher than three feet with controls and spout at the front.
5. Parking area for handicapped individuals only should be properly identified and close to the building. Ramps are

necessary if there are steps at the entrance to the building and in the pathway of the designated dance room.

The teaching techniques used with the severely handicapped are similar to those employed with other populations with a few modifications. The dance session begins by becoming acquainted with the dancers. This is achieved through the use of name tags on everyone to add more humanism to the session. The ambulatory people should pin their name tags on their waist in clear view of the wheelchair participants. The dance instructor should talk to the group about what is going to happen during the session and the dances to be learned. The general rules for the session, including the use of building, the location of the restroom and drinking fountain, should be announced.

The record player with an adjustment control that can slow the music down is ideal, as more time is needed than usual to make maneuvers with wheelchairs. A selection of music with a strong beat and easy rhythm is recommended. Allow the dancers time to listen to the music at regular speed, then slow the music to the danceable speed. Next, have the dancers clap their hands to the underlying beat. Demonstrate the dance as the dancer would be executing it. Arrange dancers into the desired formation in the room. Walk through a part of the dance with the instructor being in the view of each dancer. Because the severely handicapped are unable to maneuver their wheelchairs, ambulatory volunteers are needed to move the wheelchairs. This couple counts as one unit when adapting dances. Executing a walk step for four beats would be cued as walk, walk, walk, walk. For the nonambulatory people the cue would be roll, roll, roll, roll or roll, 2, 3, 4. We can visualize that the nonambulatory participants are receiving nothing but a nice ride if the wheelchair dance contains mainly walking steps. We need to involve them more actively. Therefore, routines are developed for involvement of the upper body. The routine may consist of slapping the hands on the thighs for the count of one, then clapping the hands together in front of the body for the count of two, snapping the fingers in the air for the count of three, and returning to the front of the body with a hand clap for the count of four. Many variations are possible, but the leader should be consistent with one pattern for each dance, keeping dancers active by moving parts of the upper body, the lower body, and/or both.

The dance should be taught in parts, separately, without music, using many repetitions; then practiced to music at the reduced tempo with many more repetitions. The session continues in this manner until the entire dance has been taught.

The instructor should continuously be giving praise and encouragement to the group. Cueing by use of a microphone or descriptive words in time to the music is most helpful to the dancers. The instructor should be enthusiastic, positive, and possess a genuine interest in the teaching of dance to others.

In instructing the severely handicapped to dance, remember to smile. A smile will soon become contagious; what can be more rewarding than a room of smiling dancers? These severely handicapped people need a person who is "special," therefore be warm, friendly, helpful, and happy!

BIBLIOGRAPHY

Harris, Jane; Pittman, Anne; and Waller, Marlys S. *Dance a While.* Minneapolis: Burgess, 1978.

Hill, Kathleen. *Dance for Physically Disabled Persons.* Washington, D.C.: American Alliance for Health, Physical Education, and Recreation, 1976.

Jensen, Mary Bee, and Jensen, Clayne R. *Folk Dancing.* Provo: Brigham Young University Press, 1973.

Moran, Joan May, and Kalakian, Leonard Harris. *Movement Experiences for the Mentally Retarded or Emotionally Disturbed Child.* Minneapolis: Burgess, 1977.

For further information on wheelchair activities, subscribe to *Sports' N Spokes,* 5201 North 19th Avenue, Suite 108, Phoenix, Arizona 85015.

For wheelchair square dancing instructions on a thirty-minute cassette tape, Colorado Wheelers, 525 Meadowlark Drive, Lakewood, Colorado 80226.

Structure 14. Dr. Peter Wisher uses the drum to convey rhythm to members of his deaf performing modern dance group at Gallaudet College.

Chapter 12

DANCE FOR THE DEAF

Peter R. Wisher

In recent years, dance as an educational medium has been receiving greater emphasis. In many ways it is evident that the dance area is booming. There is indeed an explosion of confidence in dance as a contributing factor in the educational process.

At Gallaudet College, the only liberal arts college for the deaf in the world, the performing modern dance group was created in 1955. The idea for the group first evolved when I saw the students signing the Lord's Prayer in the old chapel. It has such beautiful movement, such meaningful communication, that I knew the movement could be adapted for dance. Thus at Gallaudet College over the years we have developed a new art form. In essence it is the transformation of signs to dance movement. For example, a sign used in communication is abstracted, thus making it a dance movement. Stories, poems, and songs are choreographed and subsequently danced in this manner.

The Gallaudet Modern Dance Group has performed throughout the United States and Europe. It is living proof that deaf persons can be creative, graceful in movement, and skillful in dance. The teaching techniques used with this group seem applicable to deaf children and youth of all ages. For the hearing, dance can be considered as a supplementary vehicle in the learning process. For the deaf, it is an indispensable tool. In view of the limited learning avenues available to the deaf, it seems reasonable to assume that dance can provide a learning environment that enhances the development of self-expression, aesthetic awareness, social relationships, vocabulary, etc.

In my opinion, three areas should be considered: (1) the deaf, (2) communication, and (3) practical teaching suggestions for the teacher of the deaf.

The Deaf

It seems logical to assume that anyone interested in teaching the deaf should be aware of certain characteristics associated with deafness. The primary one is deafness per se. Inasmuch as a hearing loss varies from a mild condition to one of profound deafness, an exact definition is elusive. One estimate, in light of the above, indicates that there are approximately 2,000,000 hearing-impaired individuals in this country.

Several studies cited at the end of this chapter have indicated that an educational, social, and emotional disparity exists between the deaf and their hearing peers. One researcher reported that the deaf were retarded from four to seven years behind their hearing counterparts; others stated that normal acquisition of language was not possible for the deaf; three studies found the deaf to be socially immature, subject to impulsive behavior, and egocentric; another reported that the deaf possessed certain deficiencies with respect to abstracting and conceptualizing.

Based on over two decades of teaching the deaf, with the exception of acquisition of language, I feel that the above reported findings are of questionable validity. Of course, some deaf individuals possess the negative characteristics mentioned above, but I have found the exact opposite to be true. In fairness, I must add that my contacts have been with undergraduate students and my observations may not be true of the total population.

The most questionable deficiencies attributed to the deaf, abstracting and conceptualizing, I find totally unacceptable. Many of our students major in mathematics, drama, computer science, art, etc. In the area of dance, I have never witnessed more creativity and total involvement.

Communication

The most critical aspect, as well as the most controversial, is the manner of communication used by the deaf. After years of contacts with students and adults, I feel strongly that the so-called "simultaneous" or "total" method is the most effective. This method employs the language of signs, manual alphabet, speech, and speechreading. The best of two worlds, manual communication and speech, can be utilized.

Anyone who has an interest in teaching the deaf must acquire proficiency in manual communication. I can conceive of no way I could have achieved the success attained with the deaf dancers without resorting to this method. I might add that classes in sign language are available in most large cities, schools for the deaf, and some universities.

Practical Teaching Considerations

By no means is it possible to discuss all of the numerous aspects associated with dance and the deaf. A few that I consider essential will be presented below.

Accompaniment. After many years of experimenting, one instrument seems to be the most effective aid in teaching the deaf rhythms — the drum. All of the deaf either hear or feel basic rhythms through the use of this one instrument. Some hear the drum, but most rely on the feel of the vibrations it creates — as a metronome.

Recorded music is employed once the patterns are mastered. Of course, those individuals with some residual hearing can make use of amplified music — both as a learning device and as a source of satisfaction. The dance group at Gallaudet College has recently acquired two speakers which provide a high level of amplification. These loudspeakers placed directly on a wooden floor increase the intensity of vibrations. Also, the use of bass tones seems to enhance vibratory reception. It follows that this mechanism has proven invaluable in teaching, learning, and performing. It should be noted, however, that one profoundly deaf dancer placed her ear against one of the speakers and indicated to me that she heard nothing.

TACTILE CUES. The deaf appear to have a keen sense of awareness to any vibratory movement — visual, sound, or tactual. I have, on countless occasions, observed the deaf touch a musical instrument. From such contact, they not only obtain insight into rhythm, but also a sense of satisfaction.

In both the literature on deafness and in contacts with individuals, I have read and heard that the deaf dance to vibrations. This assumption is without doubt the most widely held belief concerning deaf dancers and the one with the least credibility. Under no circumstances can I envision a deaf person moving through space and still keeping contact with a "vibrating" floor.

INTRINSIC RHYTHM. A few years ago I became aware of a factor which I will call an intrinsic awareness of rhythm. For hearing dancers, this aspect may be considered as a useful concomitant in the area of dance; for the deaf, it is an essential element. All of a sudden I became aware of how rhythmic all of life is: heart beat, walking gait, breathing, sun rise, ad infinitum. This latent trait could serve as a useful, much-needed aid to learning in general, and as a source of self-expression, physical activity, social involvement, and as an emotional outlet.

SIGN LANGUAGE DANCE. The deaf have made a significant contribution to the creative arts in this country, as well as abroad, by incorporating signs in dances, songs, and poetry. This system of communication serves as a useful base in various forms of choreography. One definition of dance states that it is "communication through movement." In this light, the deaf have been "dancing" all their lives, since movement is so frequently employed in daily communication.

CREATIVITY. Because the deaf use movement to a great extent in communicating, it seems logical to assume that creating movements for dance would be a simple extension of this mode of communication. I must comment on a class in beginning modern dance that I am currently directing. This past week I gave them two subjects for student creation: a swinging series and "Jingle Bells." I was astounded at what happened: total involvement, social interrelationships, laughter — but most of all, the end product. Anyone who states that the deaf are lacking in abstracting abilities, in my opinion, must lack a certain amount of perception.

Because the deaf often appear to be limited in attaining optimum communication skills, they seem to possess great motivation and to derive tremendous satisfaction from participation in creative movement. One of my regrets is that educators of the deaf are not making use of this exceptional tool in the learning process with children. Some inroads are being made, but the extent is minimal.

DANCE AND SPEECH. One of the disturbing factors to me in the education of the deaf is the excessive emphasis in both time and budget placed upon speech and speechreading. For some deaf, skill in speaking and lipreading is an unattainable goal. I have met many deaf students who went to hearing schools all their lives and still did not possess a satisfactory level of oral communication.

It is not my intent to downgrade efforts to improve speech. All should strive to improve the hearing-impaired in this area. The environment provided in the dance studio seems to be ideal for teaching speech as well as use of audible sounds. I cannot recall a class in which I taught "Silent Night" that some student in class was not "singing" the lyrics. We have also sung rounds, i.e. "Three Blind Mice."

GENERAL TEACHING HINTS. Because it is impossible to detail the numerous salient points in teaching dance to the deaf, I shall comment, briefly, upon factors I feel are significant in this area.

1. The teacher should go "from the known to the unknown." Start at a point the students understand and then proceed to the unknown. It would be foolish to start with ballet movements if the students had no previous knowledge of this dance form.

2. Students "will do that which is satisfying and avoid that which is irritating." There must be a resulting satisfaction from participation. Rapport between student and teacher is of paramount importance.

3. Individual differences must be considered by the teacher. The social environment from which the student comes should also be a concern. In one area clog dancing may be of interest to students; in another, the "hustle" and disco dancing. Age and social maturation are factors to be evaluated in a dance

program.

4. Ideally, all boys and girls should participate in some form of dance, from preschool years through college. Due to the social mores in some communities, dance in general is frowned upon; in others, this opinion holds for boys only. An effort must be made for all to accept the concept that dance is a worthwhile activity in the educational process.

BIBLIOGRAPHY

Department of Medical Genetics, New York State Psychiatric Institute. *Family and Mental Health Problems in a Deaf Population.* New York: Columbia University Press, 1963.

Myklebust, Helmer. *The Psychology of Deafness.* New York: Grune and Stratton, 1964.

Report of the Proceedings of the International Congress of the Education of the Deaf and the 41st Meeting of the Convention of American Instructors of the Deaf, Gallaudet College. Washington, D.C.: U. S. Government Printing Office, 1964.

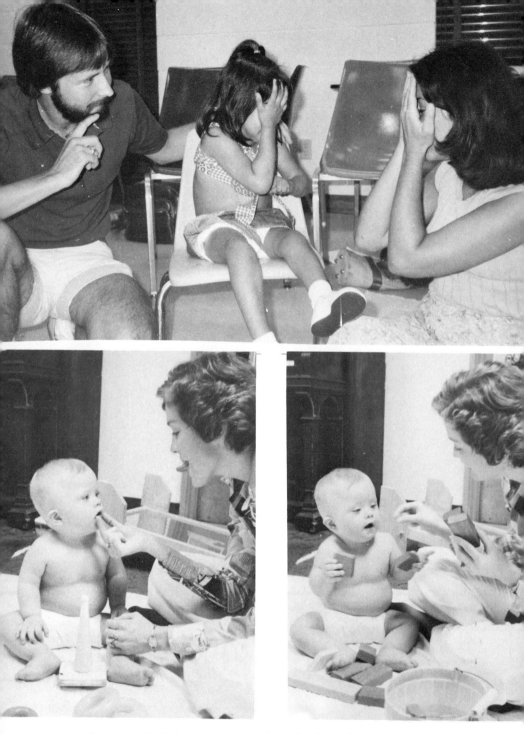

Structure 15. Body image activities to stimulate self-awareness are an integral part of early arts training. Top: Child with cerebral palsy learns a peek-a-boo sequence to music. Bottom: infant with Down's syndrome is provided tactile stimulation activities, first to find his tongue and then to feel textures of blocks with his hands.

Chapter 13

AESTHETIC AWARENESS THROUGH A MULTISENSORY APPROACH TO THE INTEGRATED ARTS

Lauren Routon

The desire of man to express himself is a basic human need. The wonder and joy of experiencing activities of an aesthetic nature belong to everyone; communication of our emotions through the arts tells us much about our culture. It is by outward expression either graphically, dramatically, or intellectually that man internalizes the things he has experienced and heightens his understanding of things. Aesthetic activities add a rich dimension to a symbolic and abstract world as he searches for order.

Anne Quan Uno

TRADITIONALLY defined as "a study of art and the nature of beauty," *aesthetics* for the severely handicapped must be interpreted as multifaceted emotional experiences that involve all of the senses: sight, sound, smell, taste, touch, and kinesthesis. Anne Uno's beautiful book *Aesthetic Activities for Handicapped Children* offers many ideas for using the creative arts to develop aesthetic awareness.

This chapter is an attempt to apply some of Uno's ideas, as well as my own, to the severely and profoundly handicapped. When working with such persons, it is best not to fragment the creative arts into music, dance, drama, and art but to blend them together so that all of the child's sense modalities are stimulated simultaneously.

Music, for instance, is often approached through making sounds with rhythmic instruments. The young severely handicapped child may, however, drop a rattle that is put in his hand or try to eat a tambourine. Clearly, background music with a strong percussive beat that elicits a desire to move is necessary. The child may initially move his entire body or "dance" to such background music rather than calling forth the fine muscle control required to manipulate rhythm instruments. Who can label such a creative arts session as either music or dance? It is obviously a combination.

Some children move more readily to words or chants than music. In this case the setting might be labeled dramatics since words usually elicit ideas. Orff-Schulwerk techniques seem to capitalize on these ideas with both chants and percussion instruments repetitively challenging a child to move. Creative dance classes for children have long used the idea of moving to familiar nursery rhymes.

Movement to Nursery Rhymes

1. The children scatter and sit on the floor or stand with much space between them. They are told they can use all the space in the room but can not touch anyone else.
2. The teacher enthusiastically tells a nursery rhyme emphasizing the movement words told in the story. "Jack and Jill *ran* up the hill to *fetch* a pail of water. Jack *fell* down, etc."

The children should be encouraged to move according to what is being said. The teacher should go slow enough to allow the children time to create their story of movement. Some severely handicapped children are so frozen into immobility that the teacher may need to take their bodies and/or limbs and manually manipulate them through the expected movements over and over again.

Severely handicapped children also often have difficulty with abstractions, i.e. running up a hill when no hill exists in the flat surface of a floor or concrete play area; fetching a pail of water when no pail is in sight. The creative teacher will therefore try to have a dance lesson featuring Jack and Jill out of doors where a small hill can be found, ideally near a water hydrant or stream of water. A bucket or pail should be readily available. Children must first be led through dancing *realities*

before they can be guided into activities of *pretending* and *coping with abstractions.*

Other Creative Arts Activities Related to Nursery Rhymes

Art activities can be integrated into a Jack and Jill series of guided discovery sessions by having children use clay to build landscapes of level land with hills. Toy dolls, clothespin figures, or other objects can then be used to simulate running up the hill and falling down.

Pictures and three-dimensional models of objects should be used to set the stage in creative arts activities. This visual aid assures that the child knows what the teacher is talking about. For instance, *pail* and many other words in nursery rhymes and verse are old fashioned and probably not a part of the child's experience or vocabulary. Most of us say *bucket.* An institutionalized child may never have experienced filling a bucket and in such cases it might be better to say "to get a *cup* of water.

Whenever possible, it is good to involve the gustatory and olfactory senses. A session on Jack and Jill should certainly include tasting the water. Aerosol cans of spray or cologne or burning incense that smells like the out-of-doors would appropriately involve the severely handicapped child more intensely in the creative arts experience.

For severely handicapped children who seldom get out-of-doors, the Jack and Jill session may be extended into nature study by asking such questions as "What do you see when you go up the hill? Trees? Flowers? Bugs? Animals? Is the ground dry or wet? Hard or soft? Smooth and nice or full of sticker burrs? What is the sky like?" Each of these questions can lead to pantomime and other drama forms. On a warm day without wind the dance/drama/music lesson may culminate in drawing, sketching, painting, or clay modeling the things one sees out-of-doors. Anne Uno's book offers many checklists of things children may be helped to see and feel when out-of-doors.

The resulting art products should be praised whether or not

they seem to capture the essence of the session. It should be remembered that the major outcome in arts activities should be the *experiences involved in doing* rather than the quality of the end product. When there is doubt what the drawing is all about, the teacher may ask the child what it is and then, with seriousness and respect, print a title at the bottom along with the child's name. This fosters further communication when other staff members see the pictures on bulletin boards and walls and subsequently go to the child-artist and say, "I saw your drawing on hills and snakes yesterday." This, then, can serve as the basis for dialogue in a world where far too little conversational material exists.

Through such multisensory sessions that combine dance, music, drama, and art, severely handicapped children can more nearly approximate the model of the creative individual described in the following verse.

THE CREATIVE INDIVIDUAL:

is aware of the way things feel to the touch.
listens to the sounds of life around him.
has a sensitivity for the way things smell.
is aware of the taste of things.
likes to construct things in materials.
prefers to rearrange old ideas into new relationships.
is observant of the world about him.
. . .
is sensitive to the beauty in man and nature.
appreciates beauty that man has made.
has a feeling for harmony and rhythm.
likes to sing, dance, and write.*

BIBLIOGRAPHY

Canter, Norma. *And A Time to Dance: Creative Movement with Retarded Children.* Boston: Plays, 1975.

*From D. W. Herberholz, and E. W. Linderman. *Developing Artistic and Perceptual Awareness.* 2nd ed. Dubuque, Iowa: William C. Brown Company Publishers, 1964, p. 6.

Cheyette, Irving, and Cheyette, Herbert. *Teaching Music Creatively.* New York: McGraw-Hill, 1969.

Robins, Ferris, and Robins, Jennet. *Educational Rhythmics for Mentally and Physically Handicapped Children.* New York: Association Press (291 Broadway, New York 10007), 1968.

Uhlin, Donald M. *Art for Exceptional Children.* Dubuque, Iowa: William C. Brown, 1972.

Uno, Anne Quan. *Aesthetic Activities for Handicapped Children.* Funded through the Texas Education Agency, no date.

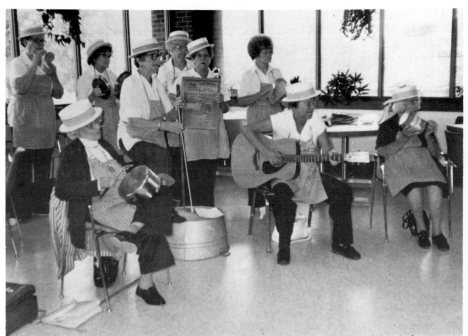

Structure 16. This senior citizen kitchen band has fun and brings much pleasure to others despite their visual and auditory problems.

Chapter 14

SO MUCH PLEASURE FROM MERE TOUCH: ARTS FOR THE VISUALLY HANDICAPPED

Sandra Ervin

I, who cannot see, find hundreds of things to interest me through mere touch. I feel the delicate symmetry of a leaf, I pass my hands lovingly about the smooth skin of a silver birch, or the rough shaggy bark of a pine . . . If I can get so much pleasure from mere touch, how much more beauty must be revealed by sight.

Helen Keller

ARTS for the blind and visually handicapped have made great strides in the last decade. There was a time when only the ears of the blind brought pleasure, and music was the art most frequently cherished. Not until the mid-1800s did embossed books begin to appear so that the blind could enjoy literature by reading braille at their own leisure rather than having to listen to someone else read aloud.

Milestones in the national library program were reached in the 1930s with the establishment of a uniform system of English braille, the development of the talking book record, and the enactment of legislation providing for regional circulating libraries for the blind and the production of braille and talking book records. Recent expansion of the library program resulted from the passage in July 1966 of Public Law 89-522, which authorized the Library of Congress to extend its free books-for-the-blind program to people who are unable to read conventional print materials because of physical limitations.

More recently art galleries and museums have begun to make their services available to the blind and visually impaired. In 1966, the first permanent tactile gallery in the United States was

119

opened. This was the Mary Duke Biddle Gallery at the North Carolina Museum of Art in Raleigh, North Carolina. So successful was this gallery that the state legislature now supports it with an annual appropriation.

Another art facility for the blind is the Wadsworth Atheneum's Lions Gallery of the Senses in Hartford, Connecticut. Originally conceived as a "touch-and-see" space for the unsighted, the facility opened in 1972 as the Tactile Gallery. In 1974, the gallery's name was changed to reflect the importance of a multisensory approach and to acknowledge the support of the Lions Organization. Pat Mulcahy, the gallery's project coordinator, offers ideas for others interested in creating multisensory galleries:

> As the program developed, it became apparent that sound is particularly important to unsighted people. Blind people do not simply touch or feel their way through life; rather, they achieve much of their sense of space and their orientation through sound.
>
> Since most unsighted people have little exposure to art and art history, we felt that a broader, multisensory approach would be more effective. Unsighted people should be introduced to the vocabulary of space, form, and composition before they are assaulted by the chronology of art history.

In 1968, the Los Angeles County Department of Parks and Recreation began a traveling tactile exhibition of sculptures called *Form in the Inner Eye*. Ed Nice, Director of the departments' Cultural Section, makes these remarks concerning the effect on the artists and viewers:

> Form in the Inner Eye challenged artists because they were forced to consider vibrations, smell, temperature, motion, and other stimuli in addition to the traditional visual criteria: rhythm, harmony, balance, and color which when considered alone prevent both artists and patrons from truly experiencing our environment.
>
> By creating the tactile sculpture exhibit, the Department of Parks and Recreation encouraged both sighted and blind people to appreciate the environment that surrounds us. We believe that through a heightened awareness of feeling and touching, people learn more about physical art objects and

learn ultimately that they too can be inwardly touched.

The most spectacular museum for the blind, as well as for other handicapped persons, is the new National Air and Space Museum of Smithsonian Institution in Washington, D.C. This is described as the most accessible cultural facility in the United States. Harold Snider, coordinator of programs for the handicapped at the Smithsonian National Air and Space Museum, coordinated the planning of the facility with the National Federation of the Blind (NFB).

This organization (located at 218 Randolph Hotel Bldg., Fourth and Court Streets, Des Moines, Iowa 50309) makes available training materials for persons in museum work. It also provides services through its 700 chapters, such as free consulting by members in areas that museums are trying to serve.

Actual involvement in the making of art products has been through vocational training. Once introduced to crafts, ceramics, and the other arts, visually handicapped persons often extend their skills during leisure time endeavors. Among the many textbooks used by art educators as a resource in teaching the blind is Victor Lowenfeld's book *Creative and Mental Growth*. In it appear illustrations of many sculptures and paintings done by persons with visual handicaps.

For many blind persons, however, the art form which offers the most pleasure is literature — reading in braille or large print books, listening to talking books or cassette tapes, or even creating poems, stories, and other forms of literature of one's own.

The author of this chapter, born with cataracts and legally blind, enjoys writing verse. The original poem which follows is about a visually impaired teenager with cerebral palsy. Considered retarded during his early years, he was not taught to read. Thanks to a dedicated teacher, he is now learning to read and write. This one example shows that no matter what age or impairment a person might have, he/she deserves an opportunity to be involved in the arts. Literature is one form of art that enables a person to become aware of the world as it is now, as it might be in the future. There is also the world of fiction for those with vivid imaginations.

THROUGH MY EYES

Although he may not see so well
Or stand up straight and tall:
He may not walk with an easy gait
Or run without a tumble or fall:

He may not speak with the purest of tone
Or pronounce words distinct or clear:
He may not read or write so well
Or try things without doubt or fear:

But there is one thing for sure
He likes to try his best:
Doing every task he is given
And folks, that's the real true test.

Sandra Gale Ervin

In order for the severely visually impaired to become involved in the world of art, many services are available to them in the United States and most of the fifty states individually.

Sources Available in the United States

AMERICAN FOUNDATION FOR THE BLIND, 15 West 16th Street, New York, New York 10011. Services provided by the Foundation are (1) publication of books, magazines, monographs, and leaflets in conventional print, large type, recorded and (limited) braille format; (2) manufacturing and recording of talking books (books on records); and (3) improving and strengthening services for visually impaired persons throughout the United States.

AMERICAN PRINTING HOUSE FOR THE BLIND, 1839 Frankfort Avenue, Louisville, Kentucky 40206. Services provided by the Printing House for the Blind are: (1) reproduction of books for grades K to 12 into large type, braille, talking books, and cassette tapes; (2) reproduction of sheet music and music books into large type or braille; and (3) manufacturing of all types of tangible apparatus.

RECORDINGS FOR THE BLIND, INC., 215 East 58th Street, New York, New York 10022. Services provided by Recordings for the Blind are: (1) recording of textbooks for the college student, primarily and (2) recording of books on reel-to-reel tape or on cassette tape.

THE LIBRARY OF CONGRESS, Division for the Blind and Physically Handicapped, Washington, D.C. 20562. Due to the enactment of Public Law 89-522, the Library of Congress is able to offer its free books-for-loan program to the blind and physically handicapped. These books are housed in regional libraries throughout the United States.

NATIONAL BLINDNESS INFORMATION CENTER, 1346 Connecticut Avenue, NW Suite 212, Washington, D.C. 20006. Call (toll free) 800-424-9770 for instant access to technical information and consultants.

LOUIS BRAILLE FOUNDATION FOR BLIND MUSICIANS, INC., 112 East 19th Street, New York, New York 10003. It is a national, nonprofit organization providing talented blind musicians with braille scores, scholarship aid, auditions, evaluation, and counseling. It also acts as an agent to obtain paid engagements for musicians.

THE NATIONAL FEDERATION OF THE BLIND, 218 Randolph Hotel Building, Des Moines, Iowa 50309. A federation of state and local organizations comprising blind people, NFB promotes legislation, evaluates present programs, and offers technical assistance to organizations interested in promoting arts and public services for the blind.

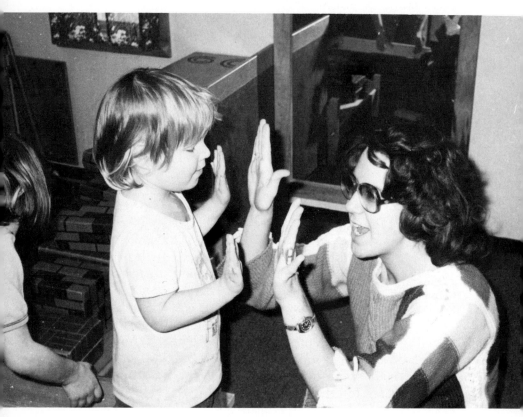

Structure 17. Deaf children learn to translate their thoughts and feelings into *signs* or hand and finger movements as part of creative dramatics instruction.

Chapter 15

CREATING A CHILDREN'S
THEATRE FOR THE DEAF

C. WARREN ROBERTSON

STARTING a children's theatre for the deaf at
Texas Woman's University was such an excellent idea that I am
surprised we did not undertake it sooner. In the first place, it
provided the Department of Speech with the opportunity of
uniting its rather divergent forces by drawing on the skills of
students and faculty both in the area of Communication Disorders and in the area of Theatre. Moreover, it provided us with
an opportunity to use the theatre not just as an instrument of
entertainment, but as a social tool, as a means of communicating with a very special audience: the hearing-impaired.

Play selection at T.W.U. always presents difficulties, since
most plays have more roles for men than for women. We over-
came this problem by selecting a fable, Fauquez's *Reynard the
Fox,* that could be played by almost any combination of men
and women. The play was an appropriate selection also in that
it is designed to play to children rather than down to them and,
in fact, provides thought-provoking entertainment for adults as
well as children. The play's unconventionality, its revelation of
the problems of human hypocrisy and self-aggrandizement, led
some to wonder if the play could be understood by hearing-
impaired children. Our subsequent discussions with hearing
and deaf children made it clear that they did in fact understand
the play well with all of the children responding to the buf-
foonery and sight gags and with the subtler points being picked
up by the more advanced audience members.

After casting the play we set about the business of learning
how to sign the lines. Only two of the eight students associated
with the production were in Deaf Education and only one of
the students, Suzy Eyesnogle, was herself deaf, and so the task

of learning the signs was monumental. As Mrs. Gladys Drake, our sign language consultant, later commented, it was like trying to learn a foreign language in six weeks. Fortunately, our naivety in this area gave us the courage to plunge ahead. Ultimately, however, we were forced to confront the fact that our signing was not adequate, and so we changed our strategy somewhat. We added Suzy to our cast of animal characters and had her introduce the play using both her voice and signs or "total communication" as we later heard this called. During the course of the action Suzy provided an ongoing commentary using signs and pantomime while most of the cast members signed only the key words of their speeches.

The decision to add Suzy to the cast was difficult for several reasons. First, we already had the problem of the audience's attention being split during portions of the play when a number of characters were on stage at the same time. This is a common shortcoming associated with amateur performances and I realized that adding a commentator would only compound the problem. Secondly, I did not want to give the actresses an excuse for not doing their best to learn their signs. In spite of these drawbacks, the decision to add Suzy to the cast turned out to be an excellent one, and perhaps proved to be the most practical and effective way for a cast of predominantly hearing actors to present a play to hearing-impaired audiences.

We approached the problem of split focus in several ways. First, we attempted to minimize extraneous movement and eliminate movement by characters who at any given moment were not speaking. Although our objective in this respect was never perfectly fulfilled, we had at least hit upon a directing principle that would be important in future theatre for the deaf productions. A second way in which we minimized the split focus was by placing Suzy in an elevated position at upstage center rather than to one side. This minimized the distance that the eye had to travel in shifting attention from character to commentator. The final way in which the split focus problem was reduced was by having Suzy sign continuously rather than intermittently. This approach meant that the audience member did not need to see if she was signing, but only looked to see what she was signing. Each audience member was given a continuous choice with regard to where to look in order to receive maximal clarification. This approach seemed rather comfortable so long as the viewer was asked to choose between two points of focus rather than three or more possible focal points.

The advantage of adding Suzy to the cast, however, went far beyond her function of translating the play's words into signs. In a very real sense she fulfilled a *choric function* providing appropriate reactions, attitudes, and comments throughout the play. In discussing Greek drama, critics have often noted the rhythm that is established as the audience's attention shifts back and forth between each dramatic episode and the danced choral *stasimon* that follows. Suzy's function was in some respects comparable to that of the Greek chorus except for the fact that her commentary was continuous rather than intermittent, a rhythmic quality, nevertheless, being established by the fact that our focus on her was intermittent. Moreover, her performance always had an organic, spontaneous quality comparable to a free-spirited dance. No two moments were ever exactly alike. In short, as the play progressed Suzy not only translated the actual lines but provided a subtext that visually made statements such as "see how vain that character is," "isn't his sense of self-importance absurd," "can you imagine someone being that stupid," "watch this and you'll see a funny trick," "wasn't that hilarious," "wasn't that sad," and so forth. The invention of the "choric translator" for the theatre for the deaf is suggestive of a new type of theatre with its own conventions and with focal control becoming the director's cardinal rule.

In retrospect, it would seem that Suzy's remarkable mimetic abilities are not just the product of her unique personality but are the studied result of dealing with her handicap. Deaf people everywhere have learned the art not just of using signs but of actually pantomiming intricate ideas and emotions. In studying Suzy's performance, one is struck by the marked similarity between what she does and what a Marcel Marceau or a Red Skelton might do. Indeed, Suzy's techniques could be studied not only by those who might want to learn the art of mime, but by those who wish to improve their acting techniques in conventional theatre productions.

The techniques which Suzy employed as our "choric translator" included exact control of the body, arms, hands, and face. She also exhibited extraordinary flexibility and an uncanny ability to quickly display a gamut of emotions and ideas. There was also economy of movement, there being almost no gesture, posture, or expression that was not expressive of some particular thought. By comparison, some actor's movements and gestures appear exceedingly sloppy. Finally, Suzy displayed the ability to freeze for a moment with an expression or gesture so that the viewer had the opportunity to take a mental picture of the exact image being portrayed. This technique gave Suzy's performance crispness and clarity. Again, the whole idea was to reinforce verbal communication with visual signs and symbols. The Greek word *theatron* means "seeing place" and it was this aspect of our craft that we attempted to emphasize.

In spite of the great strength Suzy brought to *Reynard the Fox*, we found ourselves in serious artistic difficulties during the week prior to our opening. Most of our actresses had had little theatre experience and, as a consequence, there was an inadequate sense of theatre discipline. I openly discussed my disappointment with the cast, and they responded well with considerable extra effort during this final portion of rehearsals. Moreover, Mrs. Drake helped by coaching the students on their signs. I have since concluded, however, that the project demanded too much from the students for them not to receive some form of academic credit. Without considering the time spent in private study, our total amount of time consumed in rehearsal, on the road, and in performance came to over one hundred hours — a figure that is competitive with the amount of time a student might devote to a three-hour college course.

In spite of the difficulties we had experienced, we were ready to take the play to the Waco Regional Day School for the Deaf for our opening. Brenda DeVore had completed our animal costumes, we had mastered our rather complicated make-up, and we had devised a simple set that could be carried in a small van. We were well received in Waco, with the custodian helping us set up and Mr. Bill Davis showing my wife and me the facilities while the actresses got into their make-up and costumes.

Our reception by the children surpassed our greatest hopes. Although the play lasted for two hours, the children remained supremely attentive throughout. In fact, it was our observation that those audiences that held hearing as well as nonhearing children seemed more prone to being momentarily diverted from time to time. Perhaps the Waco children's attentiveness was due in part to their strong visual orientation, or perhaps it was due more to the careful supervision they received at that school. In any case, if a child's attentions seemed to wander away from a particular task the instructor would point to his own eyes with the index and middle fingers then sweep them out, signing for the child to look in an appropriate direction.

Toward the close of the play Reynard saves the lives of his fellow animals by drawing the gunfire of the hunters — an event that the shrewd fox manages to survive. We had known that even the profoundly deaf were sensitive to vibrations but were surprised, nevertheless, when Suzy and a number of the deaf in the audience were visibly startled by our gunshot sound effects. During rehearsal, it had been extremely difficult for Suzy to correctly time pantomiming the rifle shots, but with the addition of the actual gunshot sounds, Suzy found it easy to time this particular effect.

In terms of timing her other signs and pantomimic action, she had several cues to guide her. First, she knew the general blocking and action of the play quite well. Second, she is excellent at reading lips, and finally, she could accurately interpret what the other actresses in a less perfect sense were attempting to sign.

Following this first performance, the actresses ran out through the audience, then remained in the lobby to communicate with the children. A marvelous emotion that told me "this is really worth doing" came over me as I watched the children and the cast gesturing, talking, and signing. The children interacted with all of the cast members but were especially attracted to Suzy. They seemed amazed to discover that she too really was deaf and yet could speak and communicate with such skill.

The children made it a special point to sign their names and to tell us a little bit about themselves. The theatre project seemed especially worthwhile at this point as I realized that the play had exposed the children to new words and signs and that we were inspiring them to work even harder on their communication skills.

Two little boys at the school were intrigued by my beard and one of them could not resist touching it several times, while the other boy danced about uttering a gleeful little "whoo-whoo" while pantomiming an elaborate ritual of shaving. Interestingly, I had a similar experience the following week at the Fort Worth Regional Day School for the Deaf, where a child felt compelled to touch my beard and then gave me an affectionate hug. My reaction was not just that the children needed loving care (which they seemed to be receiving), but that they also in many instances desperately needed a more perfect way of establishing meaningful human contacts. I felt that, if the play opened the door of communication ever so slightly, our time had been well spent.

In our performances at the regional day schools for the deaf in Waco, Mesquite, and Fort Worth we experienced technical difficulties for which we will be better prepared in our future productions. In the first place, most of the stages we played on were too small to accommodate all of our set pieces even though we had made a conscious effort to keep the scenery simple. We merely used what we could and eliminated the rest. Fortunately, we had rehearsed on three different stages at T.W.U. and had even held one of the dress rehearsals in a dormitory living room. This had given us experience in adjusting to playing areas of different sizes and shapes. We were not, however, prepared for the fact that the actresses could not cross unseen from one side of the stage to the other and this caused some awkwardness in our first performance. We did become skilled at smoothing over this problem, but for future productions we will plan all entrances so that they will be made from the side on which the actress has exited.

Additional technical problems included insufficient wing

space, inadequate lighting, and the lack of dressing rooms. These problems can be alleviated in the future by our carrying additional simple equipment and supplies. Folding screens could be used to hide off-stage characters, who might otherwise be seen in the wings. We already own a portable lighting control unit, which could be carried along for supplemental lighting. Finally, several mirrors could be purchased to facilitate creating dressing rooms out of teacher's lounges, nurses' stations, and other such rooms commonly available at the schools.

Technical problems such as these, however, will remain as minor, almost inconsequential, difficulties when compared with the larger issues of how to create a viable children's theatre for the deaf. A dedicated and long-range pursuit of dactylology as well as the study of pantomime and an eversharpening awareness of the principles of composition and focus should be at the heart of our developing a meaningful approach to this theatre genre. Mr. Davis put it succinctly when he stated, "we become very visual in our orientation."

Reynard the Fox was presented on five different occasions to a total of approximately 1,000 deaf, hard-of-hearing, and hearing children who seemed for the most part to immensely enjoy what they saw. It is hoped that this production will be remembered as the first step toward the creation of a successful and ongoing children's theatre for the deaf.

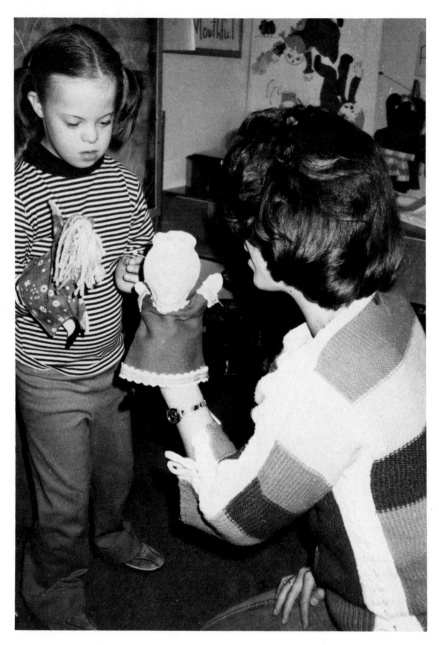

Structure 18. Puppetry is one of the most successful creative dramatic activities with young children; here a preschooler with Down's syndrome increases her vocabulary and improves communication skills through arts training.

Chapter 16

DRAMA FOR THE
MENTALLY RETARDED

RANDY ROUTON AND MICHAEL SCHNEIDER

DRAMA need not be only available for highly skilled actors or sophisticated audiences. The following is an account of how drama was used successfully as a therapeutic device with mentally retarded young men.

The men involved in putting on this play were residents of a community-based residential facility operated by a state school. They ranged in age from seventeen to twenty-eight years, and they had all spent most of their lives in an institution. Their present situation was an attempt to mainstream them into the community in a sheltered environment, thereby teaching them the skills necessary to live independently or semi-independently in a community setting.

The concepts of normalization, mainstreaming, and deinstitutionalization were the guiding principles in the formation of educational and recreational activities for the men. Included in the recreation program were activities that stressed the use of community resources and activities appropriate for the men's future life-style in a halfway house. A consideration of that life-style had to include maximum functioning potential, economical aspects, and the needs and desires of the men. Fishing, swimming, skating, baseball, using the local library, shopping, jogging, cooking, going to movies, picnics, hikes, weight-lifting, basketball, and dating were all part of the recreation programming. The possibility of dating was the inspiration for the dramatization.

Approximately one year after the men had moved into the community, twenty mentally retarded women from the same state school became community residents. Although by this time the men's level of sophistication had greatly increased

133

beyond that of the women, the men were very pleased with the possibilities that the future held. They asked the recreation leader if they could do something special for the "girls."

Notice was given that a general meeting would be held to discuss what they wanted to do. All of the suggestions were voted on and the decision to do a play and the date were made. A committee was selected to write the play, with the recreation leader appointed to serve as consultant and secretary. An attempt was made to keep the plot and lines simple and direct. A theme was chosen (western), a title ("Gunsmoke"), and a plot (which had to do with a poker game, cheating, good guys, bad guys, a shoot-out, an escape, the sheriff and somebody gets arrested, mistaken identity, an Indian that just says "How!" and the arrest of the bad guys).

The plot was broken up into three acts and the number of actors needed discerned. A second general meeting was held to present the results of the writing committee and to give the potential actors a chance to volunteer for the part of their choice. Houseparents and volunteers were assigned to help the actors come up with an appropriate costume. Emphasis was placed on helping the actors decide rather than making choices for them.

Other men were asked to help with the scenery and arrangement of the auditorium. The scenery was made with cardboard boxes that had held refrigerators and washing machines. The boxes were cut and unfolded and nailed to wooden stands. The wooden stands were 1 by 2, 1 by 4 and 2 by 4 pieces of scrap lumber. The cardboard background was then painted with one resembling the inside of a saloon and the other resembling the inside of a log cabin. The men did the sawing and nailing in the afternoons after their classes. Painting was done in the evening so they would have time to change into some old clothes.

While all of the above work was going on, volunteers were spending time with the actors in each scene going over their lines. The sequence of action was stressed more than the actual lines given. Additional volunteers worked with men making posters advertising the play and writing special invitations for those the men especially wanted to come. Advertisements were placed at the men's and women's dorms at the institution where they had previously resided and at the nearby university.

The appointed night came and all the actors were ready. They were anxious to have make-up put on and get into their costumes. Approximately sixty persons attended, some of whom were teachers, parents, friends, past and present house-parents, university students, and the women who had just moved into the community.

A prompter was standing in the wings to help with forgotten lines, and a backstage manager was there to make sure everyone was on stage on time with his guns and cowboy hat in place. One of the men wrote and gave an opening that welcomed the audience and noted the play was in honor of the women.

The play lasted fifteen minutes; the applause and bows lasted at least ten. A reception was held for all of the participants and they were each told several times what a good job they had done.

We felt there were several reasons for picking this type of activity. First, the mentally retarded client rarely gets the op-portunity to show off his talents in a mode that results in positive feedback. Because this was scheduled as a public showing, we felt it could be a great ego booster for the men. The second reason was to allow the men to have the oppor-tunity to be a part of the decision-making process. The unfor-tunately little amount of control they have over their lives must give them no small feeling of insignificance. In this play, they decided on the plot, wrote the lines, determined what the scenery should look like, gave the play a name, invited who they wanted, and arranged the chairs in the audience.

Another important aspect of this activity was that it taught the men that fun does not have to be something you buy. For no money involved, they were able to give something to someone whom they wanted to please. In doing so, they re-ceived as much themselves.

A later play was presented on another theme by the same men. One of them borrowed a movie camera and filmed parts of it. This proved to be a valuable asset. It allowed not only for the reviewing of the play, but provided unmeasurable feedback to the retarded clients that they look and act like a "normal" person. A videotape would be even more functional, because it allows for instant playback and the film can be used over and over.

BIBLIOGRAPHY

Edgerton, Robert B. *The Cloak of Competence: Stigma in the Lives of the Mentally Retarded.* Berkeley: University of California Press, 1967.
Kaempfer, Ann. "Mainstreaming Mentally Retarded Women Into a Community Recreation Program: Four Case Studies." Unpublished M.A. thesis, Texas Woman's University, 1978.
Kugel, Robert B., and Wolfensberger, Wolf. *Changing Patterns in Residential Services for the Mentally Retarded.* Washington, D.C.: President's Committee on Mental Retardation, 1969.
Nihira, Lyly, and Nihira, Kazuo. "Normalized Behavior in Community Placement." *Mental Retardation,* 1975, *13:2,* 9-13.
Perrone, Miriam. *Icarus and Other Flights: Creative Drama at Camp Sunshine.* Washington, D.C.: National Committee, Arts for Handicapped, 1978.
Ruda, Lucy. "Recreation and Leisure Preferences and Practices of Mentally Retarded Adults in a Community-Oriented Home Management Program." Unpublished M.A. thesis, Texas Woman's University, Denton, Texas, 1976.
Sherrill, Claudine, and Iwanski, Ruth Ann. "Self Concepts and Leisure Preferences of Mentally Retarded Adult Men." *Therapeutic Recreation Journal,* 1977, *11,* 23-27.
Ward, Winifred. *Playmaking with Children.* Englewood Cliffs, New Jersey: Prentice-Hall, Inc., 1957.

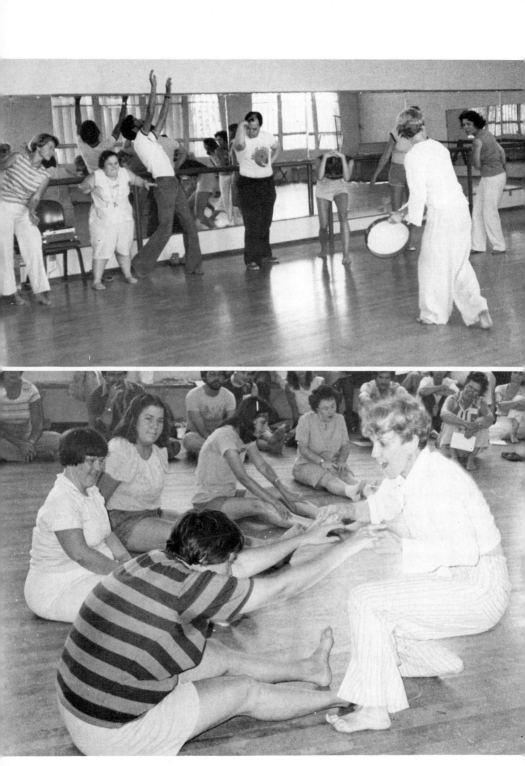

Structure 19. Anne Riordan, Chairperson of Programs for the Handicapped for the National Dance Association, leads group in movement improvisation, which combines dance and creative dramatics.

Chapter 17

ORFF-SCHULWERK: AN ADAPTATION FOR DRAMA FOR RETARDED PARTICIPANTS*

DAVID MORGAN

THE Orff-Schulwerk process offers endless possibilities for adaptation to specialty areas. In its original form, the Orff-Schulwerk method was designed as an elemental approach to music and rhythm for the schoolroom. Since its original introduction into the German school system, its simple open-ended structure has been understood by many who, having tried and experienced the process, know and believe its creative potential for learning and living.

Orff-Schulwerk has been individually adapted to many specialties. It has been used by music therapists, dance therapists, speech therapists, and even by swimming instructors. It has been used in therapeutic, clinical, and recreational settings as well as in traditional educational institutions.

Because it is a basic elemental process, it can be adapted to nearly every setting. Its basic assumptions and method have been used by some who have never heard of Orff-Schulwerk. Many assumptions of Orff-Schulwerk were implicit in creative dramatics and improvisational theatre. Although specifically designed for children between the ages of five and twelve, creative dramatics has proven very effective with mentally retarded teens and adults.

Creative dramatics may be defined as group experience in which each individual is guided to express himself for the joy of creating improvised drama as he works and plays with

*Reprinted from *Challenge*, Vol. 9, No. 1 (September-October 1973) by permission of Dr. Julian Stein, American Alliance for Health, Physical Education, and Recreation.

others. Creative dramatics emphasizes participation rather than product. The chief aim is experience — experience that fosters child growth and development, reveals needs, encourages growth of individual spirit in the presence of a group, and provides for self-realization and cooperation in an atmosphere of spirited group play. In addition, it has the potential to increase imagination, help increase verbalization, develop better listening skills, improve recall, help develop a sequential understanding of events, and give a healthy release of emotions.

Improvisation might be called creative dramatics for adults. Like creative dramatics, improvisation uses improvised dialogue and movement in creating scenes. Many of its theater games and exercises can be effectively adapted to the Orff format. Like Orff-Schulwerk, creative dramatics and improvisation emphasize learning through experience and are based on the assumptions that everyone can act, everyone can improvise, and everyone has creative potential.

Viola Spohlin, whose book *Improvisation for the Theatre* has much to offer for anyone working in drama, states in her beginning chapter —

> We learn through experience and experiencing, and no one teaches anyone anything. This is as true for the infant moving from kicking to crawling to walking, as it is for the scientist with his equations. If the environment permits it, anyone can learn whatever he chooses to learn, and if the individual permits it, the environment will teach him everything it has to teach. *Talent* or *lack of talent* have little to do with it.

Drama, like music, can be a medium for experiencing fundamental and universal truths in living — both can be comfortably adapted to the Orff-Schulwerk process. Orff-Schulwerk starts with a germ idea and takes it through four processes: improvisation, selectivity, fulfillment, and closure.

The germ idea can be as simple as a word or as complex as a story. In either case, the above procedural outline can be followed.

Applications to the Concept of Fire

An often used example of a one word germ idea for Orff-Schulwerk is *fire*. Carol Bitcon gives an example of its development in an article entitled "I Am!" presented at the 4th National Symposium of Creative Communication, Orff-Schulwerk, in 1969. Given more of a dramatic emphasis, the same germ idea went through the following development at the Recreation Center for the Handicapped in San Francisco.

The Day Trippers, a group of approximately twenty-five moderately retarded adults, had been studying insects as their theme for the month. The day before the program, there had been a big fire in San Francisco. At the beginning of the hour this event was mentioned and participants were asked if any had seen or heard about it. Several claimed they had, so a discussion was launched on how fires start. A pantomime fire was built in the middle of the circle, emphasizing the care that had to be taken not to get too close. This evolved into a chant:

If you get too close
You can burn your pants;
If you burn your pants
It'll make you dance.

To the varying beat of a drum, each participant had a chance to do a fire dance around the imaginary fire. After every participant had a turn, it was suggested as a closure that the fire be put out. The group, as was suggested in Bitcon's experience, tightly encircled the imaginary red crepe paper flames, and blew them out. During the process of the fire dance, several participants got burned. In addition to warnings and cries of sympathy that occurred when this happened, the leader produced a white smock and a stethoscope and asked if a doctor was in the house. Using the props, one of the participants checked the severity of the burns before the chant continued.

After completing the fire dance, the theme of fire was continued and the leader asked if anyone had ever heard of an insect whose house had caught fire. It took little effort to elicit this story and rhyme:

> Lady bug, lady bug
> Fly away home,
> Your house is on fire
> And your children are alone.

In the remainder of the session, a story was developed, based on answers given by participants to the leader's questions: How did the fire start? Why was Lady Bug out of the house? How was the fire put out? With some selectivity by the leader, the fire turned out to have been started by a firefly arsonist who threw a fire bomb into the house after making a call to Mr. and Mrs. Ladybug on a prop telephone, claiming he was a neighbor inviting them over. After the fire was started, all non-acting participants chanted the Lady Bug rhyme which sent the parents hurrying home where they saved their children and called the fire department. The firemen called the police and captured the fire bug and hauled him off to jail. Positive reinforcement was given to all for sincere portrayals and the session concluded with a good feeling of accomplishment. They went through the *process of improvisation* in dealing with the familiar concept of fire. With the help of the leader, they are co-authors to the *selectivity* of the most appropriate suggestions to build a story. By acting it out, they went through the *fulfillment* and natural *closure* of a finished creative product.

Depending on the ability of a group, the above described program would be simplified for more severely retarded, or expanded by eliciting suggestions from participants as to how the story could be improved. Through positive criticism, the story could be further embellished and actually performed for an audience.

Application to Newspaper Awareness

Orff-Schulwerk adapted for drama does not always need to evolve into playing out a story.

Another familiar Orff chant is —

> Extra! Extra!
> Read all about it!
> What is your news?
> What is your news?

This would be followed by —

> Newspaper! Newspaper!
> On the bench,
> Bet you can get it,
> It's a cinch!

To use this chant a scene must be set. It is a beautiful day in the park. You have just bought a newspaper and have sat down to read it. Another person enters (from the circle) and assumes a character who has reason for wanting the paper. Using this basic dramatic objective, the new person attempts to get the newspaper.

After this scene and explaining the game, the leader or another model sits on what has been set up as a bench in the middle of the circle and starts to read a real newspaper.

The chant is said by the group and any participant who wishes to start can do so. The leader offers some resistance to giving up the newspaper until the argument is sufficiently convincing. He then gives the new person the paper and leaves. The chant is repeated and the game continues as a relay around the circle. As a closure, the newspaper can be creatively destroyed.

Application to Modes of Travel

An improvisation game that can be effectively adapted to the Orff-Schulwerk method is called the *Concerto*. Although there are many variations of this theatre game, it has been most effective with handicapped participants when combined with a pantomime game. The leader prepares a grab bag before the session with pictures of various means of transportation. A chant like the following can be used:

There are other ways to travel
Than going for a walk.
Show us what you find
But — don't talk!

Everyone in the group takes a turn reaching into the bag and tries to act out the mode of transportation he picks. Each is allowed to make one sound. After everyone has had a turn, the entire group assembles in choir formation with the leader as the conductor. When pointed to, each participant, as if he were a musician in an orchestra, delivers his sound. The conductor cuts each off or allows him to continue according to his own sense of sound and rhythm. Juxtaposing varying sounds and by combining several or all of his instruments the conductor speeds up or slows down the sound piece at his whim, builds to a fitting climax, ends the piece, and takes a bow. An interesting variation of this concerto is an emotional concerto. In this game emotional sounds are used as instruments and the same procedure followed. The game also can allow participants to take turns as conductor.

Whether music or drama is the media to which Orff-Schulwerk is adapted, emphasis is on creativity. Creativity occurs when inquiry is encouraged. Creativity is the ability to form new relationships, meanings, and products by reassembling experiences and knowledge. The Orff-Schulwerk process of expanding a germ idea through phases of development, exploration, and closure can be viewed as a microcosmic example of the expansion of our entire being. When we are not expanding we are either stagnant or contracting. Too often education, especially for mentally retarded children, stresses setting limitations rather than creative expansion. Orff-Schulwerk method, in any of its adapted forms, deserves more attention from educators in this country. Through its creative process joy, which should be a part of all learning, can be attainable for all.

BIBLIOGRAPHY

Bevans, Judith. "The Exceptional Child and Orff." *Music Educators Journal* 55,7 (March 1969):41-43.
Bitcon, Carol H. *Alike and Different: The Clinical and Educational Use of*

Orff-Schulwerk. Santa Ana, California: Rosha Press, 1976.

Bitcon, Carol H., and Ball, Thomas. "Generalized Imitation and Orff Schulwerk." *Mental Retardation* 12,3 (June 1974):36-39.

Morgan, David. "Combining Orff Schulwerk with Creative Dramatics for the Retarded." *Therapeutic Recreation Journal* 9 (Second Quarter, 1975):54-56.

Editor's Note: Orff-Schulwerk is discussed further by the Cheyettes, *Teaching Music Creatively,* New York, McGraw-Hill Book Company, 1969. They indicate that the English adaptation of Orff's work with a teacher's manual was prepared by Doreen Hall and Arnold Walter. The Cheyettes define Orff-Schulwerk as "the active involvement of children in singing, rhythmic movement, and the playing of rhythmic melodic percussion instruments." The instruments employed in the Orff system include small tympani, triangle, cymbals, wood blocks, jingles, rattles, tambourine, bass drum, and small drums; and melodic percussion of soprano and alto glockenspiel, soprano and alto metalophone (a heavier type of bells); soprano, alto, and bass xylophones; a bass two-string instrument called a *bordun,* which may be played pizzicato, struck with a soft mallet, or bowed; a viola de gamba of six strings played pizzicato; and water-tuned musical glasses played with a hard mallet.

Orff-Schulwerk instruments can be ordered through Orff-Schulwerk Instrumentarium, Music for Children. U.S. Agents: Magnamusic-Baton, Inc., 6394 Delmar Blvd., St. Louis, Missouri 63130, or Magnamusic Distributors, Inc., Sharon, Connecticut 06069.

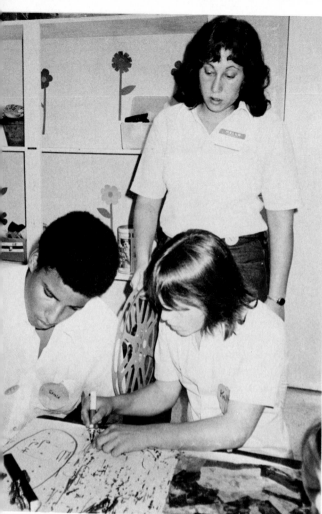

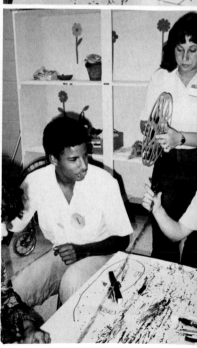

Structure 20. Markamation Activities: Students are making designs on old, bleached-out 16 mm film and later will see their original art work projected on the movie screen.

Chapter 18

A DYNAMIC RECYCLING OF FILM: MARKAMATION

MARSHA A. REID

CREATIVE programming with and for severely impaired individuals and groups is frequently limited by imagination, budget, talent, and initiative of the program staff. Markamation* may give you an infinite number of creative arts ideas as well as serving as a behavior management tool.

Markamation is a process of recycling 16mm film. The process may be done in parts or as one project. The uses of the completed film are as varied as your imagination!

It takes imagination and persistence on your part to secure *already exposed* 16mm film. The amount of film you will need initially is enough to fill a three inch reel. As you experiment more with the process, you will undoubtedly want to have a great deal of film on hand as well as differing reel sizes. Where can you get the film? Some sources depend on your locale. Public libraries may be discarding worn films. Frequently high schools, junior colleges, and universities are sources of outdated athletic scouting or training films. Television stations that use 16 mm commercial spots are frequently very willing suppliers. You probably can uncover more supply sources in your own community.

Once you get the film it must be bleached to erase existing imagery, giving the markamators a clean transparent film to decorate. After quick processing, the film is ready to be shown on a screen, a textured wall, a waving sheet, inside an empty bookcase, on a ceiling, or anywhere else you and your crew of markamators decide. Be ready for visual stimulation!

---

*Markamation is an adaptation of film animation. This particular technique was developed by David Millman while working with profoundly retarded individuals in New York City.

Preparing the Film

To prepare the exposed 16mm film for the markamators, it must be bleached, rinsed, and dried. You best know your group, so you are the best one to decide if you should prepare the film ahead of time or if there are folks you are working with who can assist or successfully complete this task.

1. Mix a solution of bleach and water in a plastic or galvanized bucket. The solution should be one-third bleach to two-thirds water. The stronger the solution, the quicker the film emulsion will dissolve.

2. Take the film off the film reel and drop the film into the bucket of bleach/water. The water may be lukewarm or cold. Let the film soak for about five minutes. You can tell the emulsion is dissolving because it will begin to "melt" off the film and form an oil slick on the water's surface.

3. With rubber gloves protecting your hands, move the film around in the bucket so the bleach hits as many exposed surfaces as possible. You can speed up the bleaching process by rubbing the film's surface. You can either remove all the film emulsion or leave parts of the movie image on the film for an interesting added effect later on.

4. When the film has been bleached to your liking, place the film in a bucket filled with cool water and rinse by agitating the film with your gloved hands. The film should be transparent and will either be clear or have a colored (blue, purple, brown) tinge.

5. Pull the film through a dry cloth towel, clean rag, or paper towels to wipe off the excess water. As you are wiping the film, put the dry part into an empty bucket to keep it from falling on the floor, picking up dirt, or being bent. Then rewind the dry film back onto the film reel by taping one end of the film to the spool with a thin piece of masking tape and inserting a pencil through the film reel to act as a rewind rod. Slowly rewind the reel by revolving it while untangling the film as it comes out of the bucket.

Plan ahead when using bleach. Some safety precautions

would include using a well-ventilated area, rubber gloves, aprons or smocks, possibly goggles or a mouth covering, and having access to cool water to rinse skin or clothing if necessary.

Getting Markamators Situated

Narrow tables end-to-end are most adequate. Make certain the table surface is clean and that the tables are covered with shelf or butcher paper. White paper is best as it allows the markamators to more easily see what they are doing. The film should be pulled down the length of the table, centered, and secured with masking tape.

The markamators should sit on both sides of the table, but not directly across from each other. This staggered fashion allows each markamator to have a section (about 2 feet) of film to mark. *Important:* Make sure that the film's sprocket holes are on the same side as the sprocket teeth of the projector. This will assure that what is drawn on the film will be projected correctly onto the screen.

Markamation

Make certain each markamator has an indelible felt marker and that additional color choices are available or to be shared. The colors build up on the film from light to dark, so a light colored marker can generally still be seen even when a darker color is put over it. Play with colors and see. Long sweeping marks, strong bold slashes, whispy little marks, fine strokes, dots, lines, dashes, completely colored areas, all sorts of doodling patterns are all possible. Scratches can be made with straight pins or needles, then colored. If words are written, the design should be repeated a minimum of five times for appearance of continuity. For example, if the word SMILE was to appear on the screen, the markamator would letter twenty-five frames: s s s s s SM SM SM SM SM SMI SMI SMI SMI SMI SMIL SMIL SMIL SMIL SMIL SMILE SMILE SMILE SMILE SMILE. The same principle applies to drawing a happy face. Draw a circle five times, then the circle and an eye five times, then the circle and both eyes five times, then the circle, both eyes, and the smile five times. The end result when the film is projected is a recognizable happy face.

After everyone has finished their section of film, the film is pulled forward (and dropped off one end of the table into a dry bucket) leaving a new, clear portion of the film to be marked. Using a clean, dry cloth, blot the film that has been drawn upon, then rewind the finished film onto an empty reel. You may wish to splice several sections of the film together eventually to make a longer running production.

Place the film reel on the projector, lower the lights, and get ready for a fantastic visual experience. The project is enhanced with music, especially if recorded music is played at a faster speed than usual!

A Tool for Behavior Management

The particular skill level(s) and behavior(s) of individuals within your group will determine if some parts of this film-making process are done in steps. There may be appropriate lead-up activities prior to markamation. Group members must know precautions when working with bleach and *permanent* felt markers. Group members should be able to follow directions or have enough aides available to assist direction following.

It is possible to give tokens for attending to tasks, sharing, following directions. It is also possible to use group members in responsible positions: filling buckets with water, pouring bleach, bleaching and rinsing the film, drying the film, rewinding the film, covering the tables, setting up the screen, arranging the "theatre," setting up the records or tape recorder, or turning off the lights. All of these tasks have been done by profoundly retarded individuals in sessions where we have used markamation. The key is in planning ahead, knowing the skills of your group, allowing for error, and assisting only when absolutely necessary.

Additional Thoughts

Markamation is an activity that can be done on the floor. Group members may need to hold a felt marker in their toes, against their chin and shoulder, or in their mouths. It may be more comfortable to be on the floor, with blankets, towels, or rugs used as bolsters to help support the markamator. The film should then be situated as close to the markamators as possible for creative success.

Markamation is designed for immediate gratification. It is a process that may take one-half hour or it could be stretched into two or more activity periods. It is suggested that you have the film prepared ahead of time, tables set up, felt markers ready to go, and the projector all ready the first time your group tries markamation. This way the film is created, rewound on the take-up reel, and put on the projector. The group will quickly be delighted at their fantastic filmmaking and probably have scores of ideas to do next.

The beauty of markamation is not the intricate cell animation, but the ability to take the variety of marks and come out with an exciting, colorful film. No artistic expertise is required. As creativity flows, so will alternative designs and uses. Besides a movie, markamation could be projected on a sheet as a backdrop for creative dramatics and shadow play; glued, after cutting the film itself, to windows or glasses for a stained glass effect; projected on a ceiling above a swimming pool for visual imagery accompanying synchronized swimming; projected on dancing bodies; and projected on the floor for movement exploration. Enjoy and have fun creating!

Structure 21. Through exploration of the contents of a stuff box, the severely handicapped child develops basic arts concepts such as understandings of shapes, sizes, and colors and expands language arts skills.

Chapter 19

CREATIVE USES OF THE STUFF BOX

J ACQUELYN V AUGHAN

As soon as the "normal" child learns to pull up, crawl, and walk, she/he is into everything within reach. Normal children explore their home environment by crawling into clothes closets and kitchen cabinets, reaching for items on tables, dressers, and anything that catches their eye. They are curious about everything they see and touch. Those of us who have observed children know that they handle these objects, beat on them, put them in their mouths, and literally explore and investigate any object.

Children learn that Dad's shoes are big and theirs are small by putting their feet inside them. They learn different textures by putting their hands in their food and touching everything else they can find. They learn to associate odors with items they find in various areas of the house: dirty clothes, newly baked bread, and wood shavings around Dad's workbench. They learn visual cues such as colors and facial expressions through this same method of observation and exploration, as well as verbal cues, because family members constantly reinforce what they are doing through positive or negative responses. They learn many concepts through this type of play, such as hard and soft, big and little, hot and cold, shapes, etc.

The Toy Box in Normal Growth
and Development

As children get older their parents find many discarded items in their toy boxes, such as bright colored yarn, wooden spoons, margarine tubs, measuring spoons, and boxes. These items are their favorite toys because they can create all kinds of "things" with them, then tear them apart and reassemble them without fear of destroying an original toy. The toy box always contains something new that Mother, Dad, Brother, or Sister has discarded, such as old shoes, milk cartons, scraps of material, shirts, and necklaces. The treasures in the toy box continue to change, being constantly filled with stimulating and interesting items.

Sensory and Motoric Deprivation
of Handicapped Children

Severely handicapped children because of their handicaps do not explore, investigate, and experiment in the same manner. As a group, they are many times denied this early form of exploration. They may not be stimulated visually because of lack of vision, may not crawl around and get into things because of lack of mobility. Intellectually they may not have reached that stage of curiosity that their "normal" peers have obtained. Parents of handicapped children may be overprotective and not allow or encourage this type of exploration because of a fear that their children might hurt themselves.

In other situations, professionals who work with these children are so concerned about the children's physical development, toileting, feeding, and self dressing that they do not give priority to creative exploration. Therefore, when the severely handicapped child does enter a habilitation or educational program, she/he is not only at a disadvantage with his/her peers because of lack of normal vision, mobility, or intellectual functioning, but also because of his/her lack of exploration, investigation, and experimentation with this type of random play. Yet it is through this form of exploration that children learn about objects and their relationship to the environment.

Use of the Stuff Box to Overcome Deprivation

Special and elementary education teachers, therapeutic recreators, and other specialists working with severely handicapped can provide the child opportunities for overcoming these disadvantages with the use of a "stuff box." A stuff box may be thought of as a "treasured" toy box: that box where items are collected and stored, items that the owner (the child) can use to assemble and disassemble projects according to the wishes of the creator. Through the use of a stuff box, the severely handicapped child can have unique play experiences that she/he may have been denied before. A stuff box, then, contains many discarded treasures usually collected by the "normal" child such as old clothing, egg cartons, empty cans, boxes, milk cartons, and plastic containers. (See list at end of article for a more extensive listing.)

For the handicapped child who is denied the normal acquisition of such items, someone has to start collecting the items for the stuff box and teach him/her how to use it. Through the manipulation, exploration, and experimentation of the contents in the stuff box, the severely handicapped child develops basic skills such as the recognition of shapes and sizes, colors, being creative, and expanding communication skills.

As with normal children, the objects in the stuff box change as the child matures. No matter what items may be included in the stuff box, they will lend themselves to multiple uses in the areas of the creative arts, while providing the severely handicapped with instant gratification and success. From the stuff box the child can create his own project without having to adhere to any set pattern, having the freedom to dismantle and reassemble without fear of punishment.

The Stuff Box as a Lead-up Activity to Rhythm and Music

In the structured environment of the classroom and/or rehabilitation setting, the stuff box becomes the focus and resource for expanding the learning experiences under the guidance of the teacher/rehabilitation specialist. The child learns to recognize materials that she/he comes into contact with every day. As an example, teacher/therapist might say, "This is a milk carton that once contained milk, like you have for lunch, smell it, feel it, look at it. Now we are going to make a noise maker (musical instrument) using the carton."

Then the teacher/therapist lets the youngsters explore the various ways of creating a noise using the carton. Depending on the age level and severity of the handicap, the teacher might provide examples of a noise maker, such as beating on it with one's hand or with a stick, putting rocks or buttons inside and shaking it, or putting rubber bands around it and "plunking" them like a guitar. Again because of the variety of the contents of the stuff box, the noise maker or musical instrument can be as simple or complex as the child's needs and ability level dictates. Other examples suggest tubes that become kazoos, cigar boxes as guitars, aluminum pans as cymbals, oatmeal boxes as drums, and plastic bottles that become rattles. In addition to making the instrument, the child can decorate it and then use it in a music or rhythm class.

The Stuff Box in Puppetry and Creative Dramatics

Not only is the stuff box an effective tool for introducing sounds and rhythms, but it can also be used for developing communication skills such as in drama. The arena of the "stage" provides an individual with an environment where the handicapped child can use inventive techniques to obtain the effect needed to communicate. As an example, the child with a speech problem may use visual verbal clues by attaching a sign with words onto a puppet that is "acting." A blind child may learn "what is a smile?" when affixing a felt cloth smile to the face of a puppet.

The teacher may begin with the simplest type of puppet by having the child glue a paper plate to a popsicle stick, tongue depressor, or paper tube and then make a face on it with finger paints, brush paints, or gluing construction paper, felt, or yarn on it. The three-dimensional face is best for the blind child because she/he can "see" the face. From this point the child can act out a story as the teacher reads, spontaneously act a story she/he is familiar with, or write an original play. The teacher can make the children aware of many other types of puppets that can be made from the stuff box, such as paper bags, sacks, wooden spoons, paper cups, and/or fabric. Such drama projects provide stimulus for the child to explore, create, and communicate with others, because with puppets one is not restricted to verbal communication.

After exploring the entire area of puppetry the teacher can then advance to a more complex level of role playing by letting the children come up with costumes and props from the stuff box to present various stories or ideas to their peer group. The children have access to old clothing for costumes as well as many articles for creating masks, animal costumes, and other apparel which gives them the opportunity to "dress up." In this way the "treasured toy box," where objects were collected and stored, now becomes a resource for "creating a person or animal." A person or animal has its own personality, which allows the child to act out different roles that support their efforts to communicate. In developing drama in this manner, the severely handicapped child is encouraged to communicate and express emotions in whatever manner she/he is comfortable without fear of being ridiculed. This vehicle of expression provides a variety of opportunities for the child to utilize his/her abilities, since the disability is no longer important because the role becomes the focus for attention.

The Stuff Box as Motivation for Movement Exploration

The stuff box provides another opportunity to explore *movement*. Movement is defined as the ability to explore one's own space. Children ask, "How tall am I? How small am I? How wide am I?" One technique is to use various sizes of cans to introduce these concepts. A child can compare a soup can (tall) with a mushroom can (small). How wide an object may be can be determined by a coffee can (wide) compared with a tomato paste can (narrow). This exploration allows the child to compare "space" relative to the size of cans found in the home.

The Stuff Box as a Source of Arts and Crafts Activities

The same items in the stuff box used in music and drama can be used as items for crafts. One of the more creative areas in the arts is in the creation of craft items. Crafts provide the handicapped child opportunity to explore and experiment with forms because she/he is not limited to those stereotyped crafts that decorate walls and shelves and themselves. As with normal children, they can also make their own toys. They can make building blocks, cars, airplanes, pull toys, shadow boxes, doll furniture, pin wheels, dolls, as examples. All these toys are a part of themselves, their own creativity. The teacher can help them explore all of these kinds of toys and they can learn why wheels go around and what makes something balance.

The stuff box can also be used for creating crafts such as spool dolls, paperweights, plaques, napkin rings, recipe holders, pins, bracelets, tote bags, "sit upons," etc. Crafts such as these provide the children with the opportunity to be creative and explore their abilities to produce a product as well as the opportunity to make a present for someone in their family or for themselves.

Normal children have a variety of opportunities to create a special gift for a member of the family or to shop for a family present. Severely handicapped children do not usually have this opportunity to shop for a special gift for a birthday using their own allowance. These children rarely have the freedom to go from store to store looking for a special gift for a family member. Yet they are aware of the process used by normal children in their selection of a special gift, which enhances their feeling of being part of the family.

With the stuff box they can make a special gift that is important to their feeling of self-worth and acceptance in the family. One can be assured that their gift is greatly appreciated by the parent, especially when the child has made it themselves. Because teachers/therapists may become more concerned with the appearance of the final product, as measured by conventional standards, they may provide more help than is necessary; the product becomes one of the teacher's creation, not the child's, and the child knows that. One of the nicest things to hear and see is a severely handicapped child hand his/her mother a paperweight and say "I made it all by myself!" It might not look like a finished product one might find created by the normal child, but to the child and parent it is special because the handicapped child had the opportunity to express herself/himself and learn to do something on his own.

Home Learnings With the Stuff Box

Because of the versatility of the stuff box and the potential it has for providing the handicapped child with the same learning opportunities as the normal child, this tool should not just be used at the school, recreation center, or rehabilitation center alone, but it should also be used at home. The teacher or therapist can help the parent understand the value of the stuff box and how their children can learn from its use. Once a handicapped child has learned some of the things that can be done with a stuff box in the educational/rehabilitation setting, the freedom to explore these "treasures" as a learning tool should be continued at home. Not only would this help parents understand the importance of treating their handicapped child the same as normal children, but they would realize they do not have to buy expensive equipment and toys for their "special" child.

Both parents and children should be encouraged to explore, experiment, and investigate their own stuff box, because through this type of play experience, they both learn. A stuff box will also provide the handicapped child other explorative outlets that are missed from just watching television. As an example, the teacher could request the handicapped child make a project for school from his/her stuff box at home. This assignment can provide the stimulus for the youngsters to use their home stuff box and assist the family in becoming more aware of its potential.

Another area of interest involves growing "things." The handicapped child can learn about plants and how they grow by saving the seeds from oranges, apples, and avocados, planting them in egg cartons and watching them sprout. Through these resources from the stuff box, they learn about life and the responsibility of caring for something alive.

In preparing a stuff box at the school/rehabilitation setting, parents should be encouraged to provide items for it. Parents involved in this way get into the habit of thinking about the potential of an article before it is discarded. Also parents become involved in the program, even if only superficially, without being concerned with expense. Further, teachers/therapists should not limit themselves to the suggested list of items noted in this article. The teacher/therapist is only limited by his/her creativity for developing this technique for learning since the author has simply scratched the surface for the potential uses and contents of the stuff box.

Normalization Contributions of the Stuff Box

If one of the primary concerns in working with severely handicapped children is "normalization," then the concern that they be exposed to the same type of development as "normal" children is an essential part of the learning process. The normal child does learn through exploration, experimentation, and manipulation of objects while crawling around the house, while the severely handicapped child rarely participates in this type of play at the infant age. It is therefore important for specialists in the therapeutic field to create these exploratory opportunities. By providing these stimuli, the teacher/therapist accelerates the learning experiences of the handicapped child thereby "closing the gap" between the child and his/her peers.

This stuff box is a unique and invaluable tool in providing these types of experiences in the areas of creative arts. It can provide a well-rounded program of drama, music, movement exploration, crafts, and games. The box becomes a major vehicle for creative expression; for developing awareness of the world around them, communication skills, and basic concepts; and for exploration of their own abilities. It gives handicapped children the same opportunities experienced by their normal peers, thus gradually diminishing one area in which they are disadvantaged with the norm. As a recreational therapist, this author has used this tool (stuff box) for several years and has found it to be one of the better methods for working with severely handicapped children.

Possible Contents of a Stuff Box

Egg cartons
Paper towel rolls/tissue rolls
Milk cartons
Empty thread spools
Scraps of fabric and yarn
Aluminum pans
Magazines and greeting cards
Margarine tubs
Oatmeal boxes
Styrofoam® food trays
Shoe boxes
Boxes — berry, cigar
Plastic bottles and containers
Large and small paper bags
Old jewelry
Newspapers
Coat hangers
Old nylons
Construction paper
Straws
Crayons
Old clothes, socks, dresses,
     hats, shoes, shirts

Popsicle® sticks
Glass jars
String
Pencils
Paper plates
Rocks
Juice cans, other cans
Buttons
Bottle caps
Paper cups
Plastic forks/spoons
Corks
Cookie cutters
Sponges
Wooden spoons
Sieves
Funnels
Flour sifters
Nuts and bolts
Soap pieces
Clothespins
Plastic lids

BIBLIOGRAPHY

Avedon, Elliott and Arje, Frances. *Socio-Recreative Programing for the Retarded.* Bureau of Publications, Teachers College, Columbia University, 1964.
Cruickshank, William M. *Cerebral Palsy: Its Individual and Community Problems.* Syracuse, New York: Syracuse University Press, 1972, pp. 261-264.

Fun in the Making. U. S. Department of Health, Education and Welfare, Office of Child Development, Washington, D.C., DHEW Publication No. (OHD) 76-31, 1973.

Hollander, Cornelius H. *Creative Opportunities for the Retarded Child.* Garden City, New York: Doubleday, Inc., 1972.

Play: Physical Coordination, Mental Creativity, Emotional Self-Control, Social Relationships. U.S. Department of Health, Education and Welfare, Social and Rehabilitation Service, Community Services Administration, Washington, D.C., DHEW Publication No. (SRS) 73-23009, 1973.

Preschool Learning Activities for the Visually Impaired Child: A Guide for Parents. Bureau of Education for the Handicapped, U. S. Office of Education, Grant #OEG-3-6-062679-1564(607), Office of the Superintendent of Public Instruction.

Structure 22. Finger painting is used to help hydrocephalic adolescent confined to wheelchair out of lethargy and to improve mental health.

Chapter 20

REALISM IN PERMITTING THE PROFOUNDLY RETARDED CITIZEN HIS RIGHT TO CREATIVE ARTS EXPRESSION

BARBARA K. ROSS

MEETING the creative arts needs of profoundly and severely mentally retarded persons is not always easy. Although some respond voluntarily to invitations to participate in creative arts activities, others remain totally inactive unless their body parts are first taken through the desired motions. Almost all severely handicapped persons require some modeling, or demonstration, in order to make socially expected responses to creative arts materials.

Presented in this chapter are some of the common behaviors exhibited by profoundly and severely retarded persons in the creative arts setting. It should be noted that profoundly retarded persons are generally so labeled because they function five standard deviations below the norm. Their intelligence quotients usually fall below 20 and many do not develop expressive language. On the other hand, severely retarded persons are so classified because they demonstrate intelligence quotients of 20 to 39; they usually develop some language and can be trained to care for their bodily needs. Only about 5 percent of all mentally retarded persons fall into the severe and profound ranges, and tremendous individual differences exist within these groups. Some, generally called idiot savants, have been known to exhibit gifted behavior in one of the arts. Illustrative of these is Shyoichiro Yamamara, whose atypical talent for drawing animal and insect pictures is described, along with illustrations, in a recent journal (Morishima and Brown, 1977).

The responses described now are those that can be expected

during the first sessions or exposures to the arts. These behaviors can be changed. Often, however, modification of behaviors involves one-to-one relationships, and the teacher or therapeutic recreation specialist in the residential facility is scheduled for ten to thirty such clients at one time. The need for volunteers to help bring arts to the handicapped is overwhelming.

Clay Activities

Profoundly Retarded Initial Responses

Places in mouth, chews, and swallows
Involves it in established manner
Drops and deliberately steps on it
Ignores it
Rejects feel of it on the skin
Wipes hands on self or therapist
Throws across room in frustration

Severely Retarded Initial Responses

Rolls in fingers
Sticks it on table
Places it in mouth or licks it
Uses it as a ball
Places objects in it
Rejects feel of it on the hands
Wipes clay on self or therapist

Begin with each person's individual response, helping him to tolerate the new texture and temperature. Be prepared in case the client tries to eat the clay. Keep a dowel or other sturdy object at hand to place between the teeth while cleaning out the mouth with fingers or washcloth. Use earth type clay rather than plastic as it passes through the digestive system with greater ease and has no chemicals to harm the body.

Finger Painting

Profoundly Retarded Initial Responses

Violently rejects feel of paint on skin
Places paint in mouth and swallows
Smears over entire body and area
Shows definite color preference
May prefer using brush instead of fingers

Severely Retarded Initial Responses

Withdraws from feel of paint on skin
Licks fingers experimentally
Smears primarily on objects
Deliberately smears on paper
Enjoys making own hand and foot print
Shows definite color preference
Place paint on floor in center of large sheet. First lead student through paint barefoot and then permit him to make tracks on a sheet. Do not wash feet until the session is through. Following the footprints session place the hands in the paint and make hand prints on the floor or a sheet. Then stand in front of a mirror and brush or rub paint on the face like make-up. If intolerance is too great, place the student in front of mirror and paint on his shirt or paint on a towel hung around the neck. Encourage the student to begin to make his own movement independent of the teacher or recreator.

Tissue Paper Art

Profoundly Retarded Initial Responses

May be frightened of large sheets
Places paper in mouth and tears it
Chews small pieces and swallows
Makes no connection between glue and paper

Squeezes glue at random in any amount
Places glue in mouth

Severely Retarded Initial Responses

May be frightened of large sheets
Tears it with hands or hands and mouth
Chews as if it were gum
Makes no connection between glue and paper
Shows no concept of amount of glue needed
Licks glue
First teach the concept of squeezing a glue bottle. Begin with smaller pieces of paper and permit the client to take any amount to place in whatever glue is on the paper. Separate piles of tissue paper by colors and permit him to mix them in any way he desires. Use both bright and dark colors. White glue may be colored with cake coloring or tempera to produce a modeled or solid color. Display all work.

Building From Rocks and Other Natural Materials

Profoundly Retarded Initial Responses

Enjoys picking up bricks or rocks
Piles two or three
Uses materials within reach and vision
Seems not to care when structure falls

Severely Retarded Initial Responses

Enjoys building structures
Piles large numbers
Searches small area for materials
Shows frustration if structure falls
Leader must interact with client and/or build a model as an example. This activity is most successful out-of-doors. Leader may reinforce building with sticks, strings, etc., to provide

variety. Encourage use of heavy objects to increase physical movement of the body.

Drawing

Profoundly Retarded Initial Responses

Breaks colors and pencils
Places colors and pencils in mouth
Chews and swallows colors and pencils
Marks randomly on all objects

Severely Retarded Initial Responses

Breaks colors and pencils
Places colors and pencils in mouth
Marks randomly on objects
Confines marks to large paper
Use felt tip, water color pens for drawing. These are less easily eaten than crayons and are nontoxic. Colors are brighter and the large pens are easily gripped. Attachments for the physically handicapped are available. Do not expect the marks to be confined to an eight by eleven inch piece of paper. Refer to *Creative and Mental Growth* by Lowenfeld for teaching progressions, beginning with scribbling.

Dramatic Activities

Profoundly Retarded Initial Responses

Lacks expressive language but can use noises and gestures
Does not reproduce situations deliberately
Willing to be led through skits
Enjoys the attention
Spontaneously acts out situations
Enjoys prop-type parts in plays

Severely Retarded Initial Responses

Uses about 300 words effectively
Acts out situations on request
May not comprehend the reproduction
Acts out familiar situations spontaneously
Prefers active parts and usually acts freely
Give student a part which coincides with his personality. Do not restrict his response to the part. Pantomime and gesture are generally more successful than speaking parts. Many nonverbal persons can learn and use signing. Orff-Schulwerk techniques are excellent.

Listening to Music

Profoundly Retarded Initial Responses

Makes definite response to sound and vibration
Tends to move body parts
Increases output in all movement activity
Loud music may produce frustration
Fast music may produce hyperactivity
Slow music may quiet client
Shows definite pattern responses

Severely Retarded Initial Responses

Makes definite responses to sound and vibration
Tends to move body parts in rhythms
Increases output in all movement activity
Loud music may produce frustration
Fast music may produce hyperactivity
Slow music may quiet client
May copy response of others around him
Music is useful in any activity either to reduce or heighten response. The type of music must be fitted to the individual student and to the activity. Music for the sake of music will heighten the student's awareness of sound, vibration, and intensity.

Producing Sounds: Rhythm Instruments

Profoundly Retarded Initial Responses

Ignores instrument placed in hand
Bangs objects together
Uses rhythm instruments on any body part
Chews rhythm instruments
Hums or uses noises to copy records
May produce own tunes

Severely Retarded Initial Responses

Bangs objects together
Uses rhythm instruments correctly
Chews rhythm instruments
Hums or uses words to copy records
May produce own tunes
Physically handicapped may use special adaptions to attach the rhythm instruments to body parts. Care must be taken that the student does not hurt his teeth or mouth by chewing on wooden instruments. Humming should be encouraged by the leader. This may be done while walking, swimming, or during any activity except running. For example, a bar of a familiar tune may be sung followed by a jump at the end.

Individual Differences Must be Respected

Although profoundly mentally retarded persons have numerous reactions in common, they are different and distinct in some aspects of motivation and performances utilizing creative type movements. Education can no longer restrict itself to rote learning and behavior modification type training. Informed persons throughout the country insist that educators of all types add a third dimension, that of developing human creativity. There is no justification for excluding the profoundly mentally retarded person from the manifestation of this concept.

The ambulatory, nonambulatory, and aged profoundly and severely mentally retarded persons all have the ability to perform creatively. Creativity has many definitions. The one idea expressed in all definitions is that of "novelty," which is derived from a rearrangement of existing knowledge or conditions. Regardless of the theory or the definitions, all measures of a person's creativity seem to be based on the product produced. This is nothing more than society attempting to place the values of the majority on the minority. The power of society, i.e. houseparents and teachers, to control creative impulses often disturbs the equilibrium of the profoundly mentally retarded person. He feels powerless, isolated, and insignificant in events that affect his life. Possibly, because of this, he may withdraw and prefer immobility to creative activity of any kind.

The key to eliciting creativity lies in the leader and her ability to broaden her own world, her concept of the profoundly mentally retarded, and her feelings concerning the worth of all individuals. Basically, a noncreative leader will do little to inspire the profoundly mentally retarded to any type of original action. The insensitive, impatient leader will teach her students to withdraw and remain immobile before she will enable them to respond creatively. If the leader is a free individual functioning as a person with feelings, fantasies, and intelligence, the freedom and growth of the student are fostered.

The leader, attempting to develop the spontaneous and creative movement of her students, may discover a number of problems. She may become discouraged with the lack of immediate response from the students. She may become disillusioned as the house-parents and others responsible for the retarded persons' care begin to complain of their increased movement and more fluent and original thinking. After all, a sitting, obedient person is easier to care for than a moving one.

These problems can, however, be overcome if the leader cares enough. Involvement in the inservice education of others who work with the severely handicapped is often necessary to change the attitudes, beliefs, and practices of the persons who structure the environment of the severely handicapped and thus can either encourage or stifle their creative development.

BIBLIOGRAPHY

American Association on Mental Deficiency. "Rights of Mentally Retarded Persons." *Mental Retardation, 11,5* (Oct. 1973) 56-58.

Grossman, H. *Manual on Terminology and Classification in Mental Retardation.* Washington, D.C.: American Association on Mental Deficiency, 1973, pp. 1-149.

Jourard, Sidney. *The Transparent Self.* Princeton, New Jersey: D. Van Nostrand, 1964, pp. 19-30, 64.

Kneller, George. *The Art and Science of Creativity.* New York: Holt, Rinehart and Winston, 1965, pp. 1-7.

Mayeroff, Milton. *On Caring.* New York: Harper and Row, 1971.

Morishima, Akira, and Brown, Louis F. "A Case Report on the Artistic Talent of an Autistic Idiot Savant." *Mental Retardation, 15* (April 1977) 33-36.

Thruston, L. *A Source Book for Creative Thinking.* New York: Scribner's, 1962, pp. 51-62.

Structure 23. Music can be a medium to motivate — to captivate — to encourage — to teach self-help skills.

Chapter 21

MUSIC AS TRAINING THERAPY FOR THE DEVELOPMENTALLY DELAYED

MARGIE REESING

HAVE you ever tried to brush a child's teeth when the mouth is clamped tightly shut? Frequently, with the child who is developmentally delayed, lack of cooperation is responsible for the inadequate training in simple basic self-help skills. Finding the means to encourage a child to help him help himself can be the key to a more successfully functioning individual. Music can be a medium to motivate — to captivate — to encourage — to teach.

Beginning with nonsensical words matched to a familiar catchy tune may be the first step in such a training program. A tune such as Mares E-Doats or Little Ducky Duddle may provide a predisposition towards a sunnier mood, setting the stage before training is actually begun. Singing a song including the child's name makes the child feel special and consequently more open to interaction between the child and the trainer. The child begins to relax, to enjoy being a part of a "game" and is, as a result, far more receptive to the learning process.

TEETH
(Come Walking With Me)

Tammy brushes her teeth
Tammy brushes her teeth
Up and down and all around
Tammy brushes her teeth.

175

BRUSHING TEETH
(Here We Go Round the Mulberry Bush)

To brush your teeth is a must every day,
Never let anything stand in the way.
Wet the toothbrush under the spout,
Take off the cap and let the tooth paste out.

Hold the brush with your left and the tube with your
    right,
Smear the paste on thick . . . What a beautiful sight.
Into your mouth this goody goes,
Taking care of your cavity woes.

Brush up and down, crossways too,
Fast and hard there's a job to do.
What a relief when you know for sure,
You are keeping the cavity wolf from your door.

Fostering a modicum of independence is one of the primary goals when working with the more severely handicapped. When an individual is able to care for his basic needs the quality of life is enriched. The repetition necessary to achieve this goal often leads to such tedium that both the trainer and the student become bored. Use of rhythmic songs, whether the trainer can sing well or not, provides a medium to break the lethargy. Putting appropriate words to familiar music can result in a handicapped child attending and participating.

PUTTING ON PANTS
(Jingle Bells)

Pick up your pants hold open wide,
Put in your feet and slide, slide, slide.
Pull them up just to your middle,
There they are fit as a fiddle.

SHOES
(Found a Peanut)

Put your toes in, put your toes in,
Put your toes in your shoes,
Push your heel down, run your finger "round"
And now you are through.

BUTTONING A SHIRT
(Little Brown Jug)

To button your shirt is quite a chore,
But you can do it in a second or more.
Put the hole over the button and work it right
    through,
Don't worry or fret or get in a stew.
Before you know it those buttons are done,
Now take off my friend and have some fun.

SOCKS

Put your toes into your socks,
Put your toes into your socks,
Wiggle your toes 'till they go on in,
Wiggle your toes 'till they go on in,
Wiggle your toes 'till they go on in,
Down into your sock.
Now pull, pull, pull,
Right over your heel.

(Put your finger in the air)
Put your toes into your socks, in your socks,
Put your toes into your socks, in your socks,
Now you catch it by the top,
And pull until it stops.
That's just how we put on our socks.

PUTTING ON A SHIRT

Put your head right in the little hole,
Put your head right in the little hole,
Put your head right in the little hole,
Peek-a-boo to you. (Tammy)

Your right arm in the sleeve it goes,
Your right arm in the sleeve it goes,
Your right arm in the sleeve it goes,
That's the way we dress ourselves.
         (Repeat using left arm)

Any kind of self-help skill can be taught by songs. One is limited only by his own imagination. The songs can be sung in a special training room in order to familiarize the child with the rhythm and the words. The trainer can then move into the dining room, bedroom, or bathroom with the child or small group of children.

The songs that have been included here are songs that have been successfully used with a group of severely/profoundly retarded children aged six to ten. The trainer had worked with these children for only a short period of time before there was a dramatic change in acquisition of self-help skills. This trainer used the piano primarily but ultimately evolved into just singing the songs without accompaniment in the actual training area. A tape recorder could be utilized to tape the music session to be replayed later in the training area.

Use of a guitar can be a very effective means of communicating with older retarded students who need these same basic self-help skills. Current songs can be adapted to the necessary self-help skill to be achieved. Music has such universal appeal that even the most severely handicapped individual usually will attend and make some response. It is only good common sense that dictates the wide use of this medium to provide more intensive training through a more interesting approach.

Other songs that have been tried by this trainer and proved successful follow.

DRINKING FROM A GLASS

Pick up your glass holding it tight,
Slowly, slowly, rising like a kite.

Now as the glass reaches your lip,
Gently give the glass a tip.

What in this world could ever taste better,
Than the cool, sweet taste of water.

WASHING FACE AND HANDS

Wet your hands in the sink and reach for the soap,
Working fingers over face like a horse in a lope.

Pick up the towel and wipe very dry,
Washing is easy if only we try.

EATING WITH FINGERS
(Jack & Jill)

Pick up food with fingers sure,
Raise them to your mouth then go back for more.

Up and down is the way it's done,
See there . . . Eating is lots of fun.

COMBING HAIR
(Baa, Baa, Black Sheep)

Pick up the comb and run through your hair,
Right side, left side, and down the middle there.
From the back of your head to the back of your neck,
By working back and forth it'll be smooth, by heck.

EATING WITH SPOON

Now, very carefully put your spoon in the food,
Dig way down and fill it real good.
Be sure and see that you spill not a drop,
From the plate to your mouth and there you stop.

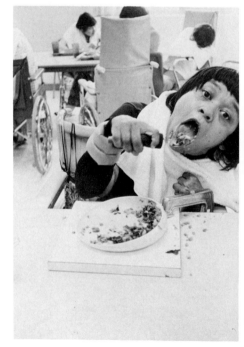

Structure 24. Scenes from the Fort Worth State School showing (top) art mural made by severely retarded clients completed and in progress and (bottom) demonstrating how manipulation of clay and other arts materials leads to increased control of eating utensils.

Chapter 22

THE ARTS AS LEARNING AND SOCIALIZATION EXPERIENCES FOR THE SEVERELY HANDICAPPED

ELLEN UHLER

$\mathbf{A}$ COLORFUL mural hangs in the reception area of Fort Worth State School. It is a landscape with a large tree, grass, the sun, and colorful vegetation on the ground. It is not a painted mural though. Instead, many brightly patterned materials have been painstakingly stitched together with thousands of big and little stitches. What is so remarkable about that? Just that it was made by students whose intelligence quotients range from twenty-five to thirty-five: students, who formerly were not considered students, who sat and watched television or stared into space, or absently performed any of the varied stereotypic behaviors (head banging, screaming, moaning, self-mutilation) for the major portion of their day.

If you were to walk into their classroom today you would see a very different picture. A small group at one table painstakingly cutting out material. Another small group sewing pieces of material together. Two or three at the ironing board pressing out materials. A hub-bub of activity . . . A feeling of warmth . . . Babbling and giggling. But mostly, you would see individuals who are interacting with other individuals, human beings, who, although severely handicapped, are maintaining the basic dignity, worth, and love to which they are entitled by birth.

You might feel a warm altruistic glow and think to yourself, "Now, isn't that nice to keep these poor unfortunates busy." But, they are not just being kept busy. They are learning! Art for them is not busy work. It is not *just* fun — it is education. Art is the medium through which they are being taught.

If we examine more closely what occurs in creating the

tapestry mural, we find incorporated into the learning process fine motor skills, language skills, cognitive skills, and social affective skills. Add to this the pleasure of creating an artistic product and it is easy to see that a great deal of true and beneficial learning takes place in this art experience.

In by-gone days, the institutionalized population has not been acclaimed for wild enthusiasm for learning. A large number of these children are extremely lethargic and disinterested in their environment. Apathy has been one of the principal obstacles to overcome. The use of music, art, puppetry, and drama appears to offer a dynamic and unifying approach to develop an increased awareness of all the senses, for it is through this ability to see, feel, hear, smell, and taste that interaction between a human being and his environment take place. The complete involvement of the individual in a purely physical, sensory activity stimulates and encourages exploration of an identification with the environment. This is the foundation of all learning. One must be able to listen, not just hear; to be aware of differences and details, not just see; to respond to differences in textures, temperatures, sizes, not just touch; to learn to utilize the sense of smell and taste for pleasure and safety purposes, not just to eat and breathe. Integration of sensory information precedes all further learning. One must reach, grasp, and hold to enable him/her to have the fine motor skills required for dressing, feeding, and toileting skills that lead to independence. One must be able to use the thumb in opposition to fingers before he/she can be taught a vocational skill, which can make him/her a contributing citizen rather than a permanent dependent in an institution at a tremendous expense to society. One must be able to function as part of a group and respect the rights of others within that group if she/he is to function within the parameters of the community.

That these behaviors, and much more, can be taught through the arts is inherent in the sensory nature of those activities. Music is a prime example. Music has long been known for its therapeutic value with the emotionally disturbed, the aged, the tired. Music as a medium for teaching is virtually unlimited.

Music creates an atmosphere conducive to self-expression motorically, affectively, and cognitively. When music activities are carefully planned and coordinated in the curriculum, body movement, spatial awareness, language, health and safety concepts, vocabulary, self-concept, and group awareness and interaction can all be incorporated. The only limitation to the use of music as a tool for teaching lies within the individual limitations of the teacher. The creative teacher, although not necessarily musically inclined herself, can use music to motivate, stimulate, relax, and maintain interest. Songs which teach a handicapped person to button, zip, and snap can be written to an existing tune and individualized according to the unique need. The tempo can be slowed down or accelerated, whichever is appropriate to the child.

If theories of advertising are true, intensity, frequency, and duration are a strong impetus in drawing attention. The chords of a guitar accompanied by the student's name being sung may provide the stimulus to attract and hold the attention of a nonresponsive child. If repeated frequently enough and for a duration of time that allows for integration of the stimuli, it can be the beginning point leading to a whole chain of responses, responses that lead to interaction with the environment.

Movement to music has been part of life since primitive days. Capitalizing on this instinctive response to beat and rhythm offers hope for teaching to all areas of exceptionality: the retarded, the emotionally disturbed, the physically handicapped, the child with learning disabilities. Music is fun and exciting and the learning experience can be made fun and exciting when it is interwoven into the curriculum in such a way as to direct learning to specific objectives. Teaching the severely spastic child to hold eating utensils in order to independently feed himself may stem from teaching him to hold a rhythm band instrument. It may take him (her) a long time to reach for and grasp that instrument but it is a lot more motivating to reach for something bright and shiny that makes some good noises than to reach for a mundane item such as a spoon. After all, when it is difficult to achieve, it is easier to be fed than to feed oneself.

Children confined to a wheelchair often have limited movement of any limb. Again, being motivated by the instinctive reaction to a beat and to rhythm often encourages use of these limited limbs, which lead to better circulation and less chance for atrophy or further deterioration. If a child's arms can be strengthened so that he can push his own wheelchair, this lessens the dependence on others to move himself freely around in his environment. He has some control, some decision making, some alternatives in his response repetoire. Through music and songs, these physical responses can be taught.

Music obviously is no panacea. Not every child can or will respond. But, just as obviously, it offers new avenues for exploration if we view the severely/profoundly/multihandicapped individuals as human beings. As human beings, they are individuals of worth and dignity with human rights to live their lives to the fullest degree possible.

Arts and crafts offer the same unlimited possibilities for learning. One does not have to create a Mona Lisa to experience the pride of creating. One does not have to depend on crayons, oils, or watercolors as the only medium, nor does one have to rely only on arms and fingers to produce an artistic creation. Feet and toes using tempora paints, or tempora paint thickened with soap flakes or thinned with detergent, can produce exotic pictures. Have you ever thought of using chocolate pudding? Then even the tongue and nose become instruments. Just putting the physically handicapped out of the wheelchair and down on the floor where she/he is not fighting gravity and exposing them to a wide variety of interesting textures, colors, and tastes may provide the stimuli to interest the severely handicapped in experimenting with his (her) environment. If the child *tries* to move his arms to make a swirl of color, or if the physical therapist or teacher moves the arms for him (her) and the child is rewarded by a design she/he has made, there is a far greater chance that she/he will attempt to move the arms again. The possibility of strengthening the arms and generalizing movements to pushing the wheelchair is increased.

Using the hands and fingers in a productive manner demands fine motor agility. The ability to pick up an object, to hold an object, to release an object at will is part of the developmental sequence we observe in the infant in the first few months of life. When neurological deficits or profound retardation occur, this normal sequence is interrupted. Motor and reflex skills, which we expect to develop naturally, must be trained. Intervention at the earliest moment possible can be instrumental in lessening the degree of handicap, in circumventing the handicap, or even at times in ameliorating the handicap. Through the arts we can provide intervention strategies.

If the teacher, parent, or therapist sets a realistic objective and then carefully analyzes the gross and fine motor skills necessary to achieve the objective, activities which stimulate the movements can be devised. For example, if the objective is to develop self-help skills that will permit a form of independence, each skill must be broken into small increments. The act of feeding oneself is a prime example. It is necessary to reach for, grasp, and release a utensil; to move the arm to bring food up and down; to have enough hand-eye coordination to get food on the spoon or fork and to the mouth and to reach across the midline. How can we develop these skills through art? Look at the first step — to reach, grasp, hold, and release. The aforementioned finger painting with a variety of textures and colors can stimulate this skill. Use of rhythm band instruments, push-pull musical toys, rolling clay, finger puppets, crayons, paints, objects such as strings, yarn, leaves, sticks, stones pushed or pulled through finger paint, aerosol shaving cream, macaroni, spaghetti, bean products pushed through finger paint, etc. These are all familiar methods in art; there is nothing new, no reinvention of the wheel. The only difference in this kind of curriculum is that the objective is to develop motor skills to enable the individual to feed himself. The means for reaching that goal are stimulating, motivating, creative, exciting, and fun. Fun for the child and fun for those working with him/her. The trainer may have to model a skill, or physically move the child's arm, hand, or fingers through the motion, gradually lessening the guidance, or may have to give

verbal prompts and cues, or may have to use concrete reinforcers (some sensory or multi-sensory rewards) on a continual
basis gradually reinforcing on an intermittent basis. In other
words, use every learning technique now known to attain the
desired results. The principles of frequency, intensity, and duration held, in addition to principles of learning, applied to a
fine arts program with realistic and measurable objectives hold
promise for a greater degree of development and independence
in a population once confined to the back ward or nursing unit
of an institution.

Application of these same principles is possible (and probably even more productive) in relation to the trainable retardate, the educable retardate, the emotionally disturbed, and
the learning disabled child. Learning does not have to be
painful, dull, unrealistic. It does have to be stimulating, exciting, fun. If it is to be learning that is lasting, conducive to
life-sustaining skills and independence, it *must* be stimulated
in such a way that the child wants to participate, is motivated
to try again and again, and is not placed in a situation where
he is right or wrong.

We do not cure mental retardation or severe handicaps
through the arts. We can provide a medium through which
each individual can express himself, one which is pleasurable
and satisfying; which can develop muscular and motor movement; which can stimulate and motivate the acquisition of
further skills leading to independence (dressing, feeding, and
toileting); which can help each individual reach the ultimate
potential of which she/he is capable, regardless of the limitations of that potential; which can provide each human being
the dignity and worth which is his right. Is that not what life is
all about?

Structure 25. Research is greatly needed to show which learning experiences in music, dance, drama, and the visual arts are most effective in changing behaviors.

Chapter 23

RESEARCH IN CREATIVE ARTS FOR THE HANDICAPPED

CLAUDINE SHERRILL

> Research is a high hat word that scares a lot of people. It needn't ... It is nothing but a state of mind — a friendly, welcoming attitude toward change. ... It is the problem-solving mind as contrasted with the let-well-enough alone mind. It is the composer mind instead of the fiddler mind. It is the "tomorrow" mind instead of the "yesterday" mind.
>
> Charles Franklin Kettering

RESEARCH, creativity, and art are inextricably linked in the self-actualizing person. All three endeavors seem to emanate from a strong inner drive to do and to be — to discover, explore, question, play with alternatives, synthesize in new and different ways, innovate, change, and originate.

Simply defined, research is the art and the science of finding answers to questions. What then is art? Robert Henri states "art, when really understood, is the province of every human being. It is simply a question of doing anything well." Carleton Noyes says "Art is creation. For the artist it is creation by expression; for the appreciator it is creation by evocation." Anne Schley Duggan, dance educator and Dean of the College of Health, Physical Education, and Recreation at the Texas Woman's University from 1927 through 1973, taught her disciples, "Art is an expression of feelings, ideas, emotions, and experiences with a definiteness of form and a high degree of skill. The art object should be enriching, uplifting, and have a quality that makes a person better from a spiritual point of view." Research undeniably is an art. It embodies the aspirations experienced by every dancer, musician, and actor who disciplines himself to hours of rehearsal in order to achieve

191

some measure of excellence and/or perfection. The striving for excellence may be a self-actualizing nature, as in *basic research*, or a dimension of the desire to communicate, to share, and ultimately to improve the quality of life as in *applied research*.

Science (derived from the Latin word *scientia*, fr *sciens*, *-entis*, present participle of *scire* to know) is defined by Webster as "knowledge obtained by study and practice." The word *science* refers also to the *processes* of gaining or creating knowledge. In the art world, it can apply to the process of creating an art product, of choreographing a dance, or producing an original play. The traditionally accepted cognitive processes involved in creating knowledge and/or art within the research context are deduction and induction.

Deduction refers to taking something known, accepted, and rather universally cited or practiced and analyzing it, subtracting from it, playing with it in new and different ways much as dancers over the years have taken movements from Graham, Wigman, or Humphrey and incorporated them into new choreographies.

Induction refers to bringing forth one's own movements, ideas, or thoughts, to improvising, or to making one's own observations rather than testing, questioning, and playing with those of others. The *scientific method*, a rather lofty contribution attributed historically to Darwin, the father of modern day research, is simply the combination of deduction and induction in continuous interaction as a researcher seeks to create an art product, i.e. anything done well.

Questions Needing Research
in the Creative Arts

The creative quality of an art and/or a science, i.e. of research itself, depends upon the presence of the behaviors enumerated in Table 1-I. Traditionally, artists have used their creative talents as a means of self-expression. Growing concern for the quality of life experienced by all persons, including the handicapped, leads to questions such as these: Can exposure to the creative arts improve the quality of life experienced by severely handicapped persons? Specifically, what behaviors can be changed through participation in the creative arts? Which learning experiences in music, dance, drama, and the visual arts are most effective in changing behaviors? How do specific handicapping conditions affect such creative behaviors as fluency, flexibility, originality, and elaboration? How do handicapped and nonhandicapped children compare with respect to artistic skills or achievements as measured by rating of their art products? What preservice and inservice education experiences should regular artist-educators have in order to effectively teach the handicapped?

Research Procedures for Finding Answers to Questions

Belief that creative arts belong to all persons, including the handicapped, and the desire to implement our beliefs commits us to active involvement in research. What procedures then are entailed in the art and science of finding answers to questions? The artistic-scientific process is characterized by five steps.

Statement of the Problem

This step begins with the selection of one specific question. It entails *deductive* reasoning as one reviews all available related literature and interviews authorities in an effort to identify what is already known and to deduce relevancies for one's own study from the existing body of knowledge. Related literature is usually found by going to the library and using a reference book like *Education Index* or a computer process like *ERIC* or *DATRIX*. Often in the creative arts, no published research exists. In such instances, the artist must rely solely on *inductive reasoning*, i.e. improvisation of ideas based upon his personal observations and experiences. Combined deductive and inductive thinking leads to listing the *limitations* of the study. These usually include quantitative statements concerning who, where, when, what, and how. This step ends with synthesizing all of the thought processes up to this point into one or two paragraphs called the Statement of the Problem.

Formulation of Hypotheses

Two types of hypotheses allow choice. If the study calls for statistical treatment, the statistical or *null hypothesis* is chosen, often worded: there is no significant difference between the two groups. If the study employs no statistics, *research hypotheses* are used. These are simply sentences, written in comfortable language, representing possible answers to the questions posed at the beginning of the investigation.

Collection, Organization, and Analysis of the Data

The method of research determines the nature of this procedure. In historical, philosophical, and much sociological research, *data* are simply the notes taken at the library or from various *primary sources* like interviews, photographs, documents in court houses, or minutes of meetings. Their organization and analysis relies upon combined deductive-inductive reflective thinking processes for synthesis into concrete findings with lucid interpretations.

In experimental research, data are generally collected twice, before and after the instructional period. Called pretests and posttests, or trials, the data can be test scores, ratings by judges, videotape documentation, or film such as that described in the article on photogrammetry. A statistical procedure called a *test of significance* is used to determine if the children actually benefitted from the instruction in or exposure to the arts.

In descriptive research, no attempt is made to change behavior, i.e. to teach or facilitate anything. Children are described just as they are and perhaps compared with other groups. If the description is statistical, only one set of data is needed. If the description is to be in narrative form, as in a case study, anecdotes may be written daily. If an analysis of the child's movement is to be made as in photogrammetry, only one filming session is required. Descriptive research, simply to discover the capacities of handicapped children, is often needed as related research before experimental studies to change behavior can be designed.

Verification or Rejection of Hypotheses

Statistical or null hypotheses are verified or rejected after completion of the mathematical or computer process called the test of significance, which yields a number like 3.71. The number is looked up in a table in the appendix of a research or statistics textbook and tells the investigator whether to accept or reject the null hypothesis.

Research hypotheses, written in comfortable language, are simply rejected or accepted after the deductive-inductive reasoning procedures enable the researcher to classify and organize the facts and evolve an interpretation.

Formulation of Conclusions

When all the data have been synthesized and reported as findings, the researcher must then draw one or two conclusions. These should be forceful statements with enough powerful facts behind them to change teaching practices in the field, to alter philosophies, beliefs, or attitudes, or to convince a funding source to provide monies for creative arts programs for the handicapped.

Comments to the Pure in Heart and Art

The arts, like all disciplines, are continuously changing. Where once all art products were believed to have form (refer back to Duggan's definition), free form or no form is now well accepted. Where once art was believed to encompass beauty and to be uplifting and spiritual, it now can be totally abstract, bizarre, discordant, ugly, or simply a happening — just as it is. Ours is the generation that defends "beauty is in the eye of the beholder." Perception is a uniquely individual phenomenon, and many modern day artists are reluctant to establish standards or criteria for evaluating art products and processes. Herein lies a grave problem for artists who would also be educators seeking all means to facilitate arts for the handicapped.

Research is deeply rooted in measurement and evaluation. To show behavioral changes in handicapped children that occur as the result of creative arts experiences between a pretest and a posttest, the artist must find some aspect of creative behavior or art performance that can be measured. Granted, this is indeed a compromise to those who believe that the arts cannot and should not be subjected to evaluation. We all believe that many kinds of behavioral changes are not easily measured, but researchers are also dreamers — committed perhaps to the impossible dream that if something exists, and we try hard enough, we can measure it. It is to this end that many researchers apply their creativity — exploring, testing, playing, inventing, revising, and discovering new and better ways to evaluate growth and development in children.

Research is perhaps the most powerful tool in all the world for getting money from administrators and funds from agencies. Persons responsible for budgetary decisions act on the basis of facts and statistics; they are most responsive to simple one and two group experimental research designs that show significant differences in children's behaviors following exposure to a creative arts program. If the artist's belief in arts for the handicapped is great enough, does not the end justify the means? If monies for expanding arts programs for children throughout the nation can best be attained by measurement, evaluation, and documentation, is it not time to experiment with these techniques in the arts?

Aileene Lockhart, well known dance educator, strongly emphasizes:

> It is a destructive bias to assume that art and science are incompatibly different, and a pessimistic outlook to assume that we must choose one or the other of the two cultures . . . the persons who have made the greatest and most lasting

impact on our world, both scientists and humanists, have been persons who could never be accused of narrowness of mind or fractionalization of knowledge.

The following chapters are designed to introduce artists and art educators to methods of collecting data, i.e. of measurement and evaluation, that seem most applicable to research in arts for the handicapped. Through venturing outside our established disciplinary boundaries, we can amass a body of knowledge that shows the arts can benefit all persons. Dance artist Anna Sokolow captures the essence of this rationale in her statement:

> The important thing is that the art being created now be related to now, our time. The artist must be influenced by his time, conditioned by life around him. If he is not, his viewpoint is limited by the past, and turns back instead of going forward. If he draws on the ever-changing life around him, his work will always be fresh and new. Art should be a reflection and a comment on contemporary life.

BIBLIOGRAPHY

Duggan, Anne Schley. Cited from class lecture notes. Texas Woman's University, Denton, Texas, 1960s.

Haywood, H. Carl. "The Ethics of Doing Research . . . And of Not Doing It." *American Journal of Mental Deficiency, 81:4,* 1977, 311-317.

Henri, Robert. *The Art Spirit.* Philadelphia: J. B. Lippincott, 1960.

Kettering, Charles Franklin. Quoted from Carter V. Good, *Introduction to Educational Research.* New York: Appleton-Century-Crofts, 1963.

Lockhart, Aileene S. "The Critical and the Creative" *The Tenth Amy Morris Homans Lecture.* Milwaukee, National Association for Physical Education of College Women (NAPECW), 1976.

Sokolow, Anna. "The Rebel and the Bourgeois." In Selma Jeanne Cohen, *The Modern Dance — Seven Statements of Belief.* Middletown, Connecticut: Wesleyan University Press, 1965.

Whitney, Frederick Lamson. "The Creative Type of Research." In *The Elements of Research.* New York: Prentice-Hall, Inc., 1942.

Structure 26. Adolescent with Down's Syndrome demonstrates trait 18.0, makes simple product by weaving, on the Behavioral Characteristics Progression (BCP), used to evaluate his learnings in the arts adapted to his ability level.

Chapter 24

BCP STRANDS FOR EVALUATING CHANGING BEHAVIORS IN MUSIC AND RHYTHMS AND ARTS AND CRAFTS

DONNA RUSSELL

AMONG the few evaluation devices that actually work with the severely handicapped is the BCP, or Behavioral Characteristics Progression, which originated in Santa Cruz, California, in 1973, and now is being used throughout Texas in all residential facilities for mentally retarded clients. The BCP is organized into fifty-nine strands, each of which denotes a specific learning area. Over 2,300 observable behavioral characteristics or traits are included within the strands, two of which focus specifically on the creative arts.

Each of the fifty-nine strands is more-or-less developmentally sequenced. Containing up to 50 specific behaviors, each strand begins with primary behaviors and progresses in small increments.

The BCP is available in three formats: (1) the observation booklet comprised of assessment charts on which the behaviors of six persons can be recorded at one time; (2) 18 by 40 inch charts that provide a complete visual picture of an individual's strengths and weaknesses; and (3) the binder that describes the behaviors in slightly more detail than do the assessment charts.

A client's progress is charted by marking or coloring in the traits that presently describe his abilities. A trait is usually colored in if the client can successfully demonstrate it three out of four times or 75 percent of the time. In this way, the BCP gives a pictorial representation of the client's past and present abilities, thereby enabling the teacher to see at a glance where improvement is needed.

The two creative arts strands from the BCP are included in

40

MUSIC & RHYTHMS

Identifying Behaviors:

Moves to music in non-rhythmic way ● Marches/dances ignoring beat ● Uses rhythm instrument but produces no pattern

Date of observation _____

	Trials					
	1	2	3	4	5	6
1.0 Mimics simple gross rhythmic hand movements, e.g. claps with music						
2.0 Entertains self playing with musical toys, e.g. push-pull type toy						
3.0 Mimics simple gross rhythmic foot movements, e.g. marks time with feet						
4.0 Moves in circular pattern						
5.0 Sways and rocks whole body using simple rhythmic movement						
6.0 Makes fine hand/foot rhythmic movements, e.g. snaps fingers, taps foot						
7.0 Plays rhythm instruments						
8.0 Marches in time to repetitious beat						
9.0 Shifts body rhythm when music tempo changes						
10.0 Participates in group songs with singing voices						
11.0 Follows/mimics others' play activities						
12.0 Hums/sings parts of familiar songs						
13.0 Plays simple rhythmic patterns on rhythm sticks						
14.0 Sings phrases of songs						
15.0 Reproduces some actions to familiar songs						
16.0 Claps to beat of familiar songs or to speech cadence/patterns						
17.0 Bounces ball (rhythmically)						
18.0 Matches notes or tones						
19.0 Imitates high and low notes or tones vocally						
20.0 Plays records at appropriate speeds						
21.0 Plays rhythm instrument in simple pattern						
22.0 Improvises body movements to follow tempo/rhythm						
23.0 Sings whole songs by rote						
24.0 Plays rhythm instrument in various rhythm patterns						
25.0 Sings parts of contemporary songs from memory						
26.0 Plays accent beat of music on rhythm instrument						
27.0 Plays a few bars of music on melody instrument						
28.0 Dances using simple steps, e.g. modern dance or waltz						
29.0 Sings simple rounds taking one part						
30.0 Performs square dancing						
31.0 Plays rhythm counterpoint on rhythm instrument						
32.0 Plays instrument or sings following conductor's direction in group, e.g. loud, soft						
33.0 Carries simple harmony to melody						
34.0 Participates in social dances with a partner						

41

ARTS & CRAFTS

Identifying Behaviors:

Scribbles but does not draw ● Tears/rips paper but produces no designs ● Uses paste ineffectively ● Has difficulty cutting with scissors

Date of observation _____

	Trials					
	1	2	3	4	5	6
1.0 Entertains self looking at picture books						
2.0 Makes one-color drawings						
3.0 Finger paints						
4.0 Colors pictures using a variety of colored crayons/pencils						
5.0 Paints pictures using a variety of colors						
6.0 Makes simple shapes from clay						
7.0 Draws/paints, telling or showing what he is doing						
8.0 Relates color to objects, e.g. colors apples red						
9.0 Entertains self with resources at hand						
10.0 Cuts/tears paper to make designs/shapes						
11.0 Pastes materials to make a collage						
12.0 Forms geometric shapes with connecting, e.g. tinker or lego, or stack toys e.g. blocks or rings						
13.0 Draws simple recognizable forms on request, e.g. man or dog						
14.0 Uses art skills to make a craft product, e.g. cut or paste						
15.0 Cuts/pastes a variety of materials to make 3D design						
16.0 Pastes colored cutouts to make a complete picture						
17.0 Divides pictures into different areas, e.g. ground and sky						
18.0 Makes simple product by weaving						
19.0 Models with clay						
20.0 Builds objects with common materials, e.g. twigs and paperclips						
21.0 Designs and constructs collages						
22.0 Uses arts and crafts skills during leisure time						
23.0 Scales objects in drawings, e.g. car larger than man						
24.0 Carves soap, balsa wood						
25.0 Entertains self with solitary games						
26.0 Uses a variety of art techniques for effect, e.g. shading						
27.0 Expresses movement in drawing						
28.0 Uses wood working skills to make a product						
29.0 Assembles plastic or wood kits						
30.0 Uses sewing skills to make a product						
31.0 Draws simple perspectives						
32.0 Copies simple art motifs/geometric designs						
33.0 Makes decorative house accessories						

this monograph. The value of the BCP for creative teachers is its concept rather than the specific strands and traits. It is often necessary to add new traits representing easier behaviors when attempting to assess the severely handicapped person. The teacher should not feel locked into any particular strand and should modify and adapt the instrument as needed. It has been found, for instance, in the Arts and Crafts strand that one specific behavior like finger painting must be developed into an entire strand with about fifty sub-behaviors in order to truly assess the changing behaviors of profoundly retarded or deaf-blind persons.

Particularly useful in helping the teacher break down an activity like finger painting into its parts are various recreation textbooks and articles that present concepts of activity analysis, such as Hayes (1971).*

BIBLIOGRAPHY

Hayes, Gene. "Activity Analysis: Finger Painting for the Mentally Retarded." *Therapeutic Recreation Journal,* 1971, 5, 133.
Lett, Mark; Uhler, Ellen; and others. *Behavioral Characteristics Progression Developmental Curriculum Guide.* Austin: Texas, Department of Mental Health and Mental Retardation, 1978.

---

*Strands 40 and 41 of the BCP were developed by the Office of the Santa Cruz County Superintendent of Schools, California, 1973. They and the other materials described herein may be purchased from VORT Corporation, P. O. Box 11132, Palo Alto, California 94306.

Structure 27. The London Trestle Tree Apparatus is one of several play environments known to stimulate originality and motor fluency among young handicapped children.

Chapter 25

OBSERVATION AND RATING
OF MOTOR CREATIVITY

CLAUDINE SHERRILL, ELLEN LUBIN,
AND LAUREN ROUTON

MOVEMENT appears to be the predominant
characteristic by which the creativity of the severely handicapped (and often nonverbal) child can be evaluated. When
presented with rhythm instruments or arts and crafts materials,
for instance, does the child move toward them? Does he use
them in one way or several? Do his responses seem random and
inappropriate, or purposeful and relevant? How does he use
time, space, force, and flow?

As part of a longitudinal study of motor creativity at the
Texas Woman's University, several studies have been completed and others are underway. The movement responses of
preschool handicapped and nonhandicapped children to novel
play apparatus such as the Lind Climber and London Trestle
Tree Equipment have been videotaped at regular intervals and
then subjected to analysis by several independent judges or
raters.

What is Motor Creativity?

The theoretical construct of motor creativity seems to have
been innovated in the early 1960s by Waneen Wyrick Spirduso.
The Wyrick test of Motor Creativity, first published in 1966,
included forms for assessment of motor originality, motor fluency, and motor creativity. The items comprising the tests
closely paralleled those on the paper-pencil tests of Torrance.
Likewise her definitions of creativity were consistent with those
of Frank Williams (see Table 1-I), as well as other leading
authorities in creativity.

205

The TWU Motor Creativity studies of young children are based on the ideas and tests of Wyrick and Torrance. All data are collected through videotape or other film techniques to allow observers an opportunity to see a movement as many times as needed. The explanations that follow show how motor creativity scores have been derived.

Motor creativity appears to encompass fluency, flexibility, originality, and elaboration as well as such affective domain behaviors as risk taking, curiosity, imagination, and courage. Wyrick, however, limited her studies only to originality and fluency and thus derived a *motor creativity score* by changing the motor fluency and motor originality scores to standard scores and averaging them. The TWU studies have paralleled this approach of Wyrick.

Motor originality is the uniqueness of movement responses. Videotapes are viewed, and every movement is tabulated according to type of movement (as walk, run, climb, hang), amount of body use (total, one arm, both legs, etc.), direction, dimension, path, focus, speed, and other movement elements appropriate to the art under study. The tabulation sheet with organized spaces for recording responses in each of these categories is, of course, prepared ahead of time. These tallies are then organized into a rank or frequency distribution so that the responses can be assigned 2, 1, or 0 points depending upon their frequency of occurrence in the total population tested. The *motor originality score* then is the sum of the 2, 1, or 0 ratings assigned to the child's individual movements.

Motor fluency is the production of as many ideas or movements as possible within a given amount of time. The movements should be relevant rather than accidental, random, or self-destructive as sometimes occurs among the severely handicapped. To derive a *motor fluency score,* the judge simply views the videotape and records every movement and/or contact with the play apparatus or arts and crafts supplies or rhythm instrument. The sum of these responses in a given period of time is the fluency score.

Research Using Videotape Techniques
to Assess Motor Creativity

Using these definitions and procedures, findings on motor creativity in early childhood are presented by Sherrill and Rowe (1975), Rowe (1976), Sherrill, Lubin, and Routon (1977), and Lubin (1978). Novel play apparatus, either the Lind Climber or the London Trestle Tree, was used in each study as the learning environment for stimulating guided movement discovery and for increasing motor creativity. Pretesting of the children's motor creativity was achieved by videotaping the initial five minutes of their movements during their first exposure to the novel play apparatus.

Sherrill and Rowe (1975) videotaped twenty-three children, ages two to six, individually in five-minute segments during their initial exposure to the Lind Climber, four weeks after the pretest, and again eight weeks after the pretest. The motor creativity scores of the eight mild/moderately retarded children were significantly lower than those of their fifteen nonhandicapped peers on all three trials. This finding was surprising because the mentally retarded children were given eight weeks of daily guided discovery sessions designed to increase fluency and originality while the nonhandicapped children played randomly with no instruction on the apparatus. All other experimental variables were controlled. While the nonparametric statistics showed the nonhandicapped group to be consistently superior, great intragroup variability existed with a few retarded children excelling in raw motor creativity scores over the nonretarded. Sherrill and Rowe concluded that retarded children, ages two to six, must have superior motor instruction of long duration in preschool prior to placement in mainstream arts settings in which motor creativity (fluency and originality) may be an instructional objective.

Rowe (1976) conducted a one-group experimental study of changes in motor creativity over a four-week period of daily individual guided discovery sessions on the Lind Climber. Subjects were thirty-two mildly mentally retarded children, ages three to six. Trial to trial significant differences were found in motor fluency and motor originality using analysis of variance techniques. The posttest scores of the retarded subjects were then compared with the baseline data of the Sherrill and Rowe (1975) study. It was found that the two groups were not significantly different on motor fluency and overall motor creativity. The posttest scores of the retarded group, however, were significantly better in motor originality than the baseline scores of the normal children.

Sherrill, Lubin, and Routon (1977) videotaped twenty children, ages three to four, on the London Trestle Tree Apparatus three times (5-minute segments) during a one-month period during which no experimental condition was introduced. The major purpose of the study was to refine the videotape analysis protocol and to determine its objectivity and reliability as a technique for assessing selected traits of motor creativity. Analysis of variance yielded objectivity coefficients of .99 and .65 for motor fluency and motor originality, showing that the two judges were evaluating the videotapes in a similar manner. Spearman Rho test-retest reliability coefficients for rater A and rater B on motor fluency and motor originality were .99 and .94 and .99 and .93 respectively, substantiating the trial to trial consistency of each rater. The videotape analysis protocol was assumed to have face validity. It was concluded that the Sherrill, Lubin, and Routon (SLR) videotape analysis protocol was a satisfactory method of assessing motor creativity in children.

Lubin (1978) videotaped changes in motor creativity among twenty-four deaf children, ages three to five, in a two-group experimental study of four weeks duration. The experimental group received daily guided movement exploration on the London Trestle Tree Apparatus while the control group played randomly. The motor creativity data derived by the SLR videotape analysis protocol were treated by multivariate factorial analysis of variance to determine significant differences between groups; no differences were found. Pre- and posttest data were collected also by the Torrance Test of Thinking Creatively in Action and Movement; this evaluation technique resulted in significant differences between the experimental and control groups. It was believed that the SLR videotape analysis protocol and the Torrance tests measured different aspects of motor creativity.

Torrance Test of Thinking Creatively in Action and Movement

Published in 1976, the Torrance Test* was developed specifically for children, ages three to seven, and has preliminary norms based on the performance of 103 children. The Torrance test consists of four sets of activities: (1) How Many Ways? — designed to sample the child's ability to produce alternative ways of moving; (2) Can You Move Like? — designed to sample the child's ability to imagine, empathize fantasy, and assume unaccustomed roles; (3) What Other Ways? — designed to sample alternative ways of putting a cup in a wastebasket; and (4) What Can You Do? — designed to sample unusual uses of cups. Activities 1, 3, and 4 are scored on motor fluency and originality; activity 2 is scored only on imagination. A total fluency score, originality score, and imagination score are attained, and a total composite score of all three is achieved also.

Torrance states that the interscorer reliability for this test is in excess of .90. An overall test-retest reliability of .84 was obtained, and face validity was assumed. At this time no published research concerning handicapped children can be found that uses the Torrance Test of Thinking Creatively in Action and Movement with the exception of that of Lubin. It is believed that the test offers great potential for investigating creative behaviors of handicapped children.

Texas Woman's University Motor Creativity Scale

The TWU Motor Creativity Rating Scale (Fig. 25-1), developed by Sherrill in 1976, is an attempt to find another way to evaluate children on the recognized components of creativity. It is still in the pilot testing stage but seems to hold promise. It is especially valuable as a training tool to help teachers under-

---

*Can be obtained by writing Dr. E. Paul Torrance, College of Education, The University of Georgia, Athens, Georgia 30602.

TWU MOTOR CREATIVITY SCALE

10 7 5 3 1 Overall	Above Average	Average	Below Average		*Originality*
	AA	A	BA	1.	Are his movement responses unusual, deviant, unexpected?
	AA	A	BA	2.	Does he experiment with his body or body parts in new, unique, different, bizarre, clever ways?
	AA	A	BA	3.	Does he use *time* (accents, speed, even and uneven) in unusual ways?
	AA	A	BA	4.	Does he use *space* in interesting, different ways (direction, dimension, curved or direct paths, focus)? Does he remain on the floor or interact with benches, tables, unexpected props in the room?
	AA	A	BA	5.	Does he use *force* (strong, weak, light, heavy) in unusual ways?
	AA	A	BA	6.	Does the *flow* of his movement seem to vary intentionally (easy, graceful, disharmonious, bound)?

10 7 5 3 1 Overall					*Fluency*
	AA	A	BA	1.	Does he make lots of attempts within the given time period?
	AA	A	BA	2.	Does he continue moving the entire time?
	AA	A	BA	3.	Do his movements seem quick, energetic, vivacious?
	AA	A	BA	4.	Are his movements relevant?

10 7 5 3 1 Overall					*Flexibility*
	AA	A	BA	1.	Are his attempts varied in nature, depicting rapidly changing ideas?
	AA	A	BA	2.	Do some reponses entail manipulation of time, space, force, and flow so that these are continuously changed?
	AA	A	BA	3.	Do some responses entail the entire body while others use body parts, extensions of body parts, or objects in the room?
	AA	A	BA	4.	Do his approaches use different muscle groups? Different sense modalities?
	AA	A	BA	5.	Does he frequently change categories of movement as walk to jump to roll to clap? Locomotor to nonlocomotor and vice versa?

10 7 5 3 1 Overall					*Elaboration*
	AA	A	BA	1.	Does he take a simple movement or idea and add on to it in several different ways? Stretch or expand it?
	AA	A	BA	2.	Do his movements reflect embellishments of several ideas?
	AA	A	BA	3.	Is he content to experiment only with his body or does he incorporate props, weights, and furnishings of the room into his exercise?
	AA	A	BA	4.	Does he add sound effects? Use his voice? Make noise?

Figure 25-1.

stand creativity in movement.

The TWU Motor Creativity Scale is comprised of basic questions under the subheadings of originality, fluency, flexibility, and elaboration. Face validity of the scale is assumed since the questions evolve from accepted definitions of the four creative behaviors believed by Torrance and other authorities to comprise creativity. For a review of these definitions, see Table 1-I.

It is recommended that the scale be used in conjunction with the videotaping of children's movement responses to a question, a problem, a novel piece of apparatus, or a stage prop. Five-minute videotapes of children individually or in couples or triads have proved sufficient to provide data for rating each child's creative behaviors in relation to his peers. It is, however, often necessary to view a videotape several times before assigning the overall numerical rating for each component of creativity. It is helpful also for the raters to have background in movement education, i.e. an understanding of the many ways a creative person can manipulate the factors of time, space, force, and flow.

Motor creativity rating, using the TWU Scale, proceeds through two stages. First the rater circles the appropriate answer to each question: *AA*, above average, which refers to about 16 percent of a large group; *A*, average, which refers to the middle 68 percent of a group as conceptualized in normal curve theory; and *BA*, below average, which refers to about 16 percent of a large group. The use of the AA, A, and BA ratings is analogous to a 3, 2, 1 point system which may be used as an alternative. When the individual questions have been answered, the rater moves into the second stage which demands synthesizing specific observations into one generalized rating, using a 10, 7, 5, 3, 1 overall numerical point scale for each component of creativity. Ten represents the highest rating and one the lowest, with ratings assigned more-or-less in accordance with normal curve expectations. Thus in a group of one hundred children, about three would receive a rating of *10*; thirteen would receive a *7*; sixty-eight would receive a rating of *5*; thirteen would receive a *3*; and about three would receive a *1*. Last, the rater adds the four overall ratings (one each for originality, fluency, flexibility, and elaboration) to determine the total motor creativity score.

The scale therefore makes possible a range of total motor creativity scores from 1 to 40. It also allows for statistical treatment of ratings on each individual component of creativity.

As in the proper use of all rating scales for assessment and/or research, the child's score should be the *average* of the ratings of three or more independent observers. At this time the TWU Motor Creativity Scale has been applied only to movement in the physical education (including dance) setting. It is believed that it holds potential also for rating motor creativity in the arts. The success of the scale depends largely upon the observational skills of the raters. Recommended readings on observational techniques therefore follow.

RECOMMENDED READINGS

Barker, R. G. *Ecological Psychology: Concepts and Methods for Studying the Environment of Human Behavior.* Stanford, California: Stanford University, 1968.

Hutt, S. J., and Hutt, Corrine. *Direct Observation and Measurement of Behavior.* Springfield, Charles C Thomas, 1970.

Lindberg, Lucile, and Swedlow, Rita. *Early Childhood Education: A Guide for Observation and Participation.* Boston: Allyn and Bacon, 1976.

North, Marian. *Personality Assessment Through Movement.* London: MacDonald and Evans, 1972.

Rowen, Betty. *The Children We See: An Observation Approach to Child Study.* New York: Holt, Rinehart, and Winston, 1973.

Webb, Eugene; Campbell, Donald; Schwartz, Richard; and Sechrest, Lee. *Unobstrusive Measures: Nonreactive Research in the Social Sciences.* Chicago: Rand McNally and Company, 1972.

Weinberg, Richard A., and Wood, Frank H. (Eds.). *Observation of Pupils and Teachers in Mainstream and Special Education Settings: Alternative Strategies.* Reston, Virginia: Council on Exceptional Children, 1975.

BIBLIOGRAPHY

Lubin, Ellen. "Motor Creativity of Preschool Deaf Children." Unpublished doctoral dissertation, Texas Woman's University, 1978.

Rowe, Joanne. "Motor Creativity of Mildly Mentally Retarded Preschool Children." Unpublished doctoral dissertation, Texas Woman's University, 1976.

Sherrill, Claudine; Lubin, Ellen; and Routon, Lauren. "Motor Creativity of Mainstream Preschool Children on the Trestle Tree Apparatus." Unpublished study funded by faculty institutional research grant, Texas Woman's University, 1977.

Sherrill, Claudine, and Rowe, Joanne. "Changes in Sensory-Motor Fluency of Young Mentally Retarded Children Engaged in a Space-Oriented Learning Program." *Proceedings of the Research Council, Southern*

District, American Alliance for Health, Physical Education, and Recreation, Mobile, Alabama, 1976. Funded by faculty institutional research grant, Texas Woman's University, 1975.

Torrance, E. P. "Thinking Creatively in Action and Movement." *Georgia Studies of Creative Behavior.* Athens, Georgia: University of Georgia, 1976.

Wyrick, Waneen. "Comparison of Motor Creativity with Verbal Creativity, Motor Ability, and Intelligence." Unpublished doctoral dissertation, University of Texas at Austin, 1966.

Wyrick, Waneen. "The Development of a Test of Motor Creativity." *Research Quarterly,* 1968, *39,* 756-765.

Structure 28. Arts sessions should be filmed periodically to create tangible records of children's progress in social, motor, and artistic behaviors.

Chapter 26

MOTION PHOTOGRAPHY: A TOOL FOR THE ANALYSIS OF MOVEMENT PATTERNS IN THE CREATIVE ARTS FOR THE SEVERELY HANDICAPPED

MARILYN M. HINSON AND TERRY LAWTON

EACH of the creative arts lends itself to movement, which can be measured. Changes in hand-eye coordination that occur through various arts and crafts can be captured on film. Likewise, the movement of the limbs in using rhythm instruments and puppets and of the total body in dance and drama can be recorded on film and analyzed for changes that seem to result from guided discovery sessions in the arts.

It is our viewpoint that motion photography, or close-range photogrammetry as it is currently called, is the most viable means we have of collecting and analyzing movement pattern data of the severely handicapped child. The following pages are intended to give some insight into method, equipment needs, a protocol for the filming session, an overview of analysis methodology, and a brief treatment of interpretation of findings. Perhaps with this background, the reader's first experience in the world of motion photography will not totally be one of trial, error, and complete confusion!

Exposure Rates

The rate at which film frames are exposed can vary from one to more than one million exposures per second according to the camera equipment available. These, of course, are the extremes in the spectrum of camera speeds. Most aspects of human motion can be analyzed at exposure rates between 64 and 500 per

216 Creative Arts for the Severely Handicapped

second. The concept of exposure rate may be clarified if it is remembered that 24 exposures per second will yield film which will not, when it is projected, distort the speed of movement. Exposure rates of less than 24 per second will accelerate motion (the "Charlie Chaplin" effect) whereas rates greater than 24 per second will provide slow motion. For movements that are inherently slow, such as walking or finger painting, exposure rates of 64 per second are quite adequate since the already slow movements need not be further slowed to any great extent to permit accurate analysis. Fast movements such as striking rhythm instruments and dancing should be filmed at rates of approximately 200 per second to optimally slow the action. Exposure rates of 500 per second are used in studies of ball velocities, golf swings, tennis serves, and so forth.

Equipment

The equipment required for high speed motion photography must, of necessity, be somewhat specialized. It is strongly recommended that representatives from the various manufacturers be consulted before final choices are made. A list of manufacturers and their products can be easily obtained from camera rental agencies.

The Camera

A sixteen millimeter (16 mm) camera is preferable to an eight or super eight millimeter camera because the size of the film, being twice as large, is easier to magnify to large image sizes. In addition, 16 mm cameras typically have more and higher exposure rate settings than do their smaller counterparts. If cost is a factor, however, a super eight camera may be used temporarily but only if it is capable of achieving a rate of at least 64 exposures per second. Other factors important to camera selection are ruggedness, ease of operation, and portability. Ketlinski (1971) provides a valuable summary of the characteristics of several camera types currently available on the market.

Film

If a super eight camera is to be used, the film of choice is an indoor or outdoor color film. A black and white film for these cameras is difficult if not impossible to purchase; since the size of the film is small, the cost of color film is not prohibitive as it is with 16 mm film. The film most often used with a 16 mm camera is a Tri-X black and white reversal film. It is a so-called "fast" film that allows its use in conditions of poor light. Purchase and processing costs of this film are about one-half that of color film. All film should be stored in a refrigerator until a few hours before use. The cold environment greatly extends shelf life.

Tripod

A sturdy and adjustable tripod is almost a must. A handheld camera will move a surprising amount because of the sway or lack of steadiness of the operator. On a tripod, the camera is stable and actually safer. It will not be dropped or stepped on while not in use, nor will it be as prone to accidental opening, which ruins the film inside. In addition, a camera on a tripod can be replaced at standardized locations by placing marks on the floor for each of the three tripod legs.

Light Meter

A light meter is used to measure the ambient light in order that lens and shutter settings can be made correctly. More and more super eight cameras are becoming available which have automatic settings; the built-in light meter sets the lens opening without intervention from the operator — a feature that is tempting to all of us. It must be remembered, however, that the operator is at the mercy of the accuracy of the camera. Since film data are costly both in terms of money and time, it is recommended that a light meter be used to verify the automatic settings.

Light meters may appear to be complicated but are actually quite simple to use. One need only set the ASA* and the shutter speed dials to the correct position, and then hold the meter next to the camera lens. When the button that activates the meter is pressed, the needle will point to the appropriate lens f stop setting. Never leave your light meter in the sun. The cells can be irreversably damaged.

Shutters

Motion picture cameras are designed around shutters that rotate behind the lens and in front of the film. A portion of the shutter is cut away so that light is allowed to pass through the lens and expose the film. If the major portion of the shutter is cut away, a great deal of light passes through and the film "sees" the object being photographed for relatively long periods of time. If the object is in motion, the film records a blur rather than a sharp image. Precise analysis of such data is, of course, severely limited. It can be seen that it is of utmost importance to know the opening of the shutter in the camera. Shutter openings are referred to by the fraction that results from dividing the amount, in degrees, the shutter is cut away by 360 degrees. For example, if a shutter has 120° cut away, it would be a one to three or 1/3 shutter (120° divided by 360°). When the shutter fraction is known, a quantity known as shutter speed can be quickly calculated by multiplying the shutter fraction by the reciprocal of the camera exposure rate per second. As an example, if a camera comprises a 1/3 shutter and is set to an exposure rate of 100 per second, shutter speed will be 1/3 times 1/100 or 1/300 seconds. A shutter speed of 1/300 indicates that every time the film "sees" the object, it will do so for 1/300 of a second. Precise analysis depends upon sharpness of image; blur must be kept to a minimum by manipulating either camera speed or shutter fraction. The following guidelines are offered to aid the reader in the

---

*ASA is a rating of the film's chemical ability to absorb light. ASA ratings of around 200 depict a "fast" film — one that can absorb light rapidly. ASA ratings of 60 to 100 are those of "slow" film. The ASA is printed on the film container.

selection of appropriate shutter speeds:

Shutter Speed	Event
1/100 sec.	Slow walking
1/300 sec.	Fast running
1/500 sec.	"Stop" a jump in mid-air
1/1000 sec.	"Stop" a golf club in mid-swing

It becomes obvious that the movement to be photographed dictates to the operator the selection of shutter speed, and since shutter speed is based upon both camera speed and shutter fraction, these factors must be kept in mind when selecting equipment. It is recommended that 1/6 or 1/9 shutters be installed in cameras that are capable of maximal exposure rates of 64 per second; and that 1/3 or 1/4 shutters be chosen for cameras capable of higher rates. Optimum results can be had, of course, if the camera allows for variable settings of shutter fractions. This feature is available, but only on the more costly cameras.

Lenses

An awesome variety of lenses are available for motion cameras, and although super eight and some 16 mm cameras come complete with lenses, it is not the typical case. When lenses must be purchased or otherwise obtained, attention must be given to the space available for photographing. Two-inch lenses are very highly recommended for sharpness of image; however, they may require the photographer to be farther removed from the object than usually available. One-inch lenses do not provide the same sharpness but do allow for more reasonable camera-to-object distances. There is some argument among motion photographers regarding the use of zoom lenses because of their sometimes questionable resolution; however, we find that if they are of high quality, they are preferable to either the one- or two-inch lenses since, by zooming in or out, the viewing area can be made satisfactory without moving the camera.

A Level and a Plumb Line

A spirit level between 18 and 24 inches long should be used to align the camera along the horizontal. Unless this is done, the camera sees the object at an angle and error will be introduced in the analysis. The plumb line, placed in the plane of motion, can serve both as a vertical reference and as a measurement scale by which film distances can be converted to real distances. Occasionally, objects such as corners of buildings, if outside, or lines formed by the intersection of walls, if inside, appear in the background of the viewing area. These can be used as vertical reference lines, and in this case, a meter or yard stick can be held in the plane of motion to provide the scale factor. The scale factor formula is quite simple and is presented below:

$$\text{scale factor} = \frac{\text{real distance}}{\text{film distance}}$$

Suppose a yard stick is photographed while held in the plane of motion to be used. Upon projection of the processed film, the length of the yard stick is measured to be two inches long. The scale factor becomes

$$\text{scale factor of one inch} = \frac{\text{three feet}}{\text{two inches}}$$

or one film inch is equivalent to one and one-half feet of real distance. Then, during subsequent film analysis, if it is noted that the object moved three film inches, it is known that the real distance moved was 1½ times 3, or 4½ feet.

Timing Devices

Some means must be provided to verify camera speed settings. Certain cameras comprise a spring tension film drive that requires frequent winding. As the spring winds down while the movement is being photographed, the camera speed can slow considerably. To offset any bias in analysis, it is recommended that a large clock or other device be placed within the viewing area of the camera. Accurate time readings can then be procured regardless of inaccuracies in speed settings. A rather recent advance in motion photography has been that of the built-in timing light generator. These small systems are housed within the camera body and emit a flash of light every one-tenth of one-hundredth of a second. The light is focused to expose only the edge of the film so the image is in no way distorted; by counting the number of flashes in a given sequence of frames, a precise determination of time can be had. Although timing light generators are potentially the most accurate means we have of determining time, they are also the most expensive.

Floodlights and Extension Cords

Indoor filming usually requires the use of floodlights. Several varieties are commercially available, but before making a selection decision, consideration must be given to the heat produced by the lights. Some floodlights can cause radiation burns if they are placed too close to the subject, and accidental touching of the bulb or housing can be quite injurious. At least two lights and preferably three are recommended for best contrast. One light should be placed approximately 30° from the plane of motion on the right and the second on the left. The third light should be placed in line with the camera. Extension cords should be of the type that have large wire — preferably number 12 — to avoid dangerous overloading of electrical circuitry.

Background Area

Some photographers recommend a light, solid color background for all filming; others urge the use of a background that will provide the greatest contrast. We prefer the latter approach, and choose background materials specific to the event to be filmed. There is no need to inscribe grid lines on the background material if a scale factor can be generated from a meter or yard stick as explained above; as a matter of fact, the yard stick method is more accurate than the background grid method. A final hint regarding background materials is offered: a card system representing the child's subject number and trial number can be placed in a corner of the viewing area. Identification of film footage will be greatly enhanced.

Film Projectors and Viewers

Most often used for film viewing and analysis is a special projector which has a heat resistant element that prevents the film from burning while the analyst views individual frames. These projectors are designed to move the film in a forward or reverse direction at various frame rates and, by increasing the projector-to-screen distance, can provide large images. (For greatest accuracy, image sizes should be one-fourth or one-fifth of life size.) The recent addition of electronic digitizers to these projectors makes them even more efficient in terms of locating joint centers. Film viewers are also in popular use by analysts. They include a projector, a viewing screen, and coordinate digitizers, which can be made to interface directly to a computer. They do have the disadvantage, however, of producing relatively small images.

The Filming Session

If the filming session is well-organized and follows standardized procedures, the time required per session can be reduced considerably. In filming areas that can be secured, equipment can be set up well before the session. If this is not possible, setup should be accomplished immediately before the session; regardless, the child should not be brought to the area until equipment has been placed and all settings have been double-checked. The time required to complete these tasks is clearly beyond the patience level of any child, and it is far better to exclude them from this routine.

Filming of most movements of concern to the therapist and teacher can be done adequately from a single camera set-up as shown in Figure 26-1. It will be seen that movement is performed in the center of the viewing area and is directed at right angles to the camera lens. The operator must confirm that the entire movement to be studied can be seen in the field of view. A practice trial by the child will not only give the operator the opportunity to confirm the sighting, but will also orient the child to the procedure expected. Several trials may be necessary, but care should be taken to avoid fatiguing the child. You are looking for the child's best effort.

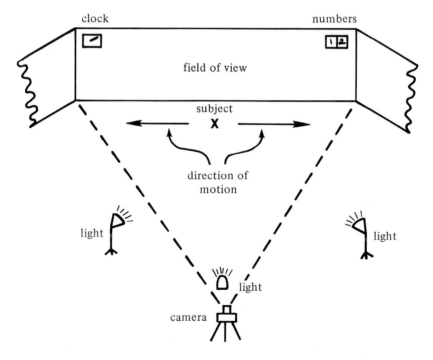

Figure 26-1. The single camera set-up.

If all aspects of the session are coordinated, a retake will not be necessary. The lights should be turned on, the clock started, the camera started, and the movement begun in sequence. The operator may say, "lights, clock, camera, action" to begin the take, and, after the child has moved completely out of the field of view, end the take by saying "all stop." It should be noted here that camera noises, bright lights, and the strangeness of the filming area can be quite upsetting to the uninitiated. If the child is fearful, several "dummy" takes may be necessary before best effort is recorded.

The procedures for subject preparation are somewhat controversial. Since typical analysis methodology involves the determination of joint centers of the child, some experts recommend that the several joints of the upper and lower limbs be marked with a white or black tape. This facilitates their location when the processed film is projected. Other motion photographers question the accuracy of such markings by suggesting that when the joint moves, the overlying skin, and therefore the tape marking, also moves. The resulting position of the mark may or may not be the joint center. We prefer to mark the children if their patience allows and then use the marks, not as absolute indicators of joint centers, but rather as guideposts that the joint center is in the close vicinity. To use no markings at all requires that the analyst be experienced and that the projected images be extremely sharp. The reader is urged to refer to a most informative article by Walton (1970) for additional information on joint markings.

Data Card

A final item in the filming protocol is that of a data card. Included on the card should be the following:

SUBJECT IDENTIFICATION: name or code number, subject number, number of trials performed, number of the trial recommended for analysis.

DESCRIPTIVE DATA: age, height, weight, etc. These data are essential to evaluations of developmental stages as well as assessments of segmental weights of limbs and centers of gravity.

CAMERA SETTINGS: camera speed, type of film used, f stop, camera-to-subject distance. In case retakes are necessary, all conditions can be replicated to insure accuracy.

SPECIAL COMMENTS: remember, a film rarely wears out, but

an operator's memory can seldom recall the events of the filming session.

PERMISSION STATEMENTS: these statements, when signed, should be attached to the data card and retained by investigator until the film is destroyed.

Analysis Methodology

Analysis of movement patterns can only be as precise as the precision of the filming session. Correct camera settings, appropriate background, and reasonable camera-to-subject distances will do much to make you beloved by the analyst. If these have been accomplished, several parameters can be measured to aid in the interpretation of movement behavior. The parameters that are typically measured follow.

Angular and Linear Displacement

This is a measure of the actual movement of the body or body part throughout the activity. Where displacement of body parts is of concern, measurements are taken in degrees or radians; if displacement of the entire body is of interest, measurements are made in linear units such as feet or meters. Each position value measured is subtracted from the initial position value; the results can be utilized to reflect the range of motion of joints as well as total movement of the center of gravity.

Angular and Linear Velocity

This parameter provides an indicator of the speed with which the body or its parts move. Angular velocity is measured in degrees or radians per second whereas linear velocity is reported in feet or meters per second. Velocity measurements are made relative to initial position values as are displacement values.

Angular and Linear Acceleration

Acceleration, either positive or negative, provides an indication as to whether the body or its part is slowing down or speeding up. Angular acceleration is measured in degrees or radians per second per second, and linear accelerations are measured in feet or meters per second per second. Both velocity and acceleration data are obtained by mathematical manipulations of the displacement data taken. Suppose a movement begins with the arm aligned at 20° above horizontal. At the end of, say, ten frames of film, the arm is positioned at 50° above horizontal. Its displacement is seen to be 50°–20° or 30°. If that displacement occurred in 1/10 of a second (measured from the clock in the view field or the timing light generator), velocity is calculated by dividing displacement, 30°, by the time involved, 1/10 second. The result indicates a velocity of 300° per second. Suppose further that an additional ten frames are advanced and we now observe that the arm is aligned at 90° above horizontal. Displacement for the second position is 90° minus 20° (initial position) or 70°. The time required for this displacement to occur was 2/10 of a second (the time required to move from 20° to 50° plus the time required to move from 50° to 90°). Velocity of the movement to 90° now becomes 70° divided by 2/10 second, or 350° per second. Acceleration may now be computed by subtracting the first velocity (300°) from the second (350°) and dividing the result by the time difference between the two velocity calculations (1/10 second). Acceleration is found to be 350°–300° divided by 1/10 or 500° per second per second. This process is continued throughout the duration of the movement and, when these points are plotted with time on the abscissa and velocity or acceleration on the ordinate, movement profiles can be generated. These are of considerable value when comparisons are to be made between children or between trials by the same child.

Center of Gravity

The mass of the body is located at a single point: the center of gravity. The location of this center changes with changes in body position. Since mobility and stability are directly related to the location of the center of gravity, it is often of interest to determine its position. A simple method for making this determination is discussed by Walton (1970) and involves the mathematical combination of the weights of the several body segments. The method is simple and can be done easily by hand if a computer is not available.

Stride Length and Stride Frequency

The length of a stride and the frequency that each foot contacts the ground are indicative of the linear velocity of ambulation. These very simple parameters can be used to determine the developmental maturity of basic movement patterns in the arts. They may also be used as measures of improvement, which occur through therapeutic programs.

Tracings and Stick Figures

These analyses are the most simple to make and are frequently most valuable. If it is only desired to determine what a child looks like while executing a motor pattern, tracings and/or stick figures may comprise the total analysis. Tracings are made by drawing a rough outline of the projected image; stick figures are made by connecting the joint center markings mentioned above.

Others

With more complicated mathematical computations that require, for efficiency, computer input and output, additional data may be obtained. Parameters such as horizontal, vertical, and the resultant forces at each joint and the moments of force or torque at the joints are examples of these additional data. Because they cannot be found by hand within a reasonable time, they will not be discussed here. For the reader who wishes to pursue this methodology, the comprehensive text provided by Plagenhoef (1971) is highly recommended.

Interpretation of Analysis

Interpretation of data provided by the analyst actually takes the form of answering the questions posed even before the film is taken. Unless advance questions are asked in a specific fashion, interpretation is likely to become rambling and tangential to the problem at hand. As examples, three questions are posed below, followed by suggestions for analysis and interpretive actions.

Question: What is the range of movement at the knee during the swing phase of a handicapped child's kick in a dance like La Raspa? In order to answer this question, the analyst need only look at two frames of the film. Locate the first and last frame that show the shank of the swing phase. Measure the angle between the thigh and the shank at the joint center. The difference between the two angles is the angular displacement or the range of motion at the knee. It can now be determined whether the range of motion is limited or within normal values. If the handicapped child demonstrates limited angular displacement, a program can be proposed to increase the range of motion. Subsequent filming sessions will evaluate any improvement with training. Obviously, this process can be generalized to any other joint in the body.

Question: Is the cause of this child's coordination problem the inability of his antagonistic muscles to contract at the proper time in the motor pattern? The answer to this question requires the determination of angular acceleration. Plagenhoef presents a simple graphic method for this determination. The angular acceleration should be determined for each frame of the film at the joint in question. A positive value indicates that the moving body part is speeding up because of the contraction of the agonist. A negative value indicates that the antagonist is contracting and thus slows down the moving body part. The analyst can now look at the pattern of positive and negative values across the frames or time. Very short times to contraction indicate that the antagonist is contracting too soon. Very long times indicate that the antagonist contracts too late. A program to develop strength or flexibility in the antagonistic muscle can now be initiated, based upon objective evidence. Subsequent filming will demonstrate whether improvement has occurred as a result of the creative arts training program.

A single leg amputee has been fitted with a prosthetic device and is still having problems with gait. Question: Is the child adjusting to the new position of the center of gravity? One of the first parameters the analyst can investigate is the location of the center of gravity with and without the prosthesis. The child may not be able to deal with the dual change in the location of the center of gravity that has occurred with the loss of the leg and then with the addition of the weight of the prosthesis. Front view film recordings and the technique posed by Walton can easily provide the answer. We know that the center of gravity should be over the base of support for greatest stability. If the center is found to be located over the child's own leg rather than over the entire base of support provided by the prosthetic device, stability is decreased. A training program could then be started that would ameliorate the problem.

With the data obtained through motion photography, individuals responsible for planning and evaluating creative arts programs can do so with objectivity. In conjunction with information gathered through other testing methods, the therapist or educator can add significantly to the evaluation of movement behaviors in each of the arts. Programs designed to increase strength and range of motion can be implemented on an individual basis — child specific. A program designed to increase the coordination of the handicapped child can be evaluated and documented as the child experiences any number of creative arts activities involving muscular coordinations. Motion photography provides, then, means of making the initial evaluations of motor patterns as well as improvement evaluations. It is the best means yet devised for making these evaluations.

BIBLIOGRAPHY

Harris, R. W. *Kinesiology, Workbook and Laboratory Manual.* Boston: Houghton Mifflin, 1977, pp. 192-210.

Hinson, Marilyn M. *Kinesiology.* Dubuque, Iowa: William C. Brown Co., 1977.

Ketlinski, R. "Can High Speed Photography Be Used as a Tool in Biomechanics." *Biomechanics.* Chicago: The Athletic Institute, 1971, pp. 59-62.

Plagenhoef, S. C. *Patterns of Human Movement, A Cinematographic Analysis.* Englewood Cliffs, New Jersey: Prentice-Hall, 1971, pp. 7-16.

Sage, G. H. *Introduction to Motor Behavior, A Neuropsychological Approach.* Reading, Massachusetts: Addison-Wesley Pub. Co., 1971, pp. 130-172.

Walton, J. A. "A Template for Locating Segmental Centers of Gravity." *Research Quarterly, 41,4,* Dec. 1970, 615-618.

Structure 29. Drum beating is one of several arts activities that develop skills that carry over into other learnings like grasping and throwing; film analysis can document the contributions of the arts to other instructional areas.

Chapter 27

DRUM BEATING TO IMPROVE OVERARM THROWING: PHOTOGRAPHIC ANALYSIS AS AN EVALUATION TECHNIQUE

Marilyn Hinson, Barbara Gench, and Terry Lawton

THE importance of accurate and complete assessment and evaluation has been emphasized recently by the passage of Public Law 94-142 and associated legislation. Not only are assessment and evaluation techniques being scrutinized as they pertain to total programs, but also as they relate to the individuals for whom these programs are designed. Perusal of the literature confirms the availability of many instruments that purport to assess and/or evaluate the individual client with validity, objectivity, and reliability; nevertheless, it is the eye of the assessor-evaluator that continues to be the most heavily relied upon tool.

Because the human eye is limited in its ability to perceive and record perceptions, several alternatives are being explored. This chapter focuses upon the use of high speed photography as a means of recording the visual data of motor performance.

Procedures

To demonstrate the value of motion photography in the creative arts, a case study was designed around an eight-year-old Down's Syndrome girl. After obtaining the necessary permissions, the filming equipment was transported to the developmental center the child attended. A grassy site appropriately lighted by the sun was selected as the movement area and the camera, a Redlake® Locam with Angenieux® 12-120 zoom lens, was placed forty feet away and at right angles to the movement direction.

When all measurements and camera settings were accomplished and recorded, the child was brought to the scene and oriented to the area. She was then given a rubber ball, six inches in diameter, and was asked to throw it overhand as had been demonstrated by the therapist. Four of these throws were filmed. A tom-tom drum was then introduced to the area and held in front of the child at the level of her waist. She was given the mallet and was asked to beat the drum. As the beating continued, the drum was gradually raised to a vertical position level with her head. This entire sequence was repeated until the child appeared to be comfortable with the task; only the final sequence was filmed. The child was again given the ball and was asked to throw it at the drum which was still being held at the level of her head but approximately fifteen feet away. Four throws were filmed for use as comparative data to the initial four throws.

All film data were analyzed on a glass top table system comprised of a Lafayette® Motion Analyzer and three 45 degree mirrors (Fig. 27-1). Tracings were made at representative positions during the prethrow, drum beating tasks, and postthrow. Composites of the tracings selected for analysis appear in Figures 27-2 to 27-5.

Results

The prethrow tracings in Figure 27-2 are particularly characterized by the child's tendency to apply force in an upward rather than a forward direction. It will be noted that the beginning position is one in which the center of gravity is quite low. Subsequent positions illustrate the elevation of the center of gravity as the child has moved to position 2c, in which there is extreme hyperextension of the spine. The release of the ball occurred at position 2d and is seen to have been accomplished with the ball high above and slightly behind the head. A comparison of positions c and d of Figure 27-2 indicates that the ball has been moved through a path that is markedly upward; the resulting projection was also upward and the target was overthrown by a considerable distance. Position f, the follow-through, confirms the fact that the child failed to apply any significant forward force to her center of gravity, so she is seen to be leaning away from the target.

There are several positive aspects of the prethrowing performance that should be noted also. The turn of the body to a position 90 degrees from the target, the forward step taken by the opposite foot, the use of the nonthrowing arm for balance are exemplary; these are all components of the successful overhead pattern.

Figures 27-3 and 27-4 are offered mainly as clarifying illustrations of the drum beating tasks. It is interesting to note, however, that the child stepped with the right rather than the left foot as she struck the horizontally held drum, but stepped with the correct foot when the drum was held vertically. Also observed in these figures is evidence of perceptual difficulty in contacting the drum.

In viewing Figure 27-5, it becomes immediately apparent that the movement errors committed during the prethrow had

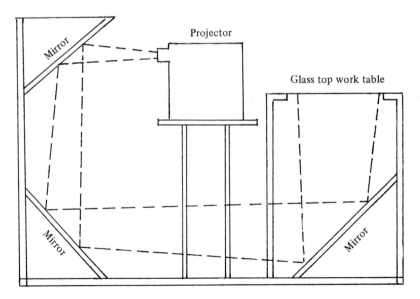

Figure 27-1. The glass top table system comprised of a Lafayette Motion Analyzer and three 45 degree mirrors.

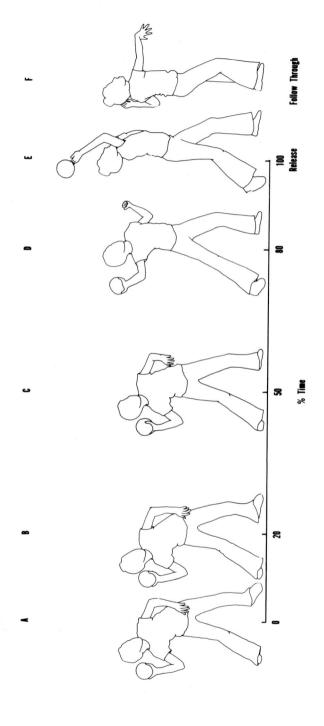

Figure 27-2. Tracings from film made at representative positions before experimental period of drum beating.

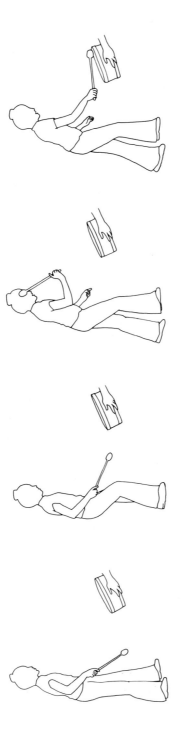

Figure 27-3. Tracings from film of drum beating tasks, first stage.

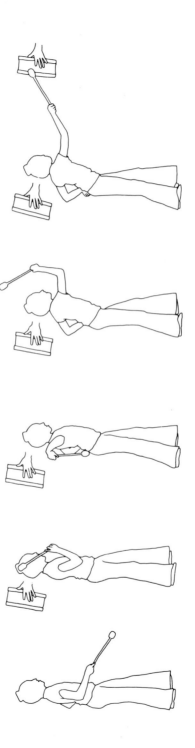

Figure 27-4. Tracings from film of drum beating tasks, second stage.

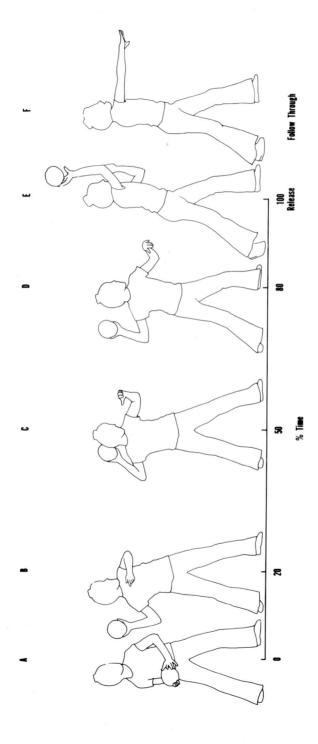

Figure 27-5. Tracings from film made at representative positions after experimental period of drum beating.

been, to some degree, corrected. The extreme hyperextension of the spine is not seen, nor is the premature release of the ball. The path of the ball was considerably lower than it was during the prethrow, and the shift of weight was more forward than upward. All in all, the postthrow appears to be rather well done.

Discussion

It appears that the creative task of drum beating as used in this study improved the overarm throw pattern of the eight-year-old Down's Syndrome girl. When it is remembered that the drum beating activity occupied only two or three minutes, it is particularly noteworthy that the changes noted above occurred. One can only postulate regarding the magnitude of the changes had the same protocol been repeated over several days; however, it seems reasonable to expect that the overarm pattern would have improved even more and that the resulting change would, perhaps, have been of a permanent nature.

The beating of a drum was selected as the creative task because of its similarity to the overarm throw pattern. Since instruction of a teaching type was not given at any time to the child, it seems that the task was well selected. Perhaps such creative activities are doubly important in programs for the severely handicapped. Not only can they be used as a means of improving motor skills, but they can also be ends in themselves as experiences designed to complement the lives of all human beings.

Structure 30. Special education and arts organizations must work together to strengthen arts training at all ages, but especially in early childhood. Here a musical toy encourages infant with Down's Syndrome to improve head control, to reach, and to grasp — all prerequisites to further learning.

ORGANIZATIONS CONCERNED WITH ARTS, SPECIAL EDUCATION, AND ARTS FOR THE HANDICAPPED

SERVICES FOR HANDICAPPED

1. Alexander Graham Bell Association for the Deaf, Inc., 1537 35th Street, NW, Washington, D.C. 20007
2. Allergy Foundation of America, 801 Second Avenue, New York, New York 10017
3. American Academy for Cerebral Palsy, University Hospital School, Iowa City, Iowa 52240
4. American Association on Mental Deficiency (AAMD), 5201 Connecticut Avenue NW, Washington, D.C. 20015
5. American Association for the Advancement of Tension Control, P.0. Box 7512, Roanoke, Virginia 24019
6. American Corrective Therapy Association, Inc., 1265 Cherry Road, Memphis, Tennessee 38117
7. American Dance Therapy Association, Suite 216-E, 1000 Century Plaza, Columbia, Maryland 21044
8. American Diabetic Association, 1 East 45th Street, New York, New York 10017
9. American Foundation for the Blind, 15 W. 16th Street, New York, New York 10011
10. American Heart Association, Inc., 7320 Greenville Avenue, Dallas, Texas 75231
11. American Instructors of the Deaf, 5034 Wisconsin Avenue, NW, Washington, D.C. 20016
12. American Lung Association, 1740 Broadway, New York, New York 10019
13. American Occupational Therapy Association, Inc., 6000 Executive Boulevard, Rockville, Maryland 20852
14. American Physical Therapy Association, 1156 15th Street, NW, Washington, D.C. 20005
15. American Printing House for the Blind, 1839 Frankfort Avenue, Louisville, Kentucky 40206
16. American Psychological Association, 1200 17th Street, NW, Washington, D.C. 20036
17. American Schizophrenia Foundation, Box 160, Ann Arbor, Michigan

48107

18. American Thoracic Society in the medical section of the American Lung Association, 1740 Broadway, New York, New York 10019

19. The Arthritis Foundation, 1212 Avenue of the Americas, New York, New York 10036

20. Association for Children with Learning Disabilities, 5225 Grace Street (Upper Level), Pittsburgh, Pennsylvania 15236

21. Association for the Education of Visually Handicapped, 1604 Spruce Street, Philadelphia, Pennsylvania 19103

22. Council for Exceptional Children, 1920 Association Drive, Reston, Virginia 22091

23. Council of Organizations Serving the Deaf Inc. (COSD), 4201 Connecticut Avenue, NW, Washington, D.C. 20008

24. Epilepsy Foundation of America, 1820 L Street, NW, Suite 406, Washington, D.C. 20036

25. Muscular Dystrophy Association of America, Inc., 27th Floor, 810 Seventh Ave., New York, New York or 1790 Broadway, New York, New York 10019

26. National Association of Hearing and Speech Agencies, 219 18th Street, NW, Washington, D.C. 20006

27. National Association for Retarded Citizens, 2709 Avenue E East, Arlington, Texas 76011

28. National Committee for Multi-Handicapped Children, 339 14th Street, Niagara Falls, New York 14303

29. National Cystic Fibrosis Research Foundation, 3379 Peach Tree Road, NE, Atlanta, Georgia 30326

30. National Easter Seal Society for Crippled Children and Adults, 2023 West Ogden Avenue, Chicago, Illinois 60612

31. National Foundation — Birth Defects, 800 Second Avenue, New York, New York 10017

32. National Foundation for Progressive Relaxation, 55 East Washington Street, Chicago, Illinois 60602

33. National Multiple Sclerosis Society, 257 Park Avenue South, New York, New York 10010

34. National Paraplegia Foundation, 333 N. Michigan Avenue, Chicago, Illinois 60601

35. National Rehabilitation Association, 1522 K Street, NW, Washington, D.C. 20005

36. National Society for Autistic Children (NSAC), 169 Tampa Avenue, Albany, New York 12208

37. National Society for Crippled Children and Adults, Inc., 2023 W. Ogden Ave., Chicago, Illinois 60612

38. National Society for the Prevention of Blindness, 79 Madison Avenue, New York, New York 10016

39. National Therapeutic Recreation Society, 1601 North Kent St., Arlington, Virginia 22209

40. National Wheelchair Athletic Association, 40-24 62nd Street, Woodside, New York 11377.
41. National Wheelchair Basketball Association (NWBA), 110 Seaton Bldg., University of Kentucky, Lexington, Kentucky 40506
42. Paralyzed Veterans of America, 7315 Wisconsin Avenue, Suite 301-W, Washington, D.C. 20014
43. President's Committee on Mental Retardation, Washington, D.C. 20201
44. Seeing Eye, Inc., Morristown, New Jersey 07960
45. United Cerebral Palsy Association, Inc., 66 East 34th Street, New York, New York 10016 or 50 West 57th Street, New York, New York 10019

GENERIC — ALL OF THE ARTS

1. Alliance for Arts in Education, John F. Kennedy Center for Performing Arts, Washington, D.C. 20566. State AAE organizations form a national communication network.
2. American Council for the Arts (previously named Associated Councils of the Arts), 570 Seventh Avenue, New York City, New York 10036. Publishes *Directory of State Arts Councils, Directory of Community Arts Councils, Directory of National Arts Organizations, Associated Councils of the Arts Reports.*
3. Arts and Humanities Division, U.S. Office of Education, 3728 Donohoe Building, 400 Maryland Avenue SW, Washington, D.C. 20202.
4. Arts in Education Program, John D. Rockefeller III Fund, JDF 3rd Fund, Room 1034, 50 Rockefeller Plaza, New York, New York 10020. Disseminates information on integrated arts programs in the schools and arts in general education (AGE).
5. Arts Management, 408 West 57th Street, New York, New York 10019. Publishes *Arts Management, The National News Service for Those Who Finance, Manage, and Communicate the Arts.*
6. Association for Handicapped Artists, 1134 Rand Building, Buffalo, New York 14203.
7. Cemrel, Inc., 3120 59th Street, St. Louis, Missouri 63139. Materials and technical assistance on aesthetic education.
8. Educational Arts Association, 90 Sherman Street, Cambridge, Massachusetts 02140. Publishes *New Ways,* a quarterly newsletter on creative education and the arts.
9. Information and Research Utilization Center in Physical Education and Recreation for the Handicapped (IRUC), an office within the American Alliance for Health, Physical Education, and Recreation, 1201 Sixteenth Street NW, Washington, D.C. 20036. Publishes *Materials on Creative Arts (Arts, Crafts, Dance, Drama, and Music) for Persons with Handicapping Conditions* and other materials.
10. National Arts and the Handicapped Information Service, ARTS, Box 2040, Grand Central Station, New York, New York 10017.

11. National Committee, Arts for the Handicapped, 1701 K Street NW, Suite 801, Washington, D.C. 20006.
12. National Endowment for the Arts, Special Constituencies, 2401 E Street NW, Washington, D.C. 20037.

ART

1. American Art Therapy Association, Inc., P.O. Box 11604, Pittsburgh, Pennsylvania 15228. Members receive the *American Journal of Art Therapy*.
2. American Association of Museums (AAM), 2233 Wisconsin Avenue, NW, Washington, D.C. 20007. Members receive *Museum News*.
3. National Art Education Association, 1916 Association Drive, Reston, Virginia 22091. Members receive *Art Education*. Also publishes *Studies in Art Education: A Journal of Issues and Research in Art Education*.
4. National Association of Schools of Art, 11250 Roger Bacon Drive, Reston, Virginia 22090.

DANCE

1. American Dance Therapy Association, Inc., Suite 230, 2000 Century Plaza, Columbia, Maryland 21044. Members receive *ADTA Newsletter* and the *American Journal of Dance Therapy*. Other significant ADTA publications include the following:

   Ninth Annual Conference Proceedings (1974). Therapeutic Process: Movement as Integration. Held in New York City. Presents papers on Theoretical Considerations in Dance-Movement Therapy; Theory and Its Application in Dance-Movement Therapy; and Research in Non-verbal Behavior and Dance Movement Therapy. Edited by Penny Bernstein.

   Eighth Annual Conference Proceedings (1973). Dance Therapist in Dimension, held in Kansas City. Contains Presentations relating to the dance therapist as Clinician, Educator, and Researcher. Keynote speeches of Warren Lamb and Joanna Greenberg are included. Edited by Sharon Chaiklin and Edna Fulton.

   Seventh Annual Conference Proceedings (1972). What is Dance Therapy, Really? This was the first national conference on the West Coast (Santa Monica) and includes presentations by Valerie Hunt, Irmgard Bartenieff, Trudi Schoop, and Janet Adler Boettiger. Edited by Barbara Freudenthal Govine and Joan Chodorow Smallwood.

   Sixth Annual Conference Proceedings (1971). Dance Therapy: Roots and Extensions, held in Washington, D.C. Contains keynote speech, "Origins in Dance," by Franziska Boas and abstracts of workshops on Tai Chi, Theatre Games, Sensory Awareness, Alexander Technique, and other related fields. Edited by Diana Cook.

Fifth Annual Conference Proceedings (1970). Process and Research, held in New York City. Milton Berger, Alexander Lowen, Martha Davis Rothstein, and Melvene DyerBennet were among conference presenters. Edited by Claire Schmais.

Combined Third (1968) and Fourth (1969) Annual Conference Proceedings. Third Annual Conference, held in Madison, Wisconsin, includes papers by Marian Chace, W. S. Condon, and Beth Kalish. Also includes ways of working with specific interest groups; autistic, individual, psychotic, aged, retarded. Edited by Sharon Chaiklin. Fourth Annual Conference held in Philadelphia, Pennsylvania, focused on Origins, Theories, and Methodologies. Pearl Primus' keynote address, "Life Crises, Dance from Birth to Death," and related arts in therapy are some of the presentations. Edited by Beth Kalish.

Monograph No. 3 (1974). Collection of ten papers on dance therapy theory; conceptualization; training; its relationship to traditional psychotherapy and Occupational Therapy; and special applications re work with blindness, a long term hospital setting, depressive states, a chronic paranoid schizophrenic, and children in a day hospital program. Edited by Fran Donelan.

Monograph No. 2 (1972). Writings on Body Movement and Communication. Collection of articles on Dance Therapy training, theory, special groups, case studies and perspectives from related professions. Includes etchings, photographs, and poetry. Edited by Fran Donelan.

Monograph No. 1 (1971). Combined publication of research papers and proceedings of the Second Annual Conference, held in Washington, D.C. in 1967. Among conference presenters were Judith Kestenberg, M.D., Paul Lippman, M.D., and Alma Kawkins; Irmgard Bartenieff, Beth Kalish and Barbara Govine are included in the seven research papers. Edited by Fran Donelan.

Bibliography (1974). Books, articles, and films on dance therapy theory, practice and research, movement fundamentals, body image, nonverbal communication, other therapeutic approaches, child development, group work, creativity and art, psychology and psychiatry and literary and cultural dimensions. Edited by Joanna G. Harris and Judy Beers.

Mirian Chace: Her Papers (1975). This volume contains biographical materials, Marian Chace's published materials, some unpublished papers, panel discussions, chapters by Edith M. Stern and Irmgard Bartenieff, and a memoriam by Eithne Tabor. Edited by Harris Chaiklin.

2. American Dance Guild, 1619 Broadway, Room 603, New York, New York 10019. Publishes *Dance Scope.*

3. AIM (Adventures in Movement), a program designed for the Handicapped for Dance, Inc., 155 Franklin Street, Dayton, Ohio 45402.

4. Committee on Research in Dance, CORD, Dance Department, Educ. 684 D, New York University, 35 W. 4th Street, New York, New York 10003. Publishes *Dance Research Journal* (formerly *CORD News*). Also has published *Dance Research Annuals, Volume I - VII*. Of this series, Volume II was entitled *Workshop on Dance Therapy: Its Research Potentials*.

5. Country Dance and Song Society of America, 55 Christopher Street, New York, New York 10019.

6. Dalcroze School of Music, 161 East 73rd Street, New York, New York 10021. Disseminates materials on Dalcroze techniques and offers certification.

7. Dance Notation Bureau, Inc., 8 East 12th Street, New York, New York 10003. Disseminates materials and provides training in Labanotation and effort-shape techniques.

8. Laban Art of Movement Guild, c/o Laban Art of Movement Centre, Woburn Hill, Addlestone, Surrey KT 15, 2QD, England.

9. Dance Horizons, 1801 E. 26th Street, Brooklyn, New York 11229. Publishes *Dance in Psychotherapy* by Elizabeth Rosen and other materials.

10. National Dance Association (NDA), an organization of the American Alliance for Health, Physical Education, and Recreation, 1201 Sixteenth Street NW, Washington, D.C. 20036. Publishes *Spotlight on Dance* (a newsletter) and many books, including the *Focus on Dance Series*. The 1974 *Focus on Dance VII* was entitled *Dance Therapy*.

11. Other popular periodicals in Dance which are not published by associations include *Dance Magazine*, Danad Publishing Co., Inc., 10 Columbus Circle, New York, New York 10019; *Dance News, Inc.*, 119 West 57th Street, New York, New York 10019; *Dance and Dancers*, Hansom Books, P.O. Box 294, 2-4 Old Pye Street (P.O. Box 294) off Strutton Ground, Victoria Street, Westminster, London. SWIP 2 LR.; and *Dancing Times*, 18 Hand Court, High Lolborn, London, W.C. 1.

DRAMA

1. American Theatre Association (ATA), 1029 Vermont Avenue NW, Washington, D.C. 20005. All members receive *Theatre News*. The American Theatre Association is subdivided into five separate associations or divisions: (1) University and College Theatre Association (UCTA). Members receive the *Educational Theatre Journal*. (2) Secondary School Theatre Association (SSTA). Members receive the *Secondary School Theatre Journal*. (3) Children's Theatre Association of America (CTAA). Members receive the *Children's Theatre Review*. (4) American Community Theatre Association (ACTA). Members receive occasional newsletters. (5) Army Theatre

Arts Association (ATAA). Members receive occasional newsletters.
2. American Society of Group Psychotherapy and Psychodrama, 39 East 20th Street, New York, New York 10003.
3. International Thespian Society, 3368 Central Parkway, Cincinnati, Ohio 45225. Publishes *Dramatics.*

MUSIC

1. American Orff-Schulwerk Association, P.O. Box 18495, Cleveland Heights, Ohio 44118.
2. Louis Braille Foundation for Blind Musicians, Inc., 112 East 19th Street, New York, New York 10003.
3. Music Educators National Conference, 1902 Association Drive, Reston, Virginia 22091. Members receive the *Music Educators Journal* and *Journal of Research in Music Education.* Associated organizations of MENC include (1) American Choral Directors Association; (2) American String Teachers Association; (3) College Band Directors National Association; (4) National Association of College Wind and Percussion Instructors; (5) National Association of Jazz Educators; (6) National Band Association; and (7) National School Orchestra Association.
4. Music Teachers National Association (MTNA, Inc.), 408 Carew Tower, Cincinnati, Ohio 45202. Members receive the *American Music Teacher.*
5. Music Services, Library of Congress, Division for the Blind and Physically Handicapped, Washington, D.C. 20542.
6. National Association for Music Therapy, Inc., P.O. Box 610, Lawrence, Kansas 66044. Members receive the *Journal of Music Therapy.*
7. National Association of Schools of Music, 11250 Roger Bacon Drive, Reston, Virginia 22090.
8. National Music Council, 250 W. 57th Street, Suite 626, New York, New York 10019. Publishes *Bulletin of National Music Council.*
9. Urban Federation of Music Therapists, New York University, 777 Education Building, Washington Square, New York 10003.

Structure 31. Large mirrors in classroom and/or movement areas enhance body image and self discovery activities, an important part of early arts training.

BIBLIOGRAPHIES

JANET LAXSON AND SHERRIL YORK

CREATIVITY

Books

Berlin, Irving N. (Ed.). *Bibliography of Child Psychiatry and Child Mental Health: With a Selected List of Films.* New York: Human Sciences Press, Behavioral Publications, 1976.

Bluhm, Donna L. *Teaching the Retarded Visually Handicapped: Indeed They Are Children.* Philadelphia: W. B. Saunders, 1968.

Blumberg, Harris M. *A Program of Sequential Language Development: A Theoretical and Practical Guide for Remediation of Language, Reading and Learning Disorders.* Springfield: Charles C Thomas, 1975.

Canner, Norma. *And a Time to Dance.* Boston: Beacon Press, 1968.

Curriculum Guide for Teachers of Trainable Retarded Children. Jefferson City: Missouri State Department of Education, 1967.

Davis, Elizabeth A. (Ed.). *Curriculum Activities Guide for Severely Retarded Deaf Students.* Indianapolis: Marion County Association for Retarded Children, 1973.

Deussen, Claire Isaacs (Ed.). *Proceedings of the Conference on Art for the Deaf, Junior Arts Center, Los Angeles.* Los Angeles: Municipal Arts Department, Junior Arts Center, 1974.

Edwards, Eleanor M. *Music Education for the Deaf.* South Waterford: Merriam-Eddy, 1974.

Fouracre, Maurice H. et al. *The Effects of a Preschool Program Upon Young Educable Mentally Retarded Children — Volume 1. The Experimental Preschool Curriculum.* New York: Columbia University, 1962.

Fukurai, Shiro. *How Can I Make What I Cannot See?* New York: Van Nostrand Reinhold, 1974.

Grayson, John (Ed.). *Environments of Musical Sculpture You Can Build. Phase I.* Vancouver: A.R.C. Publications, 1976.

Hyatt, Ralph and Rolnick, Norma (Eds.). *Teaching the Mentally Handicapped Child.* New York: Behavioral Publications, 1974.

Kinda, Crystal L. *Body Awareness for Exceptional Children Through the*

Creative Arts. Buffalo: Dok Publishers, 1976.

―――― . *Space: Spatial Awareness for Exceptional Children Through the Creative Arts*. Buffalo: Dok Publishers, 1976.

Lark-Horovitz, Betty et al. *Understanding Children's Art for Better Teaching*. Columbus: Charles E. Merrill, 1967.

Materials on Creative Arts (Arts, Crafts, Dance, Drama, and Music) for Persons with Handicapping Conditions. Washington, D.C.: American Association for Health, Physical Education and Recreation, 1975. Revised 1977.

Pattemore, Arnel W. *Art and Crafts for Slow Learners*. Instructor Handbook Series. New York: Instructor Publications, 1969.

Perry, Natalie. *Teaching the Mentally Retarded Child: Second Edition*. New York: Columbia University Press, 1974.

Reilly, Mary (Ed.). *Play as Exploratory Learning: Studies of Curiosity Behavior*. Beverly Hills: Saga Publications, 1974.

Robbins, Arthur and Sibley, Linda Beth. *Creative Art Therapy*. New York: Brunner/Maxel, 1976.

Sawrey, James M. and Telford, Charles W. *The Exceptional Individual Psychological and Educational Aspects*. Prentice-Hall Psychology Series. Englewood Cliffs: Prentice-Hall, 1967.

Shick, Richard L. and Stitch, Thomas F. (Eds.). *Curriculum Guide for Early Education of the Handicapped; Summer Sessions, 1973-1974*. Mansfield, Pennsylvania: Mansfield State College, 1974.

Trow, Wm. Clark and Haddan, Eugene E. (Eds.). *Psychological Foundation of Educational Technology*. Englewood Cliffs: Educational Technology Publications, 1976.

White House Conference on Children. *Report to the President: White House Conference on Children 1970*. Washington, D.C.: Superintendent of Documents, 1971.

Wolk, Shirley M. et al. *A Curriculum Guide for Teaching Trainable Mentally Retarded Children Experimental Copy*. Los Angeles: Los Angeles City Schools, 1964.

Zwart, Christine and Pascoe, Peter (Eds.). *Answer Me World*. London: National Society for Mentally Handicapped Children, 1975.

Periodicals

Altmann, John and Hatlen, Philip H. "New Dimensions in Sound for Blind Youth." *AFB Research Bulletin* 25 (January 1973):249-52.

Anderson, Frances E. and Barnfield, Larry S. "Art Especially for the Exceptional." *Art Education* 27 (April/May 1974):13-5.

Anthony, Gene Holton. "Creativity and the Visually Handicapped: Implications for the Industrial Arts." *Education of the Visually Handicapped* 1,4 (December 1969):122-3.

Arem, Cynthia A. and Zimmerman, Barry J. "Vicarious Effects on the

Creative Behavior of Retarded and Nonretarded Children." *American Journal of Mental Deficiency* 81,3 (November 1976):289-96.

Bell, Janice W. "Directed Creativity." *School Arts* 76,6 (February 1977):78-9.

Berger, Gertrude. "The Blind Teacher, Creativity, and the Multi-Sensory Classroom." *New Outlook for the Blind* 66,7 (September 1972):230-2.

Blackhurst, A. Edward et al. "Relationship between Mobility and Divergent Thinking in Blind Children." *Education of the Visually Handicapped* 1,2 (May 1969):33-6.

Bragg, Bernard. "The Human Potential of Human Potential: Art and the Deaf. *American Annals of the Deaf* 117,5 (October 1972):508-11.

Bush, Nancy Gale. "Ceramics Has Something for All." *Pointer* 18,1 (Fall 1973):46-9.

Cameron, Rosaline. "The Uses of Music to Enhance the Education of the Mentally Retarded." *Mental Retardation* 8,1 (February 1970):32-4.

Carter, Kyle R. et al. "The Effect of Kinesthetic and Visual-Motor Experiences in the Creative Development of Mentally Retarded Students." *Education and Training of the Mentally Retarded* 8,1 (February 1973):24-8.

Cline, Betty Smith et al. "Children Who Present Special Challenges." *Today's Education* 61,1 (January 1972):18-28.

Connolly, Austin J. "Classroom Forum." *Focus on Exceptional Children* 4,6 (November 1972):11-12.

Cooper, Joel B. and Richmond, Bert O. "Intelligence, Creativity, and Performance Abilities of EMR Pupils." *Psychology in the Schools* 12,3 (July 1975):304-308.

Craig, Helen B. and Holman, Gary L. "The Open Classroom in a School for the Deaf." *American Annals of the Deaf* 118,6 (December 1973):675-85.

Dauterman, William L. "A Study of Imagery in the Sighted and the Blind." *AFB Research Bulletin* 25 (January 1973):95-167.

Davis, William E. "Teaching Creative Writing to Educable Children." *Pointer* 18,2 (Winter 1973):90-91.

Deitering, Carolyn. "Implications for the Liturgy Creative Movement Expression. *Momentum* 5,3 (October 1974):18-23.

Ford, Barbara Gay and Renzulli, Joseph S. "Developing the Creative Potential of Educable Mentally Retarded Students." *Journal of Creative Behavior* 10,3 (1976):210-18.

Freel, Mirle E., Jr. "Art for Visually Impaired Children." *Education of the Visually Handicapped* 1,2 (May 1969):44-6.

Hargreaves, Richard. "Creativity Blues: A Personal View of a Combined Arts Course for Fourth Year Non-Examination Pupils." *English in Education* 7,1 (Spring 1973):9-14.

Haupt, Charlotte. "Creative Expression through Art." *Education of the Visually Handicapped* 1,2 (May 1969):41-3.

Irwin, Eleanor C. and McWilliams, Betty Jane. "Play Therapy for Children with Cleft Palates." *Children Today* 3,3 (May/June 1974):18-22.

Johnson, Russell M. and Millner, Joan. "A Creative-Adaptive Model of the

Intellect." *Journal of Learning Disabilities* 2,6 (June 1969):308-22.

Kokasaka, Sharen Metz. "Classroom Movement Training for the Mentally Retarded." *Education and Training of the Mentally Retarded* 8,2 (April 1973):10-14.

Kramer, Aaron and Buck, Lucien A. "Poetic Creativity in Deaf Children." *American Annals of the Deaf* 121,1 (February 1976):31-7.

Kuschel, Rolf. "The Silent Inventor: The Creation of a Sign Language by the Only Deaf-Mute on a Polynesian Island." *Sign Language Studies* 2, (October 1973):1-27.

Lance, Wayne D. "Instructional Materials for the Mentally Retarded: A Review of Selected Literature." *Education and Training of the Mentally Retarded* 10,3 (October 1975):161-6.

Landau, Barbara L. and Hagen, John W. "The Effect of Verbal Cues on Concept Acquisition and Retention in Normal and Educable Mentally Retarded Children." *Child Development* 45,3 (September 1974):643-50.

Ling, Stuart J. "Missing: Some of the Most Exciting Creative Moments of Life." *Music Educators Journal* 61,3 (November 1974):93-5.

MacDonald, Theodore H. "Basis of an Epistemology for Remedial Teaching." *Australian Journal of Remedial Education* 5,1 (March 1973):20-3.

Minty, Patricia H. and Neate, Dorothy M. "Impressions of Schools for the Deaf in Holland." *Teacher of the Deaf* 71,420 (July 1973):276-80.

Morgan, David. "An Adaptation for Drama for Retarded Participants." *Challenge* 9,1 (September-October 1973):1, 6-7.

Mossman, Maja. "Movement: The Joyous Language. Dance Therapy for Children." *Children's House* 8,5 (Spring 1976):11-15.

Nathanson, David E. et al. "Miami Snow Poets. Creative Writing for Exceptional Children." *Teaching Exceptional Children* 8,2 (Winter 1976):87-91.

Nigro, Giovanno. "Recreation and Adult Education." *Rehabilitation Literature* 35,9 (September 1974):268-71.

Ogletree, Earl J. "Eurythmy: A Therapeutic Art of Movement." *Journal of Special Education* 10,3 (February 1976):305-19.

Pollack, Sally N. et al. "Creativity in the Severely Retarded." *Journal of Creative Behavior* 7,1 (First Quarter 1973):67-72.

Ray, Henry. "Media and Affective Learning." *American Annals of the Deaf* 117,5 (October 1972):545-49.

Rubin, Judith A. "Art is for All Human Beings — Especially the Handicapped." *Art Education* 28,8 (December 1975):5-10.

Rubin, Judith and Klineman, Janet. "They Open Our Eyes: The Story of an Exploratory Art Program for Visually-Impaired Multiply-Handicapped Children." *Education of the Visually Handicapped* 6,4 (December 1974):106-13.

Scardina, Virginia. "Identifying Characteristics of Children with Dysfunction of the Left Side of the Body: Research in Sensory-Integrative

Development." *American Journal of Occupational Therapy* 28,8 (September 1974):478-83.

Schubert, Daniel S. "Intelligence as Necessary but not Sufficient for Creativity." *Journal of Genetic Psychology* 122 (March 1973):45-7.

Schwartz, Lita L. "In Response to Mohan." *Journal of Creative Behavior* 8,3 (1974):183-6.

Silver, Rawley A. "Children with Communication Disorders: Cognitive and Artistic Development." *American Journal of Art Therapy* 14,2 (January 1975):30-47.

Simons, Anneke Prins. "Viktor Lowenfeld and Social Haptics." *Art Education* 25,6 (June 1972):8-13.

Singer, Dorothy G. and Lenahan, Mary Louise. "Imagination Content in Dreams of Deaf Children." *American Annals of the Deaf* 121,1 (February 1976):44-8.

"Some Hypotheses." *Childhood Education* 51,1 (October 1974):10-5.

Swaiko, Nancy. "The Role and Value of an Eurhythmics Program in a Curriculum for Deaf Children." *American Annals of the Deaf* 119,3 (June 1974):321-4.

Taylor, Calvin W. "Developing Effectively Functioning People: The Accountable Goal of Multiple Talent Teaching." *North Carolina Association for the Gifted and Talented Quarterly Journal* 1,2 (Spring 1975):20-40.

Tiscall, William J. et al. "Divergent Thinking in Blind Children." *Journal of Educational Psychology* 62,6 (December 1971):468-73.

Weisbroad, Jo Anne. "Shaping A Body Image Through Movement Therapy." *Music Educators Journal* 58,8 (April 1972):66-9.

Wirth, Ruth. "Art for the Handicapped." *Pointer* 19,2 (Winter 1974):146-8.

Unpublished Materials

Buffmire, Judy Ann. "A Comparative Study of Creative Ability in Educable Retarded and Normal Children." Ph.D. Dissertation, University of Utah, 1969.

Chapman, Gay. "Learning in a Friendly Environment: Art as an Instructor." Paper presented at the 55th Annual International Convention, The Council for Exceptional Children, Atlanta, Georgia, April 11-15, 1977.

Council for Exceptional Children. "Exceptional Children Conference Papers: Early Childhood Education." Papers presented at the 51st Annual International CEC Convention, Dallas, Texas, April 22-27, 1973.

Ford, Barbara Gay and Renzulli, Joseph S. "Effects and Implication of Creativity Training with Mentally Retarded Youngsters." Paper presented at the American Educational Research Association meeting, San Francisco, California, April 19-23, 1976.

Khatena, Joe. "Major Directions in Creativity Research." Paper presented at the 53rd Annual Convention of the Council for Exceptional Children, Los Angeles, California, April 24, 1975.

Richards, Ruth L. and Casey, M. Beth. "Creativity and Academic Motivation Variables as Predictors of Achievement in a Two-Year College for Educationally Marginal Students." Paper presented at the Annual Meeting of the American Educational Research Association, Washington, D.C., March 30-April 3, 1975.

Richmond, Bert O. "Non-Cognitive Development of Mentally Retarded Children." Paper presented at Session I of 11th Southeastern Invitation Conference on Measurement in Education, Athens, Georgia, December 8, 1972.

White, Alan J. "A Progress Report on the Connecticut Program for Handicapped Talented Children." Paper presented at the 54th Annual International Convention, The Council for Exceptional Children, Chicago, Illinois, April 4-9, 1976.

Wiener, William K.; and Others. "Social-Emotional Development and Creative Explorations for the Handicapped Student." Paper presented at the 3rd International Symposium on Learning Disabilities, Miami Beach, Florida, 1973.

ERIC Documents

Discussion Leader's Guide: Parent/Child Home Situation. The Marshalltown Project. Revised July 1975. Marshalltown, Iowa: ERIC Document Reproduction Service, ED 136 521, 1975.

Donahue, Michael J et al. *Home Stimulation of Handicapped Children: Professional Guide. Parent/Child Home Stimulation.* Marshalltown, Iowa: ERIC Document Reproduction Service, ED 079 922, 1973.

———— . *Home Stimulation of Handicapped Children: Parent Guide. Parent/Child Home Stimulation.* Marshalltown, Iowa: ERIC Document Reproduction Service, ED 079 921, 1973.

Gallagher, Marie S. *A Comparative Study of the Most Creative and Least Creative Students in Grades 4-8 at the Boston School for the Deaf.* Randolph, Massachusetts. ERIC Document Reproduction Service, ED 031 852, 1968.

Ladner, Judith L. *Enhancement of Productive Thinking in Institutionalized Mental Retardates.* Final Report. Bronx, New York: ERIC Document Reproduction Service, ED 053 503, 1971.

Minskoff, Esther Hirsch. *An Analysis of the Teacher-Pupil Verbal Interaction in Special Classes for the Mentally Retarded.* New York, New York: ERIC Document Reproduction Service, ED 021 355, 1967.

Neisworth, John T. and Smith, Robert M. *Congenital Blindness as an Instance of Sensory Deprivation, Implications for Rehabilitation.* ERIC Document Reproduction Service, ED 015 586, 1965.

PACE in Pennsylvania 1974. A Catalog of Projects Funded in Pennsylvania Under ESEA Title III. King of Prussia, Pennsylvania: ERIC Document Reproduction Service, ED 111 087, 1975.

Parent Discussion Manual: Parent/Child Home Stimulation. The Marshalltown Project. Revised July 1975. Marshalltown, Iowa: ERIC Document Reproduction Service, ED 136 522, 1975.

Rainey, Ernestine W. *Art for Young Children.* Revised July 1974. Mississippi State University State College: ERIC Document Reproduction Service, ED 126 660, 1974.

Schrag, Howard L. et al. *The Status of Young Children in Idaho, 1974. Volume 2.* Boise, Idaho: ERIC Document Reproduction Service, ED 101 842, 1974.

A Special Conference on Arts for the Mentally Retarded At John F. Kennedy Center for the Performing Arts. Washington, D.C.: ERIC Document Reproduction Service, ED 109 843, 1974.

Tisdall, William J. et al. *Divergent Thinking in Blind Children.* Lexington, Kentucky: ERIC Document Reproduction Service, ED 023 247, 1967.

White, Alan; and Others. *Project SEARCH Multi-Arts Curriculum: Lessons Plans for Fostering Exceptional Creative Potential Among Children with Handicaps* (Working Draft). New Haven, Connecticut: ERIC Document Reproduction Service, ED 140 561, 1976.

ART

Books

Alexander, Dorothy Whitacre. *Arts and Crafts for Students with Learning Difficulties.* Elwyn, Pennsylvania: Elwyn Institute, 1968. ED 037 872.

Alkema, Charles J. *Art for the Exceptional.* Boulder: Pruett, 1971.

Anderson, Frances E. *Art for All the Children: A Creative Sourcebook for the Impaired Child.* Springfield: Charles C Thomas, 1978.

Baumgartner, Bernice B. and Schultz, Joyce B. *Reaching the Retarded Through Art.* Johnstown, Pennsylvania: Mafex Associates, 1969.

Bergen, Richard Dean. *Art Oriented Work Experience and Its Effect on Hospitalized Seriously Emotionally Disturbed Adolescents.* Doctoral dissertation, University of Kansas at Lawrence. *Dissertation Abstracts International* 33 (December 1972), 6-A. Ann Arbor, Michigan: University Microfilms, University of Michigan.

Buffalo Public Schools. *Art Projects and Activities for the Mentally Retarded.* Buffalo: Division of Curriculum Evaluation and Development, 1969. ED 039 666.

Burris, W. R. *A Handbook on the Theory and Practice of Arts and Crafts for Educable Mentally Retarded Children and Youth.* Jackson: Mississippi State Department of Education, 1962. ED 044-846.

Copeland, Mildred et al. *Occupational Therapy for Mentally Retarded Children: Guidelines for Occupational Therapy Aides and Certified Therapy Assistants.* Baltimore: University Park Press, 1976.

Council for Exceptional Children. *Arts and Crafts: Exceptional Child Bibliography Series.* Arlington: Information Center on Exceptional Children, February 1971. ED 050 525.

Fukurai, Shiro. *How Can I Make What I Cannot See?* New York: Van Nostrand Reinhold, 1974.

Gould, Elaine and Gould, Loren. *Crafts for the Elderly.* Springfield, Charles C Thomas, 1976.

Kay, Jane G. *Crafts for the Very Disabled and Handicapped.* Springfield, Charles C Thomas, 1977.

Kramer, Edith. *Art as Therapy With Children.* New York: Schocken Books, January 1972.

———. *Art Therapy in a Children's Community.* Springfield: Charles C Thomas, 1958.

Kwiatkowska, Hanna Yaxa. *Family Therapy and Evaluation Through Art.* Springfield: Charles C Thomas, 1978.

Lindsay, Zaidee. *Art and the Handicapped Child.* New York: Van Nostrand Reinhold, 1972.

———. *Art for Spastics.* New York: Taplinger, 1966.

———. *Art is for All: Arts and Crafts for Less Able Children.* New York: Taplinger, 1968.

———. *Learning About Shape: Creative Experience for Less Able Children.* New York: Taplinger, 1969.

Lisenco, Yasha. *Art Not by Eye: The Previously Sighted Visually Impaired Adult in Fine Arts Programs.* New York: American Foundation for the Blind, 1971.

Ludins-Katz, Florence and Katz, Elias (Eds.). *Creative Art of the Developmentally Disabled.* Oakland, Creative Growth, 1977.

McNeice, William C. and Benson, Kenneth R. *Crafts for the Retarded: Through Their Hands They Shall Learn.* Bloomington, Illinois: McKnight and McKnight, 1964.

McNiff, Shaun A. *Art Therapy at Danvers.* Andover, Massachusetts: Addison Gallery of American Art, 1974.

Naumberg, Marg. *An Introduction to Art Therapy.* New York: Teachers College Press, Columbia University, 1973.

———. *Dynamically Oriented Art Therapy: Its Principles and Practice.* New York: Grune & Stratton, 1966.

Pattemore, Arnel W. *Arts and Crafts for Slow Learners.* Dansville, New York: Instructor Publications, 1969.

Schmidt, Alfred. *Craft Projects for Slow Learners.* New York: John Day, 1968.

Schwartz, Alma. *Art Guide for Teachers of Exceptional Children.* Aberdeen, South Dakota: Northern State College, 1965.

Sussman, Ellen J. *Art Projects for the Mentally Retarded Child.* Springfield:

Charles C Thomas, 1976.

Sykes, Kim C. et al. *Creative Arts and Crafts for Children with Visual Handicaps.* American Printing House for the Blind, Louisville, Kentucky. Washington, D.C.: Bureau of Education for the Handicapped, 1974.

Ulman, E. and Dachinger, P. (Eds.). *Art Therapy in Theory and Practice.* New York: Schocken Books, 1975.

Wagner, Lee. *Teaching Crafts to the Mentally Retarded.* Minneapolis: T. S. Denison, 1974.

Williams, Geraldine H. and Wood, Mary M. *Developmental Art Therapy.* Baltimore: University Park Press, 1977.

Winsor, Maryan T. *Arts and Crafts for Special Education.* Belmont, California: Fearon, 1972.

Periodicals and Chapters

Alkema, Chester Jay. "Art and the Exceptional Child. Part II." *Children's House* 3 (Winter 1968):12-15.

———. "Implications of Art for the Handicapped Child." *Exceptional Children* 33 (February 1967):433-34.

Baines, M. "Art and Blind Children." *School Arts* 63 (January 1964):4-9.

Bryant, Antusa P. and Schwan, Leroy B. "Art and the Mentally Retarded Child." *Studies in Art Education* 12 (Spring 1971):50-63.

Bush, Nancy Gale. "Ceramics Has Something for All." *The Pointer* 18 (Fall 1973):46-69.

Carter, John L. and Miller, Phyllis K. "Creative Art for Minimally Brain-Injured Children." *Academic Therapy* 6 (1971):245-52.

Coombs, Virginia H. "Guidelines for Teaching Arts and Crafts to Blind Children in the Elementary Grades." *International Journal for the Education of the Blind* 16 (March 1967):79-83.

Drew, Linda N. and Reichard, Gary L. "The Use of Arts and Crafts with Educable Mentally Retarded Children." *Journal for Special Educators of the Mentally Retarded* 12 (Spring 1976):174-77.

Fahler, Dorothy. "Crafts for Parents and Their Physically Handicapped Children." *The Pointer* 17 (Winter 1972):150-53.

Fitzgibbon, Walter C. "A Rationale for Crafts for the Educable Mentally Retarded." *Exceptional Children* 32 (1965):243-46.

———. "Therapeutic Arts for the Mildy Mentally Retarded." *Digest of the Mentally Retarded* 2 (1965):205.

Francois-Michelle School. "Therapeutic Art Programs Around the World, IV. Art and Applied Art by Mentally Defective Children." *Bulletin of Art Therapy* 7 (October 1967):29-33.

Groff, Linda B. "Recreational Arts and Crafts for the Mentally Retarded." *Therapeutic Recreation Journal* 3, No. 3 (1969):29-32.

Haimes, Norma. "Guide to the Literature of Art Therapy." *American Journal of Art Therapy* 11 (October 1971-January 1972):25-42.

Harcum, Phoebe M. "Classroom Techniques: Using Clay Bodies in Multidimensional Teaching of the Retarded." *Education and Training of the Mentally Retarded* 7 (June 1973):39-45.

Harper, Grady. "Toe Painting — A Special Education Project." *Exceptional Children* 32 (October 1966):123-24.

Hayes, Gene A. "Activity Analysis: Finger Painting for the Mentally Retarded." *Therapeutic Recreation Journal* 5 (Third 1971):133+.

Henshaw, Anne. "An Experiment in Further Education." *Parents Voice* 25 (September 1975):7-8.

Jacobson, Marilyn. "Art as an Experience: An Experiment in Film." *American Annals of the Deaf* 117 (June 1972):401-402.

Jones, Peter. "Woodwork for the Visually Handicapped." *New Beacon* 59 (November 1975):285-88.

Kramer, Edith. "The Practice of Art Therapy with Children." *American Journal of Art Therapy* 11 (April 1972):89-116.

Lachman, Mildred. "The Use of Movement in Art Therapy." *American Journal of Art Therapy* 13 (October 1973):22-34.

Lovano-Kerr, Jessie and Savage, Steven. "Incremental Art Curriculum Model for the Mentally Retarded." *Exceptional Children* 39 (November 1972):193-99.

McDermott, William A. "Art Therapy for the Severely Handicapped." *American Journal of Mental Deficiency* 59 (October 1954):231-34.

McNiff, Sharon A. and McNiff, Karen. "Art Therapy in the Classroom." *Art Teacher,* 6,2 (Spring 1976):10-12.

————. "Developing Spatial Awareness in the Primary Grades Through the Integrated Art Experience." *Educational Arts Association National Conference Handbook,* Summer 1974.

McNiff, Sharon A. and Cook, Christopher. "Video Art Therapy." Paper presented at American Art Therapy Association Convention in New York, 1974. *Art Psychotherapy* 2 (1975).

McVay, R. "A Crafts Program for the Blind Children." *The New Outlook for the Blind* 60 (October 1966).

Marpet, Louis and Prentky, Joseph. "Arts, Crafts, and MR's . . ." *Digest of the Mentally Retarded* 5, No. 1 (Fall 1968):7-8.

Morishima, Akira and Brown, Louis F. "A Case Report on the Artistic Talent of an Autistic Idiot Savant." *Mental Retardation* 15,2 (Apr. 1977):33-36.

Mullins, June B. "The Expressive Therapies in Special Education." *American Journal of Art Therapy* 13 (October 1973):52-58.

Neel, Margaret. "Significance of Arts and Crafts." In *Our New Challenge: Recreation for the Deaf-Blind,* edited by Steve A. Brannan. Seattle: Northwest Regional Center for Deaf-Blind Children, 1974, pp. 86-88.

Nettlebeck, T. and Kirby, N. H. "Training the Mentally Handicapped to Sew." *Education and Training of the Mentally Retarded* 11 (February

1976):31-36.

New York State Art Teachers Association. *Art Education/Art Therapy: A Special Issue of the NYSATA Bulletin* 28,3 (May 1978).

Perlmutter, Ruth. "Constructing." *Teaching Exceptional Children* 4 (Fall 1971):34-41.

———. "Papercrafts and Mobiles." *Teaching Exceptional Children* 4 (Spring 1972):134-41.

Savini, Doris. "Ceramic Shop for Trainable Students." *Pointer* 18 (Winter 1973):126-27.

Schisgall, Jane. "The Creative Use of Multimedia (or the Shape of Strings to Come)." *Teaching Exceptional Children* 5 (Summer 1973):162-69.

Serban, George. "A Critical Study of Art Therapy in Treating Psychotic Patients." *Behavioral Neuropsychiatry* 4 (1972):2-9.

Sherman, Helen. "Hands on Hobbies." In *Our New Challenge: Recreation for the Deaf-Blind,* edited by Steve A. Brannan. Seattle: Northwest Regional Center for Deaf-Blind Children, 1975, pp. 88-97.

Silver, Rawley A. "Art and the Deaf." *American Journal of Art Therapy* 9 (January 1970):63-77.

———. "Art Breaks the Silence." *Children's House* 4,4 (Winter 1970):10-13.

———. "Cognitive Skills Development Through Art Experiences: An Educational Program for Language and Hearing Impaired and Aphasic Children." *Rehabilitation Literature* 34 (October 1973):10.

Sinclair, D. "Art Teaching for the Blind." *Teacher of the Blind* 63 (Spring 1975):65-72.

Slatoff, H. "Integrated Art Experiences for Blind Children." *The International Journal of Education of the Blind* 12 (October 1962):17-18.

Wiggin, Richard G. "Art Activities for Mentally Handicapped Children." *Journal of Educational Research* 54 (March 1961):7.

Williams, Susan A. "Film Making as a Therapeutic Medium." *Therapeutic Recreation Journal* 9 (1975):158+.

Williams, Roger M. "Why Children Should Draw: The Surprising Link Between Art and Learning." *Saturday Review* 4,2 (September 3, 1977):11-16.

Winklestein, E.; Shapiro, B. J.; and Shapiro, P. P. "Art Curricula and Mental Retarded Preschoolers." *Mental Retardation* 11 (June 1973):6-9.

Wirth, Ruth. "Art for the Handicapped." *Pointer* 19 (Winter 1974):146-48.

DANCE

Books

American Dance Therapy Association. *Annual Conference Proceedings and Monographs.* Columbia, Maryland: ADTA, 1968-present.

Bartenieff, Irmagard and Davis, Martha. *Effort-Shape Analysis of Movement:*

The Unity of Expression and Function. Bronx: Albert Einstein College of Medicine, 1963.

Bernstein, Penny. *Theory and Methods in Dance-Movement Theory*. Dubuque: Kendall/Hunt, 1972.

Canner, Norma. *. . . and a Time to Dance*. Boston: Beacon Press, 1968.

Chaiklin, Harris (Ed.). *Marian Chace: Her Papers*. Columbia, Maryland: American Dance Therapy Association, 1975.

Chapman, Ann and Cramer, Miriam. *Dance and the Blind Child*. New York: American Dance Guild, Inc., 1973.

Committee on Research in Dance. *Workshop in Dance Therapy: Its Research Potentials*. New York: CORD, 1968.

Costonis, Maureen N. (Ed.). *Therapy in Motion*. Urbana: University of Illinois Press, 1977.

Hill, Kathleen. *Dance for Physically Disabled Persons*. Washington, D.C.: American Alliance for Health, Physical Education, and Recreation, 1976.

Kratz, L. E. *Movement Without Sight*. Palo Alto, California: Peek Publications, 1973.

Laban, Rudolf. *The Mastery of Movement*. London: MacDonald and Evans, 1960.

————. *Modern Educational Dance*, 2nd rev. ed. London: MacDonald and Evans, 1963.

Laban, Rudolf and Lawrence, F. C. *Effort*. London: MacDonald and Evans, 1974.

Lefco, Helene. *Dance Therapy: Narrative Case Histories of Therapy Sessions with Six Patients*. Chicago: Nelson-Hall Co., 1977.

Mason, Kathleen Criddle (Ed.). *Dance Therapy: Focus on Dance VII*. Washington, D.C.: American Association for Health, Physical Education, and Recreation, 1974.

North, Marian. *Personality Assessment Through Movement*. London: MacDonald and Evans, 1972.

Robins, Ferris and Robins, Jennet. *Educational Rhythmics for Mentally and Physically Handicapped Children*. New York: Association Press, 1968.

Rosen, Elizabeth. *Dance in Psychotherapy*. 2nd ed. Brooklyn: Dance Horizons, 1974.

Schattner, Regina. *Creative Dance for Handicapped Children*. New York: John Day, 1967.

Schoop, Trudi. *Will You, Won't You Join the Dance? A Dancer's Essay Into the Treatment of Psychosis*. Palo Alto, California: National Press Books, 1974.

Wessel, Janet. *Locomotor and Rhythmic Skills: I Can Individualized Physical Education Curriculum Materials for Trainable Retarded*. Northbrook, Illinois: Hubbard Scientific Co., 1976.

Wethered, Audrey. *Movement and Drama in Therapy: The Therapeutic Use of Movement, Drama, and Music*. Boston: Plays, 1973.

Articles and Chapters

Adler, Janet. "The Study of an Autistic Child." *ADTA Proceedings,* Third Annual Conference (October 1968):43-48.

Anderson, Richard D. "Application of Educational Rhythmics to Therapeutic Recreation Service." *Therapeutic Recreation Journal* 5 (1971):75.

Bartenieff, Irmagard. "Dance Therapy: A New Profession or a Rediscovery of an Ancient Role of the Dance?" *Dance Scope* 7 (Fall/Winter 1972):6-18.

Bender, Lauretta and Boas, Franziska. "Creative Dance in Therapy." *American Journal of Orthopsychiatry* 11 (April 1941):235-45.

Boas, Franziska. "Psychological Aspects in the Practice and Teaching of Creative Dance." *Journal of Aesthetics and Art Criticism* 2 (1943):3-20.

Bunzel, Gertrude. "Psychokinetics and Dance Therapy." *Journal of Health, Physical Education, and Recreation* 19 (March 1948):180.

Calder, Jean E. "Dance for the Mentally Retarded." *Slow Learning Child* 19 (July 1972):67-78.

Carroccio, Dennis P. and Quattlehaum, Lawrence F. "An Elementary Technique for Manipulation of Participation in Ward Dances at a Neuropsychiatric Hospital." *Journal of Music Therapy* 6 (1969):108-109.

Chace, Marian. "Dance Alone is Not Enough . . ." *Dance Magazine* 38 (July 1964):46-47; 58-59.

_____ . "Dance as an Adjunctive Therapy with Hospitalized Mental Patients." *Bulletin of the Menninger Clinic* 17 (November 1953):219-225.

Davis, Martha. "Movement Characteristics of Hospitalized Psychiatric Patients." *ADTA Proceedings, Fifth Annual Conference* (October 1970):25-45.

Delaney, Wynelle. "The Dance Therapist Role in a Clinical Team." In *Dance Therapy: Focus on Dance VII,* edited by Kathleen Mason. Washington, D.C.: AAHPER, 1974, pp. 17-19.

Delaney, Wynelle and Sherrill, Claudine. "Dance Therapy and Adapted Dance." In *Adapted Physical Education and Recreation: A Multidisciplinary Approach* by Claudine Sherrill. Dubuque: William C. Brown, 1976, pp. 237-259.

Duggar, Margaret P. "What Can Dance Be to Someone Who Cannot See?" *Journal of Health, Physical Education, and Recreation* 39 (May 1968):28-30.

Eichenbaum, Bertha and Bednarek, Norman. "Square Dancing and Social Adjustment." *Mental Retardation* 2 (1964):105-108.

Gewertz, Joanna. "Dance for Psychotic Children." *Journal of Health, Physical Education, and Recreation* 35 (January 1964):63-64.

Goodnow, Catherine C. "The Use of Dance in Therapy With Retarded

Children." *Journal of Music Therapy* 5 (1968):97-102.

Govine, Barbara. "The Use of Movement as Adjunctive Therapy in the Rehabilitation of Psychiatric Day Patients." *Rehabilitation Services Revue* 3 (May 1965):12-15.

Grassman, Cyrus S. "Modified Folk and Square Dancing for the Mentally Retarded." *The Physical Educator* 15 (March 1958):32-35.

Hecox, Bernadette; Levine, Ellen; and Scott, Diana. "A Report on the Use of Dance in Physical Rehabilitation: Every Body Has a Right to Feel Good." *Rehabilitation Literature* 36 (January 1975):11-16.

Hering, Doris. "A Sliver of Hope. *Dance Magazine* 39 (September 1965):46-48.

Hood, Claudia. "The Challenge of Dance Therapy." *Journal of Health, Physical Education, and Recreation* 30 (February 1959):18.

Huberty, C. J.; Quirk, J. P.; and Swan, W. "Dance Therapy with Psychotic Children." *Archives of General Psychiatry* 28 (May 1973):707-713.

Jones, Clarice R. "Folk Dancing." *The Pointer* 12 (1968):18.

Kalish, Beth. "Body Movement Therapy for Autistic Children." *Journal of the American Dance Therapy Association, Inc.* 1 (Fall 1968):7-11.

———. "Working with an Autistic Child." In *Dance Therapy: Focus on Dance VII*, edited by Kathleen Mason. Washington, D.C.: AAHPER, 1974.

Keen, Heather. "Dancing Toward Wholeness." *ADTA Monograph* 1 (1971):69-99.

Kestenberg, Judith. "Suggestions for Diagnostic and Therapeutic Procedures in Movement Therapy." *ADTA Monograph* 1 (1971):5-16.

Kraft, Irvin A. and Delaney, Wynelle. "Movement Communication with Children in a Psychoeducational Program at a Day Hospital." *Journal of the American Dance Therapy Association* 1 (Fall 1968):6.

Laban, Rudolph. "The Educational and Therapeutic Value of the Dance." In *The Dance Has Many Faces*, edited by Walter Sorell. New York: Columbia University Press, 1966.

Leventhal, Marcia B. "Movement Therapy With Minimal Brain Dysfunction Children." In *Dance Therapy: Focus on Dance VII*, edited by Kathleen Mason. Washington, D.C.: AAHPER, 1974.

McGinnis, Rozanne W. "Dance as Therapeutic Process." *Therapeutic Recreation Journal* 7 (1974):181.

Matteson, Carol A. "Finding the Self in Space." *Music Educators Journal* 58 (April 1972):63-65, 135.

Mossman, Maja. "Movement — the Joyous Language: Dance Therapy for Children." *Children's House* 8 (Spring 1976):11-15.

Neel, Richard S. and Schneider, Debbie. "How My Body Looks and Moves — Lessons in Self Drawings." *Teaching Exceptional Children* 10 (Winter 1978):38-39.

Paley, A. M. "Dance Therapy: An Overview." *American Journal of Psychoanalysis* 34 (1974):81-83.

Perlmutter, Ruth. "Dance Me a Cloud." *Children's House* 6 (Winter 1974):15-

19.

Polk, Elizabeth. "Notes on the Demonstration of Dance Technique and Creative Dance as Taught to Deaf Children, Ages 7-11." *Journal of the American Dance Therapy Association, Inc.* 1 (Fall 1968):4-5.

———. "Dance Therapy With Special Children." In *Dance Therapy: Focus on Dance VII*, edited by Kathleen Mason. Washington, D.C.: AAHPER, 1974.

Riordan, Anne. "Dance for the Handicapped Pamphlet." In *NCAH Materials*. Washington, D.C.: National Committee on Arts for the Handicapped, 1977.

Roberts, A. G. "Dance Movement Therapy: Adjunctive Treatment in Psychotherapy." *Canada's Mental Health* 22 (December 1974):11.

Salus, Mariam and Schanberg, Rachel. "Body Movement and Creative Expression for the Preschool Language Handicapped Child." *ADTA Monograph* 1 (1971);38-49.

Samoore, Rhoda. "A Rhythm Program for Hearing Impaired Children." *The Illinois Advance* 1 (January 1970):15-20.

Sandel, Susan L. "Integrating Dance Therapy Into Treatment." *Hospital and Community Psychiatry* 26 (July 1975):439-440.

Schmais, Claire. "What Dance Therapy Teaches Us About Teaching Dance." *Journal of Health, Physical Education, and Recreation* 41 (January 1970):34-35, 88.

———. "What is Dance Therapy?" *Journal of Health, Physical Education, and Recreation* 47 (January 1976):39.

Schniderman, Craig M. and Volkman, Ann. "Music and Movement Involve the Whole Child." *Teaching Exceptional Children* 7 (Winter 1975):58-60.

Szyman, Robert. "Square Dancing on Wheels." *Sports 'n Spokes* 2 (November-December 1976):5-7.

Tipple, Blanche. "Dance Therapy and Education Program." *Journal of Leisurability* 2 (October 1975):9-12.

Weiner, Carole. *Dance-Movement Therapy Bibliography.* Helmuth, New York: Gowanda State Hospital, 1973. (Available from IRUC/AAHPER)

Weisbrod, Jo Anne. "Body Movement Therapy and the Visually-Impaired Person." In *Dance Therapy: Focus on Dance VII*, edited by Kathleen Mason. Washington, D.C.: AAHPER, 1974.

———. "Shaping a Body Image Through Movement Therapy." *Music Educators Journal* 58 (April 1977):66-69.

Wisher, Peter R. "Dance and the Deaf." *Journal of Health, Physical Education, and Recreation* 40 (1969):81.

———. "Therapeutic Values of Dance Education for the Deaf." In *Dance Therapy: Focus on Dance VII*, edited by Kathleen Mason. Washington, D.C.: AAHPER, 1974.

Wright, Minnie G. "The Effect of Training on Rhythmic Ability and Other

Problems Related to Rhythm." *Child Development* 8 (June 1937):159-172.

DRAMA

Books

Gilles, Emily. *Creative Drama for All Children.* New York: City Association for Childhood Education International, 1973.

Gray, Paula E. *Dramatics for the Elderly.* Doctoral dissertation. *Dissertation Abstracts International* 33, 8-A, 4192, February 1973. University Microfilms. Ann Arbor, Michigan: University of Michigan.

Kaliski, Lotte et al. *Structured Dramatics for Children with Learning Disabilities.* San Raphael, Calif.: Academic Therapy Publications, 1971.

McIntyre, Barbara. *Informal Dramatics: A Language Arts Activity for the Special Pupil.* Pittsburgh, Pa.: Stanwix House, 1963.

Philpott, A. R. *Puppets and Therapy.* Boston: Plays, 1977.

Schattner, Regina. *Creative Dramatics for Handicapped Children.* New York: John Day, 1967.

Stensrud, Carol. *Creative Dramatics: The Effects on the Oral Expression Skill of Speech and Hearing Dysfunctional Children.* Master's thesis, University of Iowa, 1975.

Wethered, Audrey G. *Movement and Drama in Therapy.* Boston: Plays Inc., 1973.

Periodicals and Chapters

Bitcon, Carol H. and Ball, Thomas S. "Generalized Imitation and Orff-Schulwerk." *Mental Retardation* 12 (June 1974):3.

Blumberg, Marvin J. "Creative Dramatics: An Outlet for Mental Handicaps." *Journal of Rehabilitation* 42 (November-December 1976):17-20, 40.

Carney, Eleanore (Ed.). "National Theatre of the Deaf." *Gallaudet Today* 1 (Spring 1971):22-23.

Clitheroe, T. K. "The Effects of Free Drama on the Interpersonal Relationships of E. S. N. Children." *Special Education* 54, 2 (1965):7-10.

Coleman, Peter. "Playmaking." *The Pointer* 20 (Winter 1975):34-35.

D'Alonzo, Bruno J. "Puppets Fill the Classroom with Imagination." *Teaching Exceptional Children* 6 (Spring 1974):3.

Davis, R. G. "Theatre Arts Training for the Severely Disabled." *Theatre News* 10 (May 1977):18.

Gervase, Ellen L. "Body Puppets in Role Playing." *The Pointer* 20 (Winter 1975):36-39.

Gitter, Lena L. "Dramatization and Role-Playing in the Montessori

Classroom." *The Pointer* 17 (Winter 1972):92-93.

Hochheimer, L. "Musical Drama Encourages Participation by Handicapped; Children Learn to Use Well the Abilities They Possess." *Chicago School Journal* 45 (1964):177-80.

Karpilow, Babette. "Drama Therapy." *Therapeutic Recreation Journal* 4 (1970):15-16, 44.

Keay, Stephen R. "Northern Suburban Special Recreation Association." *Journal of Health, Physical Education and Recreation* 44 (September 1973):63-66.

Lovelace, Betty M. "The Use of Puppetry with the Hospitalized Child in Pediatric Recreation." *Therapeutic Recreation Journal* 6 (1972):20-21, 37-38.

Malatesta, Daniel I. "The Potential Role of 'Theater Games' in a Therapeutic Recreation Program for Psychiatric Patients." *Therapeutic Recreation Journal* 6 (1972):164-66, 190.

Mazer, June L. "Producing Plays in Psychiatric Settings." *Bulletin of Art Therapy* 5 (July 1966):135-48.

Morgan, David. "An Adaptation for Drama for Retarded Participants." *Challenge* 9 (September-October 1973):1, 6-7.

————. "Combining Orff-Schulwerk with Creative Dramatics for the Retarded." *Therapeutic Recreation Journal* 9 (Second Quarter 1975):54-56.

Olson, Jack R. and Hovland, Carroll. "The Montana State University Theatre of Silence." *American Annals of the Deaf* 117 (December 1972):620-25.

Schuman, Sarah H.; Marcus, Dina; and Nesse, Dorothy. "Puppetry and the Mentally Ill." *The American Journal of Occupational Therapy* 27 (November-December 1973):484-86.

Spero, Ruth and Weiner, Carole. "Creative Arts Therapy: Its Application in Special Education Programs." *Children Today* 2 (July-August 1973):12-17.

Stensrud, Carol. "Creative Dramatics: Sensory Stimulation and Creativity for the Multiply Handicapped Child." In *Proceedings of the 1975 National Training Conference for Physical Therapists, Occupational Therapists, and Recreation Therapists*, edited by Jill Gray. Austin: Texas Education Agency, 1977.

Swerdlow, David. "Audio Drama: A Mobile Theater by the Blind." *Rehabilitation Record* 13 (May-June 1972):11-14.

Williams, Chester T. "Recreation for the Blind—A Community Drama Project." *Therapeutic Recreation Journal* 3 (1969):20-24.

Williams, R. L. and Gasdick, J. M. "Practical Applications of Psychodrama—An Action Therapy for Chronic Patients." *Hospital and Community Psychiatry* 21 (1970):187-189.

Winsten, Lynne (Ed.). "Arts for the Handicapped." *Theatre News* 10 (May 1977):1-18.

MUSIC

Books

Alvin, Juliette. *Music for the Handicapped Child.* London: Oxford University Press, 1965.

——— . *Music Therapy.* London: John Baker, 1966.

Bailey, Philip. *They Can Make Music.* London: Oxford University Press, 1973.

Bitcon, Carol H. *Alike and Different: The Clinical and Educational Use of Orff-Schulwerk.* Santa Ana, California: Rosha Press, 1976.

Cole, Frances. *Music for Children with Special Needs.* Glendale, California: Bowmar, 1965.

Coleman, Jack L. et al. *Music for Exceptional Children.* Evanston, Illinois: Summy-Birchard Co., 1964.

Cotten, Paul D. (Ed.). *A Handbook on the Theory and Practice of Music for Educable Mentally Retarded Children and Youth.* Jackson: Mississippi State Department of Education, Division of Instruction, 1968.

Dickinson, Pamela L. *Music with ESN Children: A Guide for the Classroom Teacher.* Atlantic Highlands: Humanities Press, 1976.

Dobbs, Jack P. G. *The Slow Learner and Music: A Handbook for Teachers.* New York: Oxford University Press, 1966.

Eagle, Charles (Ed.). *Music Therapy Index, Volume I.* Lawrence, Kansas: National Association for Music Therapy, Inc., 1977.

Ebey, Dorothy Helen. "Music Therapy for Children with Cerebral Palsy at the Ruth Lodge Residential School, Chicago, Illinois." Ph.D. dissertation, Chicago Musical College, 1955.

Edwards, Eleanor M. *Music Education for the Deaf.* South Waterford: Merriam-Eddy Company, 1974.

Fraser, Louise Whitbeck. *A Cup of Kindness, A Book for Parents of Retarded Children.* Seattle: Special Child Publications, 1973.

Gaston, E. Thayer, (Ed.). *Music in Therapy.* New York: MacMillian, 1966.

Ginglend, David R. and Stiles, Winifred E. *Music Activities for Retarded Children.* Nashville, Tennessee: Abingdon Press, 1965.

Graham, Richard M. *Music for the Exceptional Child.* Reston: Music Educators National Conference, 1975.

Grayson, John. *Musical Dimensions and Instruments for Realization: The Children's Playground of Musical Sculpture.* Duncan, British Columbia: Centre for Gestalt Learning, 1971.

Grayson, John E. et al. *Environments of Musical Sculpture You Can Build. Phase I.* Vancouver: Aesthetic Research Centre of Canada Publications, 1976.

Harbert, Wilhelmina K. *Opening Doors Through Music: A Practical Guide for Teachers, Therapists, Students, Parents.* Springfield: Charles C

Thomas, 1974.

Hardesty, Kay W. *Music Activities Guide for the Preschool Trainable Child, Report: Mental Retardation Training Program.* Washington, D.C.: Office of Education, 1971.

———. *Music Activities Guide for the Preschool Trainable Child.* Mental Retardation Training Program Technical Report Series 1971-1972. Columbus: Ohio State University, 1974.

Hirsch, Therese. *Music and Reeducation.* France: Neuchatel, Delachaus and Niestle, 1966.

Kesler, Buford and Richmond, Bert O. *Music Training for Severely and Profoundly Retarded Individuals.* Athens: University of Georgia, 1975.

Levin, Herbert. *Music Can Teach the Exceptional Child.* Bryn Mawr, Pennsylvania: Theodore Presser Co., 1970.

Levine, S. Joseph. *A Recorded Aid for Braille Music. Paper No. 3. The Prospectus Series.* Michigan State University, Washington, D.C.: Bureau of Education for the Handicapped, 1968.

Licht, S. *Music in Medicine.* Boston: The New England Conservatory of Music, 1946.

Massarotti, Michael C. and Slaichert, William M. *Evaluation of Sight, Sound Symbol Instructional Method.* Iowa: Pottawattamie County School System, 1972.

Michel, Donald E. *Music Therapy: An Introduction to Therapy and Special Education Through Music,* 2nd. Ed. Springfield: Charles C Thomas, 1977.

Moss, Lewellyn. *Final Report on the Study of Music as Teaching Media for Improvement of Speech of Trainable Mentally Retarded Students in Inner City Schools.* Southern Connecticut State College, Washington, D.C.: Office of Education, 1974.

New York State Education Department. *The Role of Music in the Special Education of Handicapped Children.* Albany: Division for Handicapped Children, April 1971, ED 064 853.

———. *Professional and Instructional Music Materials for Exceptional Children.* Albany: Division for Handicapped Children, October 1972. ED 071 259.

Nordoff, Paul and Robbins, Clive. *Music Therapy in Special Education.* New York: John Day, 1971.

———. *Therapy in Music for Handicapped Children.* New York: St. Martin's Press, 1971.

Podolsky, E. (Ed.). *Music Therapy.* New York: Philosophical Library, 1954.

Purvis, Jennie and Samet, Shelley (Eds.). *Music in Developmental Therapy.* Baltimore: University Park Press, 1976.

Riordan, Jennifer Talley. *They Can Sing Too—Rhythm for the Deaf.* Springfield, Virginia: Jenrich Associates, 1971.

Robins, Ferris and Robins, Jennet. *Educational Rhythmics for Mentally and*

Physically Handicapped Children. New York: Association Press, 1968.
Rosene, Paul Earl. "A Field Study of Wind Instrument Training for Educable Mentally Handicapped Children." Ph.D. Thesis, University of Illinois at Urbana-Champaign, 1976.
Schullian, Dorothy M. and Schoen, Max (Eds.). *Music and Medicine.* New York: Henry Schuman, Inc., 1948.
Soibelman, Doris. *Therapeutic and Industrial Uses of Music.* New York: Columbia University Press, 1948.
Stoesz, Gilbert. *A Suggested Guide to Piano Literature for the Partially Seeing.* New York: National Society for the Prevention of Blindness, 1966.
Stoesz, Gilbert and Bowers, Robert A. *A Piano Teacher Considers the Low Vision Child.* New York: The National Society for the Prevention of Blindness, Inc., 1965.
Tomat, Jean Hunter and Krutzky, Carmel D. *Learning Through Music for Special Children and Their Teachers.* South Waterford: Merriam-Eddy Co., 1975.
Ward, David. *Music for Slow Learners.* London, W.I. England: Advisory and Information Centre, College of Special Education, 1970.
Weber, Richard. *Musicall Series.* New York: Musicall, Inc. 1964.
Zimmer, Lowell J. *Music Handbook for the Child in Special Education.* Teaneck, New Jersey: S & S Publications, 1970.
Zimmer, Lowell Jay. *Music Handbook for the Child in Special Education.* South Hackensack: Joseph Boonvin, Inc., 1976.

Periodicals and Chapters

Alford, Robert L. "Music and the Mentally Retarded Ethnic Minority Child." *The Pointer* 19,2 (Winter 1974): 138-9.
Alley, Jayne. "Education for the Severely Handicapped: The Role of Music Therapy." *Journal of Music Therapy* 14,2 (Summer 1977):50-59.
Alvin, Juliette. "The Response of Severely Mentally Retarded Children to Music." *American Journal of Mental Deficiency* 63,6 (May 1959):988-996.
Anatasi, Anne and Levee, Raymond F. "Intellectual Defect and Musical Talent: A Case Report." *American Journal of Mental Deficiency* 64,4 (January 1960):695-703.
Ankim, Jean Carter. "Out of Silence—Music." *Music Educators Journal* 40,2 (November-December 1953):42-43, 49.
Baldwin, Lillian. "Music and the Blind Child." In *School Music Handbook.* Boston: C. C. Birchard, 1955, pp. 598-606.
Ballard, Barbara and Jones, Lloyd. "Vocal Music for the Educationally Handicapped." *Missouri School Music Magazine,* March-April 1967. Cited by *CMEA News,* California: October 1966.

Banik, Sambhu and Mendelson, Martin A. "A Comprehensive Program for Multi-Handicapped Mentally Retarded Children." *Journal of Special Educators of the Mentally Retarded* 11,1 (Fall 1974):44-49.

Barber, Eleanor. "Music Therapy with Retarded Children." *Australian Journal of Mental Retardation* 2,7 (September 1973):210-213.

Bellamy, Tom and Sontag, Ed. "Use of Group Contingent Music to Increase Assembly Line Production Rates of Retarded Students in a Simulated Sheltered Workshop." *Journal of Music Therapy* 10,3 (Fall 1973):125-136.

Beer, A. S. "Music and the Exceptional Child." *Music Educators Journal* 37 (November-December 1950).

Beryk, Sophia V. "Resources for Blind Students and Their Teachers." *Music Educators Journal* 48,2 (November-December 1965):75-77.

Bevans, Judith. "The Exceptional Child and Orff." *Music Educators Journal* 55,7 (March 1969):41-43:125-127. Reprinted in *Education of the Visually Handicapped* 1,4 (December 1969):116-120.

Birkenshaw, Lois. "Consider the Lowly Kazoo. *Volta Review* 77,7 (October 1975):440-441.

————. "Teaching Music to Deaf Children." *Volta Review* 67 (May 1965):352-358, 387.

————. "A Suggested Program for Using Music in Teaching Deaf Children." In *Proceedings of the International Conference on Oral Education of the Deaf*. Northampton, New York: The Conference, 1967.

Bitcon, Carol H. and Ball, Thomas S. "Generalized Imitation and Orff-Schulwerk." *Mental Retardation* 12,3 (June 1974):36-39.

Blair, Donald and Brooking, Mair. "Music as a Therapeutic Agent. *Mental Hygiene* 41 (April 1957):228-237.

Blos, Joan W. "Rhymes, Songs, Records, and Stories: Language Learning Experiences for Preschool Blind Children." *New Outlook for the Blind* 68,7 (September 1974):300-307.

Bokor, Clark R. "A Comparison of Musical and Verbal Responses of Mentally Retarded Children." *Journal of Music Therapy* 13,2 (Summer 1976):101-108.

Bolander, Betty. "A Special Skill Adapted to the Needs of the Group." *Intercom* 27 (Summer 1975):6-7.

Boyle, Constance M. "Dalcroze Eurhythmics and the Spastic." *Spastics' Quarterly* 3 (March 1954):5-8.

Braswell, Charles et al. "The Influence of Music Therapy on Vocational Potential." *Journal of Music Therapy* 7,1 (Spring 1970):28-38.

Breinholt, Verna and Schoepfe, Irene. "Music Experiences for the Child with Speech Limitations." *Music Educators Journal* 47,1 (September-October 1960):45-46, 48, 50, 52.

Brick, Rose Marie. "Eurhythmics: One Aspect of Audition." *Volta Review* 75,3 (March 1973):155-160.

Brim, Charlotte L. "Music, Vital Capacity, and Post-Respirator Patients."

Music Educators Journal 37 (January 1951):18-19.

Browne, Hermina E. "Panel: What and Why of Music Therapy in Mid-Atlantic Region." *Yearbook of Music Therapy* (1955):157-160.

Bruce, Robert. "Music Therapy: How It Helps the Child." *Journal of the International Association for Pupil Personnel Workers* 19,2 (March 1975):74-79.

Cameron, Rosaline. "The Uses of Music to Enhance the Education of the Mentally Retarded." *Mental Retardation* 8,1 (February 1970):32-34.

Carey, M. "Music for the Educable Mentally Retarded." *Music Educators Journal* 46 (February 1960):72.

Cassity, Michael David. "Nontraditional Guitar Techniques for the Educable and Trainable Mentally Retarded Residents in Music Therapy Activities." *Journal of Music Therapy* 14,1 (Spring 1977):39-42.

Cheslik, Deloris. "Music Instruction for the Visually Handicapped." *Music Educators Journal* 48,2 (November-December 1961):98-100.

Clark, Lois. "Musical Rhythm Motivation." *Journal of Psychiatric Nursing and Mental Health Services* 6,5 (September 1968):287-293.

Clarke, Janet and Evans, Elizabeth. "Rhythmical Intention as a Method of Treatment for the Cerebral Palsied Patients." *Australian Journal of Physiotherapy* 19,2 (June 1973):57-64.

Cole, F. E. "Music Serves the Exceptional Child." *California Journal of Elementary Education* 24 (May 1956):233-234.

Connor, Frances P., and Talbot, Mabel E. "Music Experiences." *Digest of the Mentally Retarded* 2,1 (Fall 1965):12-19, 31.

Conway, Janice Lyle. "A Rhythm Band for Mental Patients." *American Journal of Occupational Therapy* 3 (January-February 1949):246.

Coogan, Kathleen. "Music — An Exceptional Medium for Exceptional Children." In *Education for the Exceptional. 3: Mental and Emotional Deviates and Special Problems.* Boston: Porter Sargent, 1956, p. 488.

Corrington, L. R. "Acoustic Rhythm Program" *Proceedings of the Thirty-Third Meeting of the Convention of American Instructors of the Deaf.* St. Augustine, Florida: n.p., 1947.

Costello, P. "Music for the Deaf." *Volta Review* 66 (February 1964):92-93.

Cotter, Vance W. "Effects of Music on Performance of Manual Tasks with Retarded Adolescent Females." *American Journal of Mental Deficiency* 76,2 (September 1971):242-248.

Cox, J. C. "Music in the Junior High School Special Curriculum." *Music Educators Journal* 46 (April-May 1960):58+.

Cruickshank, W. M. "The Challenge of the Exceptional Child." *Music Educators Journal* 38,6 (June-July 1952):18.20.

Deakins, E. "Music for the Mentally Handicapped." *Illinois Education* 38 (March 1950):267-269.

Decuir, Anthony A. "Vocal Responses of Mentally Retarded Subjects to Four Musical Instruments." *Journal of Music Therapy* 12,1 (Spring 1975):40-43.

Dileo, Cheryl Lynn. "The Use of a Token Economy Program with Mentally Retarded Persons in a Music Therapy Setting." *Journal of Music Therapy* 12,3 (Fall 1975):155-160.

Dinklage, H. "Therapeutic Charms of Music." *Music Educators Journal* 51 (April 1965):129-131.

Dobbs, Mary Carolyn. "Retarded Children Do Respond to Good Music." The *School Musician Director and Teacher* 40,6 (February 1969):60.

Doepke, Katherine G. "Retarded Children Learn to Sing." *Music Educators Journal* 54,3 (November 1967):89-91.

Dolan, M. Catherine. "Music Therapy: An Explanation." *Journal of Music Therapy* 10,4 (Winter 1973):172-176.

Dorow, Laura Gilbert. "Conditioning Music and Approval as New Reinforcers for Imitative Behavior With the Severely Retarded." *Journal of Music Therapy* 12,1 (Spring 1975):30-39.

_____ . "Televised Music Lessons as Educational Reinforcement for Correct Mathematical Responses With the Educable Mentally Retarded." *Journal of Music Therapy* 13,2 (Summer 1976):77-86.

Douglas, C. W. "Chamber Music for the Mentally Gifted." *Music Educators Journal* 53 (January 1967):95.

Dryer, Jerome and Dix, James. "Reaching the Blind Child Through Music Therapy." *Journal of Emotional Education* 8,4 (April 1968):202-211.

Eddy, Clark. "No Fingers to Play a Horn." *Music Educators Journal* 58,8 (April 1972):61-62.

Engle, A. and Engel, Co. "The Effect of Musical Distraction Upon the Performance Efficiency of Children." *Journal of Educational Research* 56 (September 1962):45-47.

Erickson, Lorraine B. "Piano Playing as a Hobby for Children with Problem Hands." *Inter-Clinic Information Bulletin* 11,6 (March 1972):6-17.

_____ . "Keyboard Fun for Children with Osteogenesis Imperfecta and Other Physical Limitations." *Inter-Clinic Information Bulletin* 12,4 (January 1973):9-17.

_____ . "Never say 'You Can't Do That' to an Amputee!" *Inter-Clinic Information Bulletin* 13,10 (July 1974):13.14.

Fahey, Joan Dahms and Birkenshaw, Lois. "Bypassing the Ear: The Perception of Music by Feeling and Touching." *Music Educators Journal* 58,8 (April 1972):44-49, 127-128.

Fauth, B. L. and Fauth, W. W. "Rhythm." *American Annals of the Deaf* (November 1954):391-396.

Feinberg, Saul. "Creative Problem-Solving and the Music Listening Experience: Ideas for an Approach." *Music Educators Journal* 61,1 (September 1974):53-60.

Fielding, Benjamin B. "Two Approaches to the Rehabilitation of the Physically Handicapped Music Project. *Exceptional Children* 20 (May 1954):336-341.

Fields, Beatrice. "Music as an Adjunct in the Treatment of Brain-Damaged

Patients." *American Journal of Physical Medicine* 33 (October 1954):273-283.

Fitzgerald, Viola M. "All Slow Learners Enjoy Music." *Instructor* 63 (May 1954):52.

Fraser, L. W. "Reaching the Brain Damaged Child Through Music." In *Music Therapy.* Lawrence, Kansas: The Allen Press, 1958.

Fursland, Muriel. "Music is Her Life." *Parents Voice* 24,2 (June 1974):21.

Galloway, Herbert F. "A Comprehensive Bibliography of Music Referential to Communicative Development, Processing, Disorders, and Remediation." *Journal of Music Therapy* 12,4 (Winter 1975):164-196.

Galloway, Herbert F. and Bean, Marjorie F. "The Effects of Action Songs on the Development of Body-Image and Body-Part Identification in Hearing-Impaired Preschool Children." *Journal of Music Therapy* 11,3 (Fall 1974):125-134.

Garrison, J. H. "Magic of Music." *Texas Outlook* 46 (April 1962):38.

Gerard, Barbara A. "A Survey of Music Activities in Schools for the Handicapped in the New England Area." Master's thesis, Boston University, 1955.

Gilbert, Janet Perkins. "Mainstreaming in Your Classroom: What to Expect." *Music Educators Journal* 63,6 (February 1977):64-75.

Gilles, Dorothy and Kovitz, Valerie. "Helping Learning Disabled Music Students." *Clavier Magazine* 12 (September 1973): reprint ed.

Gilliland, Esther Goetz. "Functional Music for the Exceptional Child in the Special Schools of Chicago." *School Music Handbook.* Boston: C. C. Birchnard, 1955, pp. 585-591.

Gilmore, M. E. "Rhythm, Language and the Deaf Child." *Volta Review* (February 1966):160-165.

Glick, Lester G. "This Country Has Only 600 Music Therapists. Where Can They Serve Best?" *Music Educators Journal* 56,9 (May 1970):67-68.

Gollnitz, G. "Fundamentals of Rhythmic-Psychomotor Music Therapy. An Objective-Oriented Therapy for Children and Adolescents with Developmental Disabilities." *International Journal of Child Psychiatry* 41,4/5 (April/May, 1975):13-134.

Goodenough, Forest and Goodenough, Dorothy. "The Importance of Music in the Life of a Visually Handicapped Child." *Education of the Visually Handicapped* 2,1 (March 1970):28-32.

Goodglass, H. "Musical Capacity After Brain Injury." In *Music Therapy.* Lawrence, Kansas: The Allen Press, 1963.

Grayson, John. "A Playground of Musical Sculpture." *Music Educators Journal* 58,8 (April 1972):50-54.

Greene, Bonnie. "Opening Locked Doors with Music." *Children's House* 7,4 (Fall 1974):6-10.

Greene, Robert J.; Hoats, David L.; and Hornick, Adelbert J. "Music Distortion: A New Technique for Behavior Modification." *Psychological Record* 20,1 (Winter 1970):107-109.

Guberina, P. "The Use of Phonetic Rhythms in the Verbotonal System." *Proceedings of the International Conference on Oral Education of the Deaf.* Washington, D.C.: The Volta Bureau, 1967.

Harbert, Wilhemina K. "Music Techniques Applied in Disordered Speech-A Case Report by the Music Worker." In *Music Therapy.* Lawrence, Kansas: The Allen Press, 1954.

————. "Music Education for Exceptional Children." *Music in American Education—Music Education Source Book II.* Chicago: Music Educators National Conference, 1955.

Harrison, W. et al. "Effect of Music and Exercise Upon the Self Help Skills of Non-Verbal Retardates." *American Journal of Mental Deficiency* 71 (Spring 1966):279-282.

Herbert, Gwynneth F. "Education Through Music." *Slow Learning Child* 21,1 (March 1974):15-23.

Herlein, Doris G. "Music Reading for the Sightless: Braille Notation." *Music Educators Journal* 62,1 (September 1975):42-45.

Herron, Carole Jane. "Some Effects of Instrumental Music Training on Cerebral Palsied Children." *Journal of Music Therapy* 7,1 (Summer 1970):55-58.

Hochheimer, L. "Musical Drama Encourages Participation by Handicapped; Children Learn to Use Well the Abilities They Possess." *Music Educators Journal* 51 (September 1964):85-86.

Hummel, Cora J. "The Value of Music in Teaching Deaf Students." *Volta Review* 73,4 (April 1971):224-228, 243-249.

Humphrey, Hubert. "Message from Mrs. Hubert Humphrey." *Illinois Music Journal* 23 (November 1965):32-33.

Johnson, Janet M. and Phillips, Linda L. "Affecting the Behavior of Mentally Retarded Children with Music." *Music Educators Journal* 57,7 (March 1971):45-46.

Jorgenson, Helen and Parnell, Martha K. "Modifying Social Behaviors of Mentally Retarded Children in Music Activities." *Journal of Music Therapy* 7,3 (Fall 1970):83-87.

Joseph, Harry and Heimlich, Evelyn P. "The Therapeutic Use of Music with 'Treatment Resistent' Children." *American Journal of Mental Deficiency* 64 (1959):41-49.

Kalish, Beth. "Body Movement Therapy for Autistic Children." *American Dance Therapy Association Conference Proceedings* 1,1 (October 1968).

Kaplan, M. "Music Therapy in the Speech Program." *Exceptional Children* 22 (December 1955):112-117.

Klas, Brenda and Klas, Leroy. "Accordion Seems Under-Rated in Classroom" *Special Education in Canada* 49,1 (Fall 1974):25.

Klinger, H. and Peter D. "Techniques in Group Singing for Aphasics." In *Music Therapy.* Lawrence, Kansas: The Allen Press, 1963.

Knolle, Lee. "Sioux City's Special Brass Band: An Instrumental Program for the Mentally Retarded." *Music Educators Journal* 60,2 (October

1973):47-48.

Kondorossy, Elizabeth J. "Let Their Music Speak for the Handicapped." *Music Educators Journal* 52,4 (February-March 1966):115-116, 119.

Korduba, Olga M. "Duplicated Rhythmic Patterns Between Deaf and Normal Hearing Children." *Journal of Music Therapy* 12,3 (Fall 1975):136-146.

Kral, Carole. "Musical Instruments for Upper-Limb Amputees." *Inter-Clinic Information Bulletin* 12,3 (December 1972):13-26.

Larsen, A. "Music for Saul." *Illinois Music Journal* 22 (December 1964):52+.

Larson, Betsy Ann. "A Comparison of Singing Ranges of Mentally Retarded and Normal Children with Published Songbooks Used in Singing Activities." *Journal of Music Therapy* 14,3 (Fall 1977):138-143.

Larson, Cedric. "Music Therapy—A New Occupational Horizon." *Etude* 71 (August 1953):19-20.

Leonhard, K. and Berendt, Hildegard. "Musikalische Leistung Idiotin (Musical Performance of a Severely Mentally Retarded Girl)." *Confinia Psychiatrica* 11,12 (December 1968):106-118.

Lesak, Eleanor. "Music Activities for the Severely Mentally Retarded and Pre-School Mentally Retarded." *Mental Retardation: Selected Conference Papers*. Springfield: Illinois Mental Health Department, 1969.

Levin, Herbert D. and Levin, Gail M. "Instrumental Music: A Great Ally in Promoting Self-Image." *Music Educators Journal* 58,8 (April 1972):31-34.

Lewis, Mary Francis. "A Handbell Choir for Blind Students." *New Outlook for the Blind* 68,7 (September 1974):297-299.

Liebman, Joyce and Liebman, Arthur. "On Stage, Everybody." *Music Educators Journal* 60,2 (October 1973):45-46.

Lienhard, Marta E. "Factors Relevant to the Rhythmic Perception of a Group of Mentally Retarded Children." *Journal of Music Therapy* 13,2 (Summer 1976):58-65.

Ling, Stuart J. "Missing: Some of the Most Exciting Creative Moments of Life." *Music Educators Journal* 61,3 (November 1974):40, 93-95.

Lorenzen, Hans and Jokl, Ernst. "Piano Music for the One-Handed with Remarks on the Role of Art in Rehabilitation." *American Corrective Therapy Journal* 28,1 (January-February 1974):11-23.

Luckey, R. E. "Adult Retardates' Responsiveness to Recordings as a Function of Music Therapist Participation." *American Journal of Mental Deficiency* 71 (January 1967): 109-111.

Luckey, R. E. et al. "Severely Retarded Adults' Response to Rhythm Band Instruments." *American Journal of Mental Deficiency* 71 (January 1967):616.

Lunt, Ingrid. "Rhythm and the Slow Learner." *Special Education* 62,4 (December 1973):21-23.

Mailhot, Alice. "Musical Instruments for Upper-Limb Amputees." *Inter-Clinic Information Bulletin* 13,10 (July 1974):9-12, 14-15.

Matteson, Carol A. "Finding the Self in Space." *Music Educators Journal*

58,8 (April 1972):63-65.

May, E. "Music for Children with Cerebral Palsy." *American Journal of Physical Medicine* 35 (October 1956):320-323.

May, Elizabeth. "Music for Deaf Children." *Music Educators Journal* 47,3 (January 1961):39-40, 42.

McClelland, Etta. "Music for the Trainable Mentally Retarded." *Deficience Mentale/Mental Retardation* 20,1 (January 1970):18-20.

McCord, H. "Background Music: A Possible Aid in Teaching Adult Reading Improvement." *Journal of Developmental Reading* 5,1 (Autumn 1961):60-61.

McDermott, Elizabeth P. "Music and Rhythms: From Movement to Lipreading and Speech." *Volta Review* 73,4 (April 1971):229-232.

McGuire, L. "Music for the Blind Child." *National Catholic Education Association Bulletin* 59 (August 1962):488-490.

Metzler, Roberta Kagin. "The Use of Music as a Reinforcer to Increase Imitative Behavior in Severely and Profoundly Retarded Female Residents." *Journal of Music Therapy* 11,2 (Summer 1974):97-110.

Michaux, L; Duche, D.; Stein, C.; and LePage. "Early Musical Disposition in a 5 Year Old Girl with Backwardness in Intelligence and Language Development." *Revue de Neuropsychiatrie Infantile et d'Hygiene Mentale de l'Enfance* 5 (May 1957):284-291.

Michel, Donald E. and May, Nancy Hudgens. "The Development of Music Therapy Procedures with Speech and Language Disorders." *Journal of Music Therapy* 11,2 (Summer 1974):74-80.

Miller, Ann. "Growing with Music — A Program for the Mentally Retarded." *Exceptional Children* 20 (April 1954):305-307, 310-311.

Miller, D. Merrily. "Effects of Music-Listening Contingencies on Arithmetic Performance and Music Preference of EMR Children." *American Journal of Mental Deficiency* 81,4 (January 1977):371-378.

Mills, Sherry Rae. "Band for the Trainable Child." *Education and Training of the Mentally Retarded* 10,4 (December 1975):268-270.

Mooney, Muriel K. "Blind Children Need Training, Not Sympathy." *Music Educators Journal* 58,8 (April 1972):56-59.

Morrison, Douglas. "Sounds Familiar." *Times Educational Supplement (London)* (14 February 1975), p. 37.

Muranake, Yoshio and Homma, Kazuko. "Music Reading with the Optacon." *Bulletin* (March 1976):9-20.

Murphy, Mary Martha. "A Large Scale Music Therapy Program for Institutionalized Low Grade and Middle Grade Defectives." *American Journal of Mental Deficiency* 63,2 (September 1958):273.

———. "Rhythmical Responses of Low Grade and Middle Grade Mental Defectives to Music Therapy." *Journal of Clinical Psychology* 13 (October 1957):361-364.

Music Educators National Conference. "Music in Special Education." *Music Educators Journal* 58,8 (April 1972):5-143.

Mylecraine, Mary. "Library Serves Blind Students." *Music Journal* 29,9 (November 1971):13-15.

Newacheck, Vivian. "Music Aids the Slow Learner." *Ohio Schools* 30 (May 1952):252+.

Newham, W. H. "Music Therapy." *Times Educational Supplement (London)* (1 May 1964) p. 1173.

Nocera, Sona D. "Special Education Teachers Need a Special Education." *Music Educators Journal* 58,8 (April 1972):73-75.

Obaldia, Mario de and Best, Gary A. "Music Therapy in the Treatment of Brain-Damaged Children." *Academic Therapy* 6,3 (Spring 1971):263-269.

O'Toole, C. M. "Music for the Handicapped Child." *Music Educators Journal* 48 (June 1962):73-76.

Palmer, M. F. "Musical Stimuli in Cerebral Palsy, Aphasia, and Similar Conditions." In *Music Therapy*. Lawrence, Kansas: The Allen Press, 1953.

Paul, Rochelle and Staudt, Virginia M. "Music Therapy for the Mentally Ill: A Historical Sketch and a Brief Review of the Literature on the Physiological Effects and on Analysis of the Elements of Music." *Journal of General Psychology* 59 (October 1958):167-176.

Peters, Martha L. "Music and the Exceptional Child." *Therapeutic Recreation Journal* 2,3 (Third Quarter 1968):3-8.

———. "Music Sensitivity — A Comparison of Mongoloid and Normal Children." *Journal of Leisure Research* 1,4 (Fall 1969):289-295.

———. "A Comparison of the Musical Sensitivity of Mongoloid and Normal Children." *Journal of Music Therapy* 7,4 (Winter 1970):113-123.

Peterson, Carol Ann. "Sharing Your Knowledge of Folk Guitar with a Blind Friend." *New Outlook for the Blind* 63,5 (May 1969):142-146.

Pilcher, Maxine. "Resources for Teaching Music to the Blind." *Music Educators Journal* 51,2 (November-December 1964):67-68.

Pirtle, Marilyn and Seaton, Kay P. "Use of Music Training to Actuate Conceptual Growth in Neurologically Handicapped Children." *Journal of Research in Music Education* 21,4 (Winter 1973):292-301.

Pitman, Derek J. "The Musical Ability of Blind Children." *Research Bulletin No. 11.* American Foundation for the Blind (October 1965):63-80.

Polk, Elizabeth. "Notes on the Demonstration of Dance Technique and Creative Dance as Taught to Deaf Children." *Journal of the American Dance Therapy Association* 1,1 (January 1968):4.

Reardon, Diane M. and Bell, Graham. "Effects of Sedative and Stimulative Music on Activity Levels of Severely Retarded Boys." *American Journal of Mental Deficiency* 75,2 (September 1970):156-159.

Reid, Dennis H. et al. "The Use of Contingent Music in Teaching Social Skills to a Nonverbal Hyperactive Boy." *Journal of Music Therapy* 12,1 (Spring 1975):3-18.

Rejto, Alice. "Music as an Aid in the Remediation of Learning Disabilities."

Journal of Learning Disabilities 6,5 (May 1973):286-295.

Richman, Joel S. "Background Music for Repetitive Task Performance of Severely Retarded Individuals." *American Journal of Mental Deficiency* 81,3 (November 1976): 251-255.

Ring, Nigel D. "Miscellaneous Aids for Physically Handicapped Children." *Inter-Clinic Information Bulletin* 12,3 (December 1972):1-12.

Roan, Margaret Z. "Music Can Help the Crippled Child." *Crippled Child* 29 (April 1952):10-11, 28-29.

Robison, Doris E. "There's Therapy in Rhythm." *Music Educators Journal* 57,7 (March 1971):42-44, 95, 97-100.

Ross, Dorothea M.; Ross, Sheila A.; and Kuckenbecker, Shari L. "Rhythm Training for Educable Mentally Retarded Children." *Mental Retardation* 11,6 (December 1973):20-23.

Rowland, Hershel. "Much Alike: A Little Different." *Music Educators Journal* 51,3 (January 1965):93-94.

Samoore, Rhoda. "A Rhythm Program for Hearing Impaired Children." *The Illinois Advance* (January 1970):1-3, 15-20.

Saperston, Bruce. "The Use of Music in Establishing Communication with an Autistic Mentally Retarded Child." *Journal of Music Therapy* 10,4 (Winter 1973):184-188.

Scheerenberger, Richard. "Description of A Music Program at a Residential School for Mentally Handicapped." *American Journal of Mental Deficiency* 57 (April 1953):573-579.

———. "Presenting Music to the Mentally Retarded." *Music Educators Journal* 41,2 (November-December 1954):23-25.

Schneider, E. H. "The Use of Music with the Brain Damaged Child." In *Music Therapy*. Lawrence, Kansas: The Allen Press, 1954.

Schomer, Morton J. "A Perceptual Development Program for the Music Therapist." *Journal of Music Therapy* 10,2 (Summer 1973):95-109.

Schorsch, Sister M. Josepha. "Music Therapy for the Handicapped Child." *Education* 70,7 (March 1950):434-439.

Sears, William W. (Ed.). *Journal of Music Therapy — Special Issue: Research Abstracts*. Lawrence, Kansas: The National Association for Music Therapy, June 1964.

Seybold, Charles D. "The Value and Use of Music Activities in the Treatment of Speech in Delayed Children." *Journal of Music Therapy* 8,3 (Fall 1971):102-110.

Shepherd, Louis T., Jr. and Simons, Gene M. "Music Training for the Visually Handicapped." *Music Educators Journal* 56,6 (February 1970):80-81.

Sheridan, Wilma. "Music and Rhythms for the Deaf-Blind." In *Our New Challenge: Recreation for the Deaf-Blind,* edited by Steve A. Brannan. Seattle: Northwest Regional Center for Deaf-Blind Children, 1975, pp. 88-97.

Sherwin, Albert C. "Reactions to Music of Autistic (Schizophrenic)

Children." *American Journal of Psychiatry* 109 (May 1953):823-831.

Slavit, N. "Music Unifien Class." *Instructor* 72 (September 1962):40.

Snow, William Benham and Fields, Beatrice. "Music as an Adjunct in the Training of Children with Cerebral Palsy." *Occupational Therapy and Rehabilitation* 29 (June 1950):147-156.

Stainback, Susan B. et al. "Effect of Background Music on Learning." *Exceptional Children* 40,2 (October 1973):109-110.

Steele, Anita Louise. "Music in a Special Way." *Children Today* 2,4 (July-August 1973):8-11.

Steele, Anita Louise et al. "The School Support Program: Music Therapy for Adjustment Problems in Elementary Schools." *Journal of Music Therapy* 13,2 (Summer 1976):87-100.

Stern, Virginia. "They Shall Have Music." *Volta Review* 77,8 (November 1975):495-500.

Sternlicht, M.: Deutsch, M. R.; and Siegel, I. "Influence of Musical Stimulation Upon the Functioning of Institutional Retardates." *Psychiatric Quarterly Supplement* 41 (Part 2 1967):323-329.

Stevens, E. and Clark, F. "Music Therapy in the Treatment of Autistic Children." *Journal of Music Therapy* 6,4 (Winter 1969):98-104.

Stevens, Emily A. "Some Effects of Tempo Changes on Stereotyped Rocking Movements of Low-Level Mentally Retarded Subjects." *American Journal of Mental Deficiency* 76 (July 1971):76-81.

Stubbs, Barbara. "A Study of the Effectiveness of an Integrated, Personified Approach to Learning with Trainable Mental Retardates." *Journal of Music Therapy* (Fall 1970):77-82.

Sturdivant, Catharine. "The Little Music Makers." The Best of *Challenge*, Vol. I. Washington, D.C.: American Alliance of Health, Physical Education, and Recreation, 1974, pp. 71-72.

Swaiko, Nancy. "The Role and Value of an Eurhythmics Program in a Curriculum for Deaf Children." *American Annals of the Deaf* 119,3 (June 1974):321-324.

Talkington, Larry W. and Hall, Sylvia M. "A Musical Application of Premack's Hypothesis to Low Verbal Retardates." *Journal of Music Therapy* 7,3 (Fall 1970):95-99.

Thompson, Myrtle F. "Music Therapy at Work." *Education* 72 (September 1951):42-44.

Thomson, L. "Piano Playing for the Mentally Retarded." *Music Journal* 17 (September 1959):62-64.

Thresher, Janice M. "A Music Workshop for Special Class Teachers." *Exceptional Children* 36,9 (May 1970):683-684.

Underhill, Karen K. and Harris, Lawrence M. "The Effect of Contingent Music on Establishing Imitation in Behaviorally Disturbed Retarded Children." *Journal of Music Therapy* 11,3 (Fall 1974):156-166.

Uslan, Mark M. "Teaching Basic Ward Layout to the Severely Retarded Blind: An Auditory Approach." *New Outlook for the Blind* 70,9

(November 1976):401-402.

Van Oudenhouven, N. J. and Van Der Aart, W. J. "Auditory Discrimination Learning and Transfer in Imbeciles." *British Journal of Mental Subnormality* 14,2 (Fall 1968):98-100.

Van Uden, A. "An Electrical Wind Instrument for Severely or Totally Deaf Children." *Volta Review* 55,5 (May 1953):241.

_____ . "Instructing Prelingually Deaf Children by the Rhythms of Bodily Movement and of Sounds, by Oral Mime and General Bodily Expression — Its Possibilities and Difficulties." *Proceedings of the International Congress of Educators of the Deaf and the Forty-First Meeting of the Convention of American Instructors of the Deaf.* Washington, D.C.: Gaullaudet College, 1963.

_____ ."A Sound-Perceptive Method." In *The Modern Educational Treatment of Deafness,* edited by Sir Alexander Ewing. Manchester, England: University Press, 1960.

Vernazza, Marcelle. "What Are We Doing About Music in Special Education?" *Music Educators Journal* 53,8 (April 1967):55-58.

Vernetti, Carol J. and Jacobs, John F. "Effects of Music Used to Mask Noise in Learning Disabilities Classes." *Journal of Learning Disabilities* 5,10 (November 1972):533-537.

Vettese, Joseph. "Instrumental Lessons for Deaf Children." *Volta Review* 76,4 (April 1974):219-222.

Wagner, Michael J. "Brainwaves and Biofeedback: A Brief History: Implications for Music Research." *Journal of Music Therapy* 12,2 (Summer 1975):46-58.

Walker, Doris E. "When It Comes to Music, They See the Light." *The Pointer* 19 (Winter 1974):127.

_____ "Play-a-long, Sing-a-long with the Hi Hopes." *The Pointer* 20 (Winter 1975):57-60.

Walker, John B. "The Use of Music as an Aid in Developing Functional Speech in the Institutionalized Mentally Retarded." *Journal of Music Therapy* 9,1 (Spring 1972):1-12.

Wallert, M. "In Slow Gear: Music for the Disadvantaged Child." *Instructor* 72 (May 1963):18+.

Ward, David. "Music for Slow Learners." *Special Education/Forward Trends* 3,3 (September 1976):23-26.

Wasserman, Norma M. "Music Therapy for the Emotionally Disturbed in a Private Hospital." *Journal of Music Therapy* 9,2 (Summer 1972):99-104.

Wasserman, N. et al. "The Musical Background of a Group of Mentally Retarded Psychotic Patients: Implications for Music Therapy." *Journal of Music Therapy* 10,2 (Summer 1973):78-82.

Weber, R. "Teaching Unteachables Through Instrumental Music." *Music Journal* 23 (November 1965):35+.

_____ "Can They Remember? Growth of the Retarded Mind Through

Music." *Music Journal* 24 (November 1966):32+.

Wiegl, Vally. "Music as an Adjunctive Therapy in the Training of Children with Cerebral Palsy." *Cerebral Palsy Review* 15 (October 1954):9-10.

———— "Music for the Retarded." *Music Journal* 27,1 (January 1969):56-57.

Welsbacher, Betty T. "More Than a Package of Bizarre Behaviors. The Neurologically Handicapped Child." *Journal for Special Educators of the Mentally Retarded* 11,2 (Winter 1975):84-86, 93.

Whiting, H. S. "Effect of Music on Hospital Accident Rate." *American Journal of Mental Deficiency* 51 (January 1947):397-400.

Wiley, Don. "Teaching Music to the Blind." *Clavier* 7,8 (November 1968):14-17.

Willemain, T. R. and Lee, F. F. "Tactile Pitch Feedback for Deaf Speakers." *Volta Review* 73,9 (December 1971):541.

Wingert, M. Lucille. "Effects of a Music Enrichment Program in the Education of the Mentally Retarded." *Journal of Music Therapy* 9,1 (Spring 1972):13-22.

Wiser, B. D. "Instrumental Music for the Retarded Child." *School Musician* 31 (Fall 1960):40-41.

Wojan, K. J. "Eurythmics for Children from Nursery Through Middle School." *Proceedings of the International Congress of Educators of the Deaf and of the Forty-First Meeting of the Convention of American Instructors of the Deaf.* Washington, D.C.: Gallaudet College, 1963.

Wolf, Enid Gordon: Ruttenberg, Bertram; Levin, Herbert; and Levin, Gail. "A Song for Lolita." *Music Educators Journal* 55,9 (May 1969):50-53.

Wolpow, Raymond I. "The Independent Effects of Contingent Social and Academic Approval Upon the Musical On-Task and Performance Behaviors of Profoundly Retarded Adults." *Journal of Music Therapy* 13,1 (Spring 1976):29-38.

Worthington, Donna. "Therapy with Cerebral Palsied Children." *Music Journal* 27,9 (November 1969):66.

Zimny, G. H. and Weidenfeller, E. W. "Effects of Music Upon GSR of Children. *Child Development* 33 (December 1962):891-896.

Zine, Barbara et al. "Free Play Responses of Profoundly Retarded Children to Prerecorded Broadcast Children's Songs." *Journal of Developmental Disabilities* 1,2 (Spring 1975):17-22.

INDEX

A

Academic concepts, 33, 152, 157, 159, 160, 184-191
Accessibility, 8, 23, 55, 100-101, 121
Accompaniment, 79-80, 94, 101-102, 107, 155-156, 178
Adaptive behaviors, 33
Advocacy, 9, 14, 17, 21, 67-73
Aesthetics, 85, 113-117, 245
Art galleries, 119-121
Art therapy, 36, 246
Arts and crafts, 37, 39, 54, 115, 121, 146-151, 158-159, 166-169, 182, 184, 186, 198, 201, 205
Assessment, 19-20, 21, 22, 39, 41, 60, 79, 199-202, 207-212, 215, 225-229, 233-240
Autism, 19, 35-36, 76, 244
Awareness, 79, 85, 112-117, 120, 142-143, 160, 170

B

Behavioral Characteristics Progression, 39-42, 198-202
Behavior management/modification, 25, 32, 39-40, 42, 150, 166, 171, 188
Blind, 119-123, 156, 243-244, 249
Body image, 27, 112, 153-161, 250
Braille, 119, 121-123, 243, 249
Brain injury, 34

C

Camera equipment, 216-222, 223, 233-235
Carry over values, 43, 159-161, 232
Cerebral palsy, 30, 35-37, 99, 112, 121, 185, 243, 245
Choric function, 127
Clay, 39, 166, 182, 201
Communication, 26, 33, 105-107, 116, 125-130, 132, 157

Community leadership, 23, 62, 69-71
Community resources, 7, 23, 58, 59, 61, 69-71, 119-121
Creative process
  behaviors, 5, 192-193
  individual, 116
Creativity, 3, 47, 108-109, 144, 172
Cultural arts activities, 15, 49, 71-73, 119-121

D

Dance, 192, 200, 215-216
Dance forms
  ballet, 58
  dance/movement therapy, 77-81, 138
  deaf, 104-110
  square, 93-96
  wheelchair, 99-102
Dance therapy, 36, 74, 76-82, 84, 139, 246-247
Deaf, 104-110, 124, 125-131, 243-244
Deaf-blind, 35, 38, 202
Deduction, 192, 193, 195
Developmental stages
  creative process, 53-54
  play, 50-53
  symbol formation and creative growth, 53
Down's Syndrome, 74, 112, 132, 198, 233-240, 242-245
Drama
  creative drama, 62, 80-81, 114, 124, 125-131, 133-136, 138-145, 156, 169-170, 184, 215
  cultural arts activities, 15, 49, 71-73, 119-121
  movement exploration, 6, 75-81, 85-92, 114-115, 157, 160-161
  Orff-Schulwerk, 114, 139-145, 170, 249
  puppetry, 12, 39, 132, 156-157, 184, 187, 215

283